Social Work
& Human
Development

Sara Miller McCune founded SAGE Publishing in 1965 to support the dissemination of usable knowledge and educate a global community. SAGE publishes more than 1000 journals and over 800 new books each year, spanning a wide range of subject areas. Our growing selection of library products includes archives, data, case studies and video. SAGE remains majority owned by our founder and after her lifetime will become owned by a charitable trust that secures the company's continued independence.

Los Angeles | London | New Delhi | Singapore | Washington DC | Melbourne

5th Edition

Social Work & Human Development

Janet Walker

SAGE | **Learning Matters**

Series Editors:
Jonathan Parker and Greta Bradley

Learning Matters
An imprint of SAGE Publications Ltd
1 Oliver's Yard
55 City Road
London EC1Y 1SP

SAGE Publications Inc.
2455 Teller Road
Thousand Oaks, California 91320

SAGE Publications India Pvt Ltd
B 1/I 1 Mohan Cooperative Industrial Area
Mathura Road
New Delhi 110 044

SAGE Publications Asia-Pacific Pte Ltd
3 Church Street
#10–04 Samsung Hub
Singapore 049483

First published in 2003 by Learning Matters Ltd.
Reprinted in 2003
Reprinted in 2004
Reprinted in 2005 (twice)
Reprinted in 2006
Second edition 2007
Third edition 2010
Reprinted in 2011
Fourth edition 2014

Editor: Kate Keers
Development editor: Lauren Simpson
Production controller: Chris Marke
Project management: Deer Park Productions,
Tavistock, Devon
Marketing manager: Camille Richmond
Cover design: Wendy Scott
Typeset by: C&M Digitals (P) Ltd, Chennai, India
Printed in the UK

Library of Congress Control Number: 2017935031

British Library Cataloguing in Publication Data

A catalogue record for this book is available from the
British Library

ISBN: 978-1-4739-8980-1
ISBN 978-1-4739-8981-8 (pbk)

At SAGE we take sustainability seriously. Most of our products are printed in the UK using FSC papers and boards.
When we print overseas we ensure sustainable papers are used as measured by the PREPS grading system.
We undertake an annual audit to monitor our sustainability.

Contents

Acknowledgement

I am indebted to my colleague and long-time friend Karin Crawford for our journey together in producing previous editions of the book. Her knowledge, skills, contribution and support has been critical to the writing of the content. I wish to express my sincere gratitude and appreciation to her; she contributed in so many ways to make this book happen.

About the author

Janet Walker is Deputy Head in the School of Health and Social Care at the University of Lincoln, where she has responsibility for leading, developing and supporting teaching, learning, practice and research in health and social care and social work. She has experience of research and support for teaching and learning in England, with other European countries and worldwide, developing teaching and learning in social care and social work, including a European joint Erasmus Mundus Master programme in Advanced Development in Social Work. Prior to working in academia, Janet gained substantial experience in practice, as a social work practitioner and manager.

Foreword

I am delighted to provide a foreword for this fifth edition of *Social Work and Human Development*. For more than a decade now, social work students have enjoyed and benefited from the ever-widening range of texts published by SAGE/Learning Matters in the *Transforming Social Work Practice* series, and this book stands as an exemplar of all that is best about this type of publication – being at the same time accessible yet never simplistic, relevant to practice yet never unacademic, contemporary yet offering the longer view of how our understanding of the human condition has been contested, constructed and variously understood.

All social work programmes have to meet the requirements of the Professional Capabilities Framework. Within the context of such change, qualifying programme providers have had to review the content of their courses to identify the core elements of the curriculum. One way of looking at these essential areas of knowledge is to think of them as 'threshold concepts' (Cousin, 2006). A threshold concept is, by definition, *transformative* (in that once understood, a threshold concept changes the way in which the student views the discipline) and also *troublesome* (in that knowledge can be troublesome when it is alien, incoherent and counterintuitive).

The attempts to apply the notion of threshold concepts to the discipline – and practice – of social work usually begin with *human growth and development*, including ideas about attachment, separation, loss and change – in short, human experience across the life course. Put another way, these threshold concepts contribute to the Aristotelian *episteme* of social work, meaning scientific or empirical knowledge based upon first principles.

Whenever another serious case review questions the competence of social workers (and other professionals) to 'do the job', the implicit allegation is that practitioners lack the capacity to benchmark the well-being or vulnerability of an individual child or young person against the 'normal' childhood experience of others (and to act as a consequence of these differences). Whilst the notion of a 'normal' childhood is necessarily difficult and contested, the idea that social workers need to understand growth and development, along with the concepts of milestones and transitions, is largely beyond doubt.

At the other end of the life course spectrum, social workers increasingly need to understand the later life course, along with the impacts of ageing, grief and loss, diminished capacity, dementia and long-term conditions.

This new and updated version of Janet Walker's text will once again enable the social work student to begin the transformative process of engaging with core threshold concepts relating to the life course and to human experience that inform effective practice across all social work service domains.

Nigel Horner
Head of School of Health and Social Work
University of Lincoln

Introduction to the fifth edition

This book is about human development across the life course, looking at how patterns of growth, stability and change impact on people's life course. It examines and applies theoretical concepts and ideas, policy and practice initiatives, and legislation and research that inform professional practice. A life course perspective is intended to support you to understand the whole of life from birth to death as a progressive and developmental path, with opportunities for growth and change across all facets. Critically it invites you to apply ideas about human development to practice situations through the use of exercises and case studies, and asks you to reflect on the implications for professional practice and your personal and professional values.

This fifth edition of *Social Work and Human Development* is written primarily for students studying for their degree in social work who are beginning to develop their knowledge, skills and understanding of the requirements for professional practice. Whilst it is primarily aimed at those who are at the beginning of their studies, it will be useful for subsequent years depending on how a programme is designed, what is being studied, and especially as students move into learning in practice.

This book should appeal to people who are considering a career in social work or social care, but are not yet studying for a degree in social work. It will also assist students undertaking a range of social, health and education-related courses in further and higher education. Additionally nurses, occupational therapists and other allied professionals will be able to gain insight into human development across the life course and the role and requirements for social work, particularly to support the collaborative context of practice. Newly qualified social workers undertaking their Assessed and Supported Year in Employment (ASYE) (DfE, 2013a) may find that this book can assist them with their programme of assessment against the Professional Capabilities Framework (PCF) (TCSW, 2012a), supporting their reflection on the skills, knowledge and capabilities and strengthening their professional competence. It will also support social workers in meeting the *Knowledge and Skills Statements for Social Workers in Adult Services* (DH, 2015) and *Knowledge and Skills Statements for Child and Family Social Work* (DfE, 2015). Experienced and qualified social workers, especially those contributing to practice learning, or carrying out their own professional development as a requirement of their continuing registration with the Health and Care Professionals Council (HCPC), aligned to the relevant levels of the PCF (TCSW, 2012a), will be able to use this book for consultation and revision. This will also support social workers and others contributing to practice learning – for example, to gain understanding of the expectations of the qualifying degree in social work and as a teaching aid – and those seeking to demonstrate that they meet the *Practice Educator Professional Standards for Social Work* (TCSW, 2012b).

In developing this edition I have sought to maintain the principal of human growth and development as encompassing the whole life course, and that an understanding of human growth and development is a central element of social work education and practice. The emphasis is on integrating contemporary practice with theoretical concepts of life course development, highlighting the importance of diversity. Further, through using a life course perspective the intention has been to seek to emphasise the way in which our lives are shaped by the social, political, cultural and economic environment. Each chapter has been revised to ensure it links to current developments and the context of practice and experiences. Diagrams, activities, case studies and research information have been reviewed and added to. Reading sections at the ends of chapters have been developed to include recent materials.

Requirements for social work education

Social work education in the United Kingdom ensures that students develop the knowledge, skills, values, ethics and processes for professional practice, with qualified social workers educated to at least honours degree level. Social work is a profession that is practised all over the world, operating in complex, demanding and uncertain human environments – with its international definition seeking to encapsulate the principles of social work:

> *The social work profession facilitates social change and development, social cohesion,*
> *and the empowerment and liberation of people. Principles of social justice, human rights,*
> *collective responsibility and respect for diversities are central to social work. Underpinned*
> *by theories of social work, social sciences, humanities and indigenous knowledges, social*
> *work engages people and structures to address life challenges and enhance wellbeing.*

> (Point in time definition endorsed by the International Federation
> of Social Workers (IFSW) and International Association of
> Schools of Social Work (IASSW), 2013)

This definition seeks to encapsulate social work's concern for the needs, interests and well-being of people, groups and communities to define together the outcomes they seek and the preferred methods to achieve this. Social workers will intervene in a wide variety of human situations; they are more likely to undertake their practice with people who are vulnerable and at risk, who are struggling in some way to participate fully in society. Whilst the practice of social work seeks to be supportive, empowering and enabling, there is also the need to ensure the protection and safeguarding of vulnerable and at risk individuals. The central focus is on the needs, interests and well-being of the child, adult or family. Part of this involves maintaining a view of the person in their environment, through an understanding of the physical, psychological and cultural dimensions of their well-being. This needs to take into account the importance and impact of their family, neighbourhood and community relationships, as well as the wider political and social environments, which may have contributed to the person's marginalisation.

Social workers need to be highly knowledgeable and skilled to work competently and effectively. They have to draw on a wide range of theoretical approaches with different people in different contexts, assessing needs, planning and intervening within their social context, constructively challenging individual, institutional and structural discrimination. They should work in partnership with people who use services and carers, seeking to empower and emancipate individuals. Effective collaboration with other professionals is an essential component of good social work practice. It is critical that social work students develop a rigorous grounding in, and understanding of, theories and models for social work. Such knowledge helps social workers to assess what they must do, when they must do it, how they must do it, and then to justify the decisions that have been made, all the while recognising that social work is a complex activity in which each situation is unique, with no absolute 'rights' or 'wrongs' of practice in place.

This book aims to contribute to the intentions of the Social Work Task Force (2009) and Social Work Reform Board (SWRB) (2012) to improve the quality and consistency of the social work degree, further supported by the Munro Review (2011), which emphasised the importance of investing in the next generation of social workers to improve the quality of practice. The book aims to meet the standards and expectations set out by professional regulatory bodies, specifically the Quality Assurance Agency for Higher Education (QAA), The (former) College of Social Work (TCSW) and the Health and Care Professionals Council (HCPC).

It will meet subject skills in the Quality Assurance Agency (2016) academic benchmarks for social work. The *Subject Benchmark Statement for Social Work* as an applied academic subject at honours level sets out expectations concerning the subject knowledge, understanding and skills of an honours graduate in social work, as well as the teaching, learning and assessment methods employed in their education and the standards expected of them at the point of graduation. This includes understanding the nature of social work and developing a knowledge and understanding of: social work services, service users and carers; the service delivery context; values and ethics; and social work theory and the nature of social work practice. In addition social work graduates should acquire and integrate in problem solving, communication, working with others, personal and professional development, and technological and numerical skills. One of the main themes of the Subject Benchmarks is *'the centrality of the development of knowledge and skills for social work in relation to assessment and intervention, at all stages of the life course'* (QAA, 2016, p. 4).

The HCPC, as part of its provision, has developed standards of proficiency for social work in England. Its *Standards of Proficiency* (HCPC, 2017) are the threshold standards for safe and effective practice within the profession, setting out what a social worker in England must know, understand and be able to do following the completion of their social work degree. Alongside the standards of proficiency, the HCPC also sets separate standards for conduct, performance and ethics and for continuing professional development. Social workers in England must meet the HCPC's standards to stay on the Register. The HCPC uses these standards to decide whether or not a social worker is fit to practise.

The book will meet the PCF for Social Work (TCSW, 2012b); the Appendix provides an overview of the Framework. The PCF provides a comprehensive framework of what should be expected of students at every stage of their education and training from entry to final qualification, and for continuing professional development following qualification. It aims to provide a holistic approach to identifying and assessing learning needs and outcomes, and to enable students to understand how they can meet and demonstrate these outcomes. The PFC has nine domains (or areas) within it. For each of these there is a main statement and an elaboration. Then at each level within the PCF, detailed capabilities have been developed explaining how social workers should expect to evidence that area in practice. The nine capabilities should be seen as interdependent, not separate. The first four levels relate to student social workers. These represent the 'level' of capability a social work student should be demonstrating at different points in their social work training:

1. *Professionalism* – Identify and behave as a professional social worker, committed to professional development.

2. *Values and ethics* – Apply social work ethical principles and values to guide professional practice.

3. *Diversity* – Recognise diversity and apply anti-discriminatory and anti-oppressive principles in practice.

4. *Rights, justice and economic well-being* – Advance human rights and promote social justice and economic well-being.

5. *Knowledge* – Apply knowledge of social sciences, law and social work practice theory.

6. *Critical reflection and analysis* – Apply critical reflection and analysis to inform and provide a rationale for professional decision-making.

7. *Intervention and skills* – Use judgement and authority to intervene with individuals, families and communities to promote independence, provide support and prevent harm, neglect and abuse.

8. *Contexts and organisations* – Engage with, inform and adapt to changing contexts that shape practice. Operate effectively within own organisational frameworks and contribute to the development of services and organisations. Operate effectively within multi-agency and interprofessional settings.

9. *Professional leadership* – Take responsibility for the professional learning and development of others through supervision, mentoring, assessing, research, teaching, leadership and management.

By the completion of qualifying programmes, newly qualified social workers should have demonstrated the knowledge, skills and values to work with a range of user groups, the ability to undertake a range of tasks at a foundation level and the capacity to work with more complex situations; they should be able to work more autonomously, whilst recognising that the final decision will still rest with their supervisor; they will seek appropriate support and supervision.

The former College of Social Work, in collaboration with social work educators, has developed curriculum guides for social work. This book draws on these guides, in particular the curriculum guide for 'Human growth and development' (Boylan and Ray, 2012).

In essence, this book will focus on developing your knowledge and understanding of human development throughout the life course and its importance and relevance to social work practice. An action-orientated approach helps to facilitate an evaluation, review and reflection of your learning and practice. Case studies, which focus on different aspects of the human life course, will be used throughout to enhance this process and illustrate key learning points. Additionally, theory and research summaries are provided to underpin this developing knowledge with theories, models and evidence.

Book structure

Understanding the way in which individuals develop before birth, as babies, children and adolescents through to young, middle and older adulthood towards death, is fundamental to social work practice. Social workers work with people across the life course. Having an understanding of such knowledge supports them in assessing and planning to meet individual needs. It allows them to be sensitive and appropriate in their communication with people and in the services they offer and provide. It is important that social workers have an understanding of human development to work effectively with other disciplines and demonstrate a professional literacy commensurate with their status. This book will demonstrate how theories of human life course development inform social work practice in key areas.

Throughout it you will examine how an understanding of the theories of human life course development is necessary to establish effective partnerships with people who use social work services, with other professionals, and when using the law to protect and enhance service-users' rights. The importance of taking a biographical approach, listening to the narrative stories of individuals and their constructions of their own lives, is highlighted. This is underpinned by recognising the importance of diversity and difference. Links will be made to the skills needed at various stages of development, including communication and working with other professionals. Additionally, other key elements of the prescribed curriculum, such as the knowledge of child development and legal intervention to protect, will be incorporated. Throughout the chapters you will be encouraged to examine your own views and perspectives and to interrogate the origins of these.

The book takes a case-study approach throughout, with case studies being used to illustrate and draw out key points, to aid and reinforce learning. You will also be provided with summaries of relevant contemporary research, suggestions for further reading and current government guidance and policy documents, all of which will give evidence for and support best practice. The emphasis in this book concerns your achieving the requirements of the curriculum and developing knowledge that will assist you in meeting the Professional Capability Standards (TCSW, 2012a) for social work.

The seven main chapters cover human development through the life course. In the first chapter you will be introduced to the reasons why knowledge and understanding of human development throughout the life course are important to social work practice. The chapter starts by outlining the importance of recognising the impact that personal values and your own life events can have upon practice. You will also consider the concept of life events and transitions. The chapter makes the links between practice and inquiries into social and health care that have come into the public domain. By introducing you to a range of theoretical approaches to human development and the significance of knowledge from other disciplines, it creates the links to the specific practice-focused chapters that follow.

Chapter 2 develops the introduction to theoretical models for understanding development across the life course. This chapter will outline the theoretical approaches commonly used by social workers and other professionals when working with people in a variety of settings, across the whole life course. The connections, similarities and differences between the theories are examined and you will compare and contrast models and apply these to practice situations. The chapter will suggest that no single theory alone can explain the complexity of human life course development. Having introduced a range of perspectives and developmental theories in this chapter, those that follow will focus on specific phases in the human life course. These practice-focused chapters will build on this introduction to theories, examining particular approaches and their usefulness to social work practice with individuals at certain age points along the developmental spectrum of their lives.

Chapters 3 and 4 focus on human development and social work practice with children. They are intended to support you in developing your understanding and ability to critique theories that explain human development taking a cognitive approach, and theories taking a biological and physical perspective. In particular they explore physical, social and emotional development, including developing themes in relation to the critical issues of attachment, vulnerability and resilience. This will introduce issues in relation to child protection and related issues of legal intervention. The chapters examine the role of the family and adults, especially parents and carers, in supporting the development of children. They demonstrate how an understanding of development needs to be placed in the context of patterns of interactions – the ecological approach.

In Chapter 3 you will explore life course development knowledge in social work practice with infants, young children and their families. This chapter will set out knowledge in respect of early child development. You will examine pre-natal, peri-natal and neo-natal periods of life development and consider the relative importance of hereditary factors and environmental factors in determining an individual's development. This chapter will specifically develop your understanding and ability to critique theories that explain human development taking a cognitive approach, and theories taking a biological or physical perspective.

Chapter 4 looks at using life course development knowledge in social work practice with older children and their families. The chapter will specifically develop your understanding and ability to critique theories that explain human development taking a systemic approach.

In Chapter 5 you will look at life course development knowledge in social work practice in respect of young people in their teenage or adolescent years. The chapter will explore issues related to the transition to adulthood and the particular significance that this may have for young people with disabilities. You will develop your understanding and ability to critique theories that explain human development taking a behavioural and social learning approach.

In Chapter 6 life course development knowledge in social work practice with people in early and middle adulthood is examined. You will focus on developing your understanding of human life course development and the significance of transitions in adult life. Drawing on situations related to adults experiencing physical disability, adults with learning difficulties and adults who have caring responsibilities, the chapter will consider how transitions present opportunities for growth and development or, conversely, potential crisis points. This chapter will specifically develop your understanding and ability to critique theories that explain life course development in stages or phases. This chapter and Chapter 7 have been developed to enable you to frame your learning in the context of current social work practice with adults and older people. Most significantly, you will read about the focus of policy and practice in services for adults and how knowledge of human life course development supports your practice within this policy context.

Chapter 7 examines ways in which an understanding of the theories of human development is necessary for effective social work practice with older people and their families. It considers older age in terms of opportunities for growth and development and addresses issues related to ageing, older age and how it is constructed in our society. An exploration of the significance of transitions in later life will enable you to consider effective ageing and end-of-life issues. This chapter will further develop your understanding and ability to critique theories that explain life course development in stages or phases.

Chapter 8 offers concluding remarks and signposts. At this stage you will be invited to review the learning outcomes set at the outset and encouraged to review your progress by charting and monitoring your learning, taking developmental needs and reflections forward to other books within the series.

Learning features

This book is interactive. You are encouraged to work through the book as an active participant, taking responsibility for your learning, in order to increase your knowledge, understanding and ability to apply this learning to practice. You will be expected to reflect creatively on how your immediate learning needs can be met in the area of understanding human development and how your professional learning can be developed in your future career.

Case studies throughout the book will help you examine theories and models for social work practice. Activities have been devised that require you to reflect on experiences, situations and events and will help you review and summarise the learning undertaken. In this way your knowledge will become deeply embedded as part of your development. When you come to practise learning in an agency, the work and reflection undertaken here will help you improve and hone your skills and knowledge.

This book will introduce knowledge and learning activities for you as a student social worker to demonstrate how theories of human life course development inform social work practice in key areas.

Professional development and reflective practice

This book places great emphasis on developing skills of reflection and analysis about, in and on practice. Reflective practice is a critical skill for social work practice that will allow you to constantly examine and improve your practice skills in the ever-changing complexity of practice situations. Critical reflection is an approach to analysing practice and experiences to identify the conscious and unconscious assumptions embedded in personal and professional practice.

Some definitions

We reflect in order to learn or we learn as a result of reflecting. (Moon, 2004, p. 186)

The goal of reflective learning is a transformation of perspective (Mezirow, 1991), a significant shift in perspective that allows professionals not only to critically review their practice, but which also helps them to work in a more responsive, creative, and ultimately more effective manner. (Redmond, 2004, p. 1)

Reflective practice involves the ability to be aware of the 'theory' or assumptions involved in professional practice, in order to close the gap between what is espoused and what is enacted, in an effort to improve both. (Schön, 1991)

For Schön (1983/1987) professional knowledge involves both rules ('technical rationality') and professional action ('reflection in action'). Reflective practice therefore involves the ability to be aware of the 'theory' or assumptions involved in professional practice in order to close the gap between what is espoused and what is enacted, in an effort to improve both. A reflective approach encompasses a recognition of the intuitive, the artistic and the creative in professional practice (Fook, 1996). Reflection is concerned with consciously looking at and thinking about our experiences, actions, feelings and responses, and then interpreting or analysing these in order to learn from them (Boud *et al.*, 1994). Critical reflection therefore uses a reflective process of uncovering and unsettling hidden or implicit (taken-for-granted) assumptions, for example how power is created or maintained, how social justice is promoted and so on.

This book will assist you in developing a questioning approach that looks in a critical way at your thoughts, experiences and practice, as well as key theories and models that explain human development and the life course. As a result of these deliberations, the book seeks to heighten your skills in taking a critical approach and reflecting on your work within the context of contemporary professional practice. Reflection is central to good social work practice, but only if action and further development result from these reflections.

Reflection about, in and on your practice is not only important during your education to become a social worker, it is also considered to be central to social work throughout your career (for example in supporting you in critical reflection and challenge through professional supervision; supporting you to deal with ethical dilemmas; and reflecting on professional judgement of complex issues in relation to safeguarding and working with others). Further, the PCF expects integration of critical reflection across all its domains, and the ability to apply critical reflective skills is a key aspect of social work practice and development. Reflective practice is seen as a key activity to support you with your continuing professional development, therefore maintaining your registration with the HCPC (HCPC, 2012b).

As you undertake reading and work on the chapters in this book, you are invited to reflect on your learning and the implications for your practice. You could address the following questions as you complete each chapter.

Reflection point

- What do I know, or can I do now, that I did not know or could not do before I did this section of studying?
- Is there anything I do not understand or want to explore further?
- What else do I need to know to extend my professional development and learning in this area?

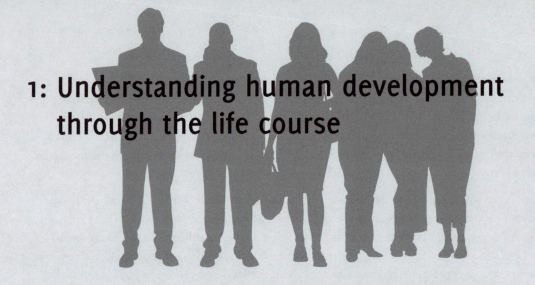

1: Understanding human development through the life course

Achieving a social work degree

This chapter will help you begin to meet the following capabilities, to the appropriate level, from the Professional Capabilities Framework:

- **Knowledge**
  - o Apply knowledge of social sciences, law and social work practice theory.
- **Critical reflection and analysis**
  - o Apply critical reflection and analysis to inform and provide a rationale for professional decision making.
- **Professionalism**
  - o Identify and behave as a professional social worker, committed to professional development.
- **Rights, justice and economic well-being**
  - o Advance human rights and promote social justice and economic well-being.
- **Professional leadership**
  - o Take responsibility for the professional learning and development of others through supervision, mentoring, assessing, research, teaching, leadership and management.

It will also introduce you to the following academic standards as set out in the social work subject benchmark statement:

3.1.4 Social work theory.
3.1.5 The nature of social work practice.

Introduction

In this first chapter, some of the key terms and perspectives that the book will develop in respect of life course development and social work practice are set out. The importance of human growth and development is outlined, in particular how it relates to social work practice. We shall be considering your own life course, how it has developed and how an understanding of this can help you in your social work practice. This chapter will cover why it is important to recognise your personal values and be aware of the impact that these may have on your practice. The critical importance of reflective practice will form an element of this discussion. The chapter will also look at some of the broad debates on human development as an introduction to the next chapter, which will examine in more detail different theoretical perspectives on how human beings become the people they are. It will show how the contribution of other professionals can enhance developmental knowledge, improving the social work response and thereby improving practice. In order to demonstrate the importance of knowledge and skills in human development for social work, this chapter will make the links between practice and public inquiries into health and social care practice in relation to specific cases.

Social work practice involves interactions with and between people, which are influenced by each person's life course and their experience and perceptions about their own life. Social workers need to understand people and how they develop, and place people's life situations in the context of the expectations of normal life course development. This will enable the worker to appreciate that a person's experience, their growth, development and life experiences have a direct impact on who they are and how they see their world.

The social work profession is based on the supposition that people can be helped and supported to change and grow as a result of their experiences. Service users consistently identify the importance of the knowledge, approach, relationships and the personal qualities of social workers (Beresford, 2007; Seden and Ross, 2007; Beresford et al., 2008; Manthorpe and Martineau, 2008; Doel, 2010; Oliver, 2010; Beresford et al., 2011; Winter, 2011). Working with service users involves comprehensively looking at the past, present and future of people's lives (Katz et al., 2012). The life course is conceptualised as a series of age-linked transitions that are embedded in social institutions – for example family, schools, work, church, government – and history, as conditions that influence the life course across time and place (Bengston et al., 2012). Therefore, in order for you to be sensitive and appropriate in your communications with people and in the services you offer and provide, you need to appreciate and understand their life course and what makes them who they are. Understanding how people grow and develop is central to the role and tasks of a professional social worker.

Social work is an activity that requires an ability to thrive and embrace dilemmas, conflicts, uncertainty and not knowing; practice is central to shaping the identity of social work:

> *Social work derives from the society of which it is part. The preoccupation of social work with people and their social circumstances creates its main occupational risk – a lack of specificity, an inherent ambiguity.*

(Butrym, 1976, p. ix)

In acknowledging the constantly changing context of social work organisations and social work practice, Cree and Davis stress that:

> *the necessary qualities of social workers do not change: their ability to listen to people, to advocate on behalf of others and see them in the context of their whole lives. These are qualities that stand out in social work.*

(2007, p. 12)

Life course development and social work practice

Development goes on throughout life. Because human beings are complex, the study of life course development is inter-disciplinary, drawing on many disciplines. These include biology, genetics, history, psychology, sociology, anthropology, philosophy, medicine and education.

As you learn about human development through this book and your further reading, you will come across a number of terms that may appear to describe similar concepts. In this section you will be introduced to some of the key words that are commonly related to this topic. The interpretation of those words and how they are used in this book will be explained.

Throughout the book a life course perspective is taken. This will be expanded upon in the next chapter when you consider theoretical approaches to the study of human development. Taking a life course perspective means adopting an approach that considers the whole of a person's life as offering opportunities for growth, development and change. You will notice that the words 'life course' are used; however, in other texts you will find the words 'life span' and 'life cycle' applied in similar contexts. Léonie Sugarman (2001) writes from a psychological perspective and adopts the term 'life-span development' as she discusses 'life-span developmental psychology'. Paul Baltes (1987), also a developmental psychologist, describes the concept of a 'life-span perspective'. You will read more about his ideas in Chapter 2. In contrast Erik Erikson (1997), another theorist whose approach is explored in the following chapters, writes about the 'life cycle' from a psychosocial approach. The term 'psychosocial' describes an approach that considers both the individual psychology and the social context of people's lives on their individual development. The psychosocial perspective enables social workers to consider the influences of the relationship between the internal world of the service user and the social environment in which they live (Howe, 2009; Oko 2011). Erikson describes the concept of 'life cycle' as implying *'some kind of self-completion'* (1997, p. 9). The use of the word 'cycle' brings the notion of time and progression to life development, but it can be criticised for implying a circular process whereby in the later years of life there is a return to the dependency of childhood. Development is a lifelong concept and people's life course is rarely linear in its progression; further, our lives are shaped by political, economic, social, cultural and economic factors. Thus from psychosocial and sociological perspectives, the term 'life course' has become favoured and is the term that we shall adopt for the remainder of this book.

In order to develop your understanding of social work and human development the chapters that follow will introduce you to a range of theories, research and ideas. However, the underpinning philosophy of a life course perspective is emphasised, and its application to social work practice is developed through an understanding of the narrative approach. This narrative approach – or biographical approach as it is sometimes called – focuses on the individual's experiences through their own first-hand account of their life. Narrative social work can be defined as a 'conversation' between theory and practice, which can then lead to development in both social workers and service users (Roscoe *et al.*, 2010). Within this book you will develop your knowledge and ideas by studying human life course development in the context of individuality and difference. You will learn about development in respect of people of differences in age, gender, levels of ability, race, ethnic and cultural background. However, where it has not been possible to cover each of these topics in detail, the significance of the narrative approach coupled with a whole of life course perspective is that stereotypical assumptions are challenged and diversity is valued. The narrative approach is explained further in Chapter 2.

Summary of definitions and key concepts

Development A complex, continuous and progressive series of changes that occur as a result of maturation and experience.

Life course The progression and path an individual takes from conception to death.

Life course perspective A viewpoint that considers the whole of a life (from conception to death) as offering opportunities for growth, development and change.

Life cycle An alternative term used to describe the life course; this is now considered to be an out-of-date term.

Life span An alternative term used to describe the life course, often used in developmental psychology.

Narrative or biographical approach A way of working with individuals that focuses on the importance of their own first-hand account of their life, their experiences and the meanings they attach to them. Narrative social work can be viewed as a 'conversation' between theory and practice.

The ideas explained above will be considered in more detail as you progress through this book. In the next section you will consider your own life course, and what this has meant to you from your personal perspective, much as you would take a narrative approach with a service user.

Understanding your own life experiences

To understand the impact of human growth and development on social work practice we will begin by asking you to look at your own life course development. Examining your own life, and the experiences that have influenced it, is an important stage in learning the significance of life course development. By understanding and making sense of your own life experience, you will be able to appreciate the importance of key events in shaping you as a person. We will begin by exploring that development.

Activity 1.1

Think about your own life, your childhood and the time you were growing up. By following the activities below, you will represent your life in a diagram:

- Draw a line to represent the 'ups' and 'downs' of your life so far.
- Now place those life events against the peaks and troughs of your line.
- Consider the line you have drawn, and identify for each of these points the main influencing factors – in other words what made the change happen, and were you able to make choices?

When you have completed this, consider your thoughts and feelings at these times (for example, 'happy', 'sad', 'excited', 'uncertain').

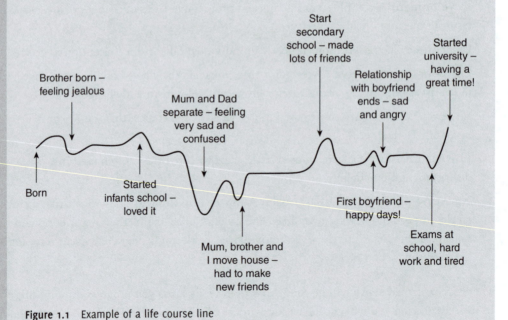

Figure 1.1 Example of a life course line

Comment

Every person completing this activity will have drawn a different diagram. However, if you have the opportunity to compare the life course line that you have drawn with another person, perhaps another student, you are likely to find a number of common themes. Figure 1.1 is an example that we have completed.

You will find the concept of life road maps developed in Chapter 2 of *Social Work Practice* (Parker and Bradley, 2014).

You may recognise many similarities that may be linked to events that have occurred at certain ages – for example, we are all dependent upon others for the first few years of our lives, and there may be other similar milestones in our lives, such as starting school, moving to secondary school, or biological developments such as puberty and so on. There will also be differences that may be linked to your history, age, class, gender, culture, disability and/or ethnicity – such as living in the same town all your life or moving around; the influence of family life events such as marriage, children or divorce; the impact of your race and culture on your upbringing and so on. Thinking about your own life, and making sense of the experiences you have had, will be invaluable in gaining some insight into the impact of your life course on your development and growth as a person.

You may feel that you have had a fairly uneventful life, or conversely that a lot has happened in your life. However, we have all experienced changes and obstacles. What you have been doing in this activity is identifying the personal and social impact of life events. These can also be called 'periods of transition', which are phases or stages within a person's life course when people move through life events.

All people will experience transitions in their lives. An example of this might be the impact that arises from choosing to go to university.

Activity 1.2

Think about the impact of making the decision to study at university. What influenced your decision? What impact has this had on your life and life style? What impact do you hope that gaining a qualification will have for your future life course?

Comment

Some of the issues you might have raised may be related to your family, friends, finance, where you live and so on. What will be apparent here is that this decision can be described as a major life decision as it will have been influenced by your past life experience, will have impacted on your immediate experience, and will significantly influence and impact on your future life experiences.

Understanding the impact of transitions within a person's life course is important for social work practice in order to help us understand other people's lives. Although people may experience the same life event, their response to the transition and the decisions they make will be different. People will have different perceptions of what is happening to them as they move through a transition in their lives, and thus their response and the learning they gain from it will be different. For example, you may have enjoyed school, tolerated it or hated it. This could be due to your academic ability, the influence of your peers or the attitude and response of a particular teacher. People's response to these transitions may be different – for example, a response to 'hating' a particular teacher may have been that you took no part in the learning or it may have been to work hard to 'show them' what you could do. Biological and historical timings have consequences for our behaviours, outcomes and well-being. Thinking of life development in stages or points of crisis, which we all attempt to move through successfully, can assist us in understanding the challenges faced by people at various points in their lives.

You may be aware of people who have complex life issues but appear to cope with them, and other people who seem to be unable to cope with any issues within their lives. As social workers we need to recognise the opportunities to work with people through transition as an opportunity to grow. We also need to try to enable people to use these events to trigger change and move on and develop. People can have crises and still have happy and fulfilling lives. Additionally, there is the opportunity to support people through, for example: providing services; linking them with other people in similar positions for sharing and support; working with communities to promote change.

Case study 1.1 is an example of a major life transition.

Case study 1.1

Following a violent outburst from her children's father, resulting in her receiving broken ribs and a broken arm, Christine has moved into her mother's home with her children, Ashley (2 years) and Chloe (3 months). Ashley is 'clingy' and demanding. Christine finds it difficult to 'bond' with Chloe; she is fretful and difficult to feed. She is lonely and depressed, missing her friends and home. Christine's mother is very concerned about her daughter, and the children and the consequences for their future. Recently the children's father has been texting her, remonstrating with her to come home, stating that this was a one-off incident caused by stress at work, and would never happen again. He states that he wants to see the children. Christine does not want to return but feels too depressed and 'exhausted' to make any decisions.

Activity 1.3

Think about (reflect on) Case Study 1.1:

- Write down the thoughts and emotions that you have experienced in considering this case.
- How might the individuals involved in this case be feeling?
- Which issues seem to be the significant ones? As a social worker for this case what might you be trying to achieve? What could be the consequences of this for Christine/her children/the children's father/Christine's mother/yourself?
- What do you need to do in order to make things better/improve the situation/resolve the situation/feel better/get on better?
- What broader issues need to be considered if any action is to be successful? What might be the consequences of this action?

Comment

In the above activity you are being invited to reflect on the case which may have raised a whole range of different emotions: concern, shock, anger, helplessness, fear. You may have considered 'practical' aspects of help (e.g. access to legal advice) as well as 'emotional support' issues (e.g. support for Christine in coming to terms with her previous, current and future situation; issues in relation to the psychological, social and emotional welfare of the children). You could have found this a difficult activity, and practically you may be feeling that you need further information, including evidence from research and supervision, and advice from experienced key professionals, to address some of these questions.

Life course development demonstrates some key principles (Bengston *et al.*, 2012). Our lives are embedded in relationships with others and influenced by them. There is an interconnectedness of lives, particularly across the generations; for example, the factors that influenced our grandparents' choices may have an influence on where you live, the work your family is involved in, the language you speak. Historical and social events can create opportunities and constraints that can impact on choices and behaviours, changing the direction of lives.

People make choices within the opportunities and constraints of their own lives – for example, the family, community and cultural aspects that influence and impact on our lives. As social workers we do need to recognise and promote opportunities to support people as active agents in their own lives. For example, as social workers we should respect, uphold, and defend each person's physical, psychological, emotional and spiritual integrity and well-being; respect, promote and support

(Continued)

(Continued)

people's dignity and choice (as far as this does not threaten the rights, safety and legitimate interests of others); and empower people to be involved in decisions affecting their lives (British Association of Social Work (BASW), 2012). Human development, relationships and events have consequences throughout our lives, for example as their being cumulative in providing advantages and disadvantages. Structural inequalities can have a profound impact on people's lives. For example, the Joseph Rowntree Foundation report 'Monitoring poverty and social exclusion 2016' (Tinson *et al.*, 2016) identifies the alarming concentration between poverty and disability, the risks of poverty for the growing numbers of people living in the private rented sector, and the continuing rise in poverty for those who work. The Marmot Report, commissioned by the Secretary of State for Health, examines the most effective evidence base for reducing health inequalities in England. Marmot identifies that *'inequalities in health arise because of inequalities in society – in the condition in which people are born, grow, live, work and age'* (2010, p. 16).

An important aspect of your practice as a social work student and a social worker is that of 'reflective practice' (Schön, 1983/1987). The notion of reflection is evident in many different disciplines (for example, for education or health professionals). Reflective practice means fundamentally thinking about (reflecting on) your approach before, during and after any intervention. It seems to include such complex activities as 'learning from experiences', 'thinking about', 'turning back on self', and 'deconstructing'. Schön (ibid.) describes technical rationality (rules) and professional artistry (reflection in action), and for him very often the 'theory' or rules espoused by practitioners are quite different from the 'theory' or assumptions embedded in the actual practices of professionals. Reflective practice therefore involves an ability to be aware of the 'theory' or assumptions involved in professional practice in order to close the gap between what is espoused and what is enacted in an effort to improve both. Fook (2002) suggests that reflective practice involves learning from experience by examining fundamental assumptions and reintegrating experiences (as well as reformulating meaning and principles for living), resulting in new guidelines for action.

Case study 1.1 continued

Following a visit by the Health Visitor to support Christine and monitor the children, Christine allowed her to contact the local Family Support Team. The social worker visited and provided support and advice. They have planned together ways in which Christine and her children can move forward with their lives: this has included opportunities to talk about her feelings and

⟶

concerns; seeking legal advice in relation to the children's welfare; identifying a playgroup for Ashley; and help with seeking her own accommodation. In addition the social worker has arranged for Christine to attend a support group at the Women's Centre, providing her with an opportunity to share her experiences with people in a similar position, to learn ways to cope and to develop strategies for the future.

As social workers we also need to recognise the impact of our own role and decisions as they impact on people's lives and major life transitions. Potentially, professional intervention itself can have an impact on a person's life development (for example, where someone who experiences mental ill health is made the subject of a compulsory admission to hospital under the mental health legislation). Whilst this may be in the best interest of their safety and the safety of others, the potential impact on that individual's life and life course could be enormous. Equally, a lack of social work intervention or poor practice, when working with young people moving from foster or residential care to independence, can impede their progress through this important transition period. Therefore the potential for social work interventions to interrupt and damage individual life courses is considerable.

Reflective practice is concerned with thinking about (reflecting on) the best approach before, during and after any intervention. Thus, as a social worker, you recapture the experience, think about your practice in the situation, and then evaluate it. This requires you to be aware of the knowledge, experience and skills that inform your actions and decisions and how you apply them to your practice. Personal and professional values will underpin every aspect of this practice.

The impact of values on understanding human development

As we have seen so far, our own life experiences help us understand a great deal about the experience, shape and course of our lives. This experience has helped to shape the person that we each become and our responses and choices. Our beliefs and values are deep-rooted and impact on the way we live our lives. It is critical that we recognise and acknowledge that impact on our professional practice as it could shape our attitudes and responses to others.

Being aware of the impact of people's life experiences on their values, beliefs and their own identity can also help us make sense of other people's lives and life courses (for example, through understanding and sharing experiences with others, such as the experience of going to school, being a teenager, studying at university and so on). However, we should not make assumptions that our experiences are the same as everyone else's. Everyone's experience is unique and his or her interpretation of it will be different. Whilst our own experiences are important, this is not sufficient in itself as a criterion on which to base our understanding of others. We cannot assume that we know everything on the basis of those experiences. At a personal level, for example, it may be hard to understand how an adult can sexually abuse a child or how one person can be violent towards another. It is important that we recognise how our own life experiences impact on our understanding of other people's situations and shape our personal values, beliefs and assumptions of others.

To give you an example of how a particular value and belief, which has developed through a person's life course experiences, may impact upon their thoughts and practices as a social worker or student, we shall briefly consider religion. Gilligan and Furness (2006) reported on research undertaken with social work students and practitioners to explore the role of religion and spirituality in social work practice. The following research summary utilises short extracts taken from their research findings.

Research summary

As humans, we internalise many of our early beliefs. Our actions and behaviour tend to be shaped by our experiences and to some extent by the dominant religious legacies that have become enmeshed with and translated into the cultural traditions, rituals and customs of communities.

(Gilligan and Furness, 2006, p. 625)

A (further) comparison of responses from students to specific interventions suggests a fairly consistent pattern between particular groups; 64 per cent of the Muslim students considered 'The use of religious or spiritual language or concepts' as potentially appropriate, in contrast to only 25 per cent of Christian students and 36 per cent of those holding no current beliefs. Also, a higher number of Muslim students considered 'Recommending participation in a religious or spiritual program' and 'Participation in a client's rituals as an intervention' as potentially appropriate. This difference seems likely to result from the fact that religious beliefs and customs are central to the lives of Muslims and that they are, as a result, more likely to recognise the potential importance of religion and spirituality in the lives of others. However, while most of the Christian students saw the intervention 'Helping clients develop ritual as an intervention (e.g. visiting graves of relatives, house blessings, etc.)' as potentially appropriate, most Muslim students did not, possibly because of the essentially euro-centric nature of the examples offered.

(ibid., pp. 631–632)

In summarising the findings of their research into the role of religion and spirituality in social work practice Gilligan and Furness state that:

> *there is a clear need for all social work practitioners and educators to give greater priority to exploring the potential significance of religious and spiritual beliefs in their training, in their professional practice and in the lives and perspectives of service users and colleagues. Social workers need to be able to respond appropriately to the needs of all service users, including those for whom religious and spiritual beliefs are crucial. 'Culturally competent' practice depends, amongst other things, on an understanding and appreciation of the impact of faith and belief.*
>
> (ibid., p. 617)

In a later research study with social work students undertaken by Mulder (2015), he highlights that a lack of knowledge can generate religious discrimination, potentially restricting the quality of service delivery. Participants also noted the need for cultural competence in working with populations of diverse spiritual and religious traditions and practices.

The significance of taking account of and valuing difference in people's life courses, cultures, own beliefs and experiences was highlighted through the report into the death of Victoria Climbié.

Case study 1.2

Victoria Climbié died on 25 February 2000, aged 8 years and 3 months. Her aunt and partner were subsequently convicted of her murder and are serving sentences of life imprisonment. A number of professionals had contact with Victoria, her aunt and partner, including Social Services. On 20 April 2001, Lord Laming was appointed by two secretaries of state to conduct three statutory inquiries. Together they would become known as the Victoria Climbié Inquiry (Laming, 2003). This report has raised significant practice issues and has also been the conduit for a widespread reform of services for children and families (see *Every Child Matters: Change for Children* (DfES, 2004)). Evidence from the Victoria Climbié Inquiry indicated that a lack of understanding of cultural difference, by a range of different professionals, contributed to the death of this child (Laming, 2003, cited in Gilligan and Furness, 2006, p. 634).

Cultural competency is a balance between ethnocentrism and cultural relativism (Korbin, 2007). 'Ethnocentrism' is the belief that your own cultural beliefs and practices are preferable and superior to all others. The danger here is that there is an assumption of a single standard for practice and that it imposes the beliefs or behaviours of the dominant culture on all the population. We may therefore misidentify cultural practice as poor practice. Cultural relativism is the belief that every culture must be viewed as equal to all others and that culturally sanctioned behaviours cannot be judged by the standards of another culture. We therefore may assume that all behaviours and beliefs are culturally relevant.

Cultural competence in life course development allows us to keep a focus on the needs of the service users. We need to be able to distinguish between a healthy child or adult and one whose development is being impaired because of their circumstances (for example, because of abuse or neglect). Further, whilst we need to be sensitive to, acknowledge, respect and take account of culture and diversity, we also need to see past this to identify any actual or potential impairment to health and development. In complex circumstances, such as were identified in the circumstances that led to the death of Victoria Climbié, this can be challenging; however, being culturally sensitive and competent as a professional social worker is essential.

Cultural competency evolves over time through the process of attaining cultural knowledge, and becoming aware of when cultural mores, values, beliefs and practices are being demonstrated; sensitivity to these behaviours is consciously occurring, and one purposely utilises culturally-based techniques in practice with service users and in service delivery. Cultural competence involves such things as developing relevant knowledge and skill; being sensitive, open-minded and respectful; seeking appropriate advice and support; and being aware of the impact of oppression, racism and racial abuse on others and how to challenge this.

Case Study 1.3 highlights the case of Steven Hoskin, who was murdered by people who targeted him because of his learning disability.

Case study 1.3

In July 2006, Steven Hoskin was found dead at the bottom of a 100-foot railway viaduct in St Austell, Cornwall. On the night of his death, he had been tortured by five people for hours before his death, suffering various injuries inflicted upon him. His murder was a culmination of an ongoing series of abuses occurring over a period of months. Steven was a 38-year-old man with learning disabilities and numerous agencies and organisations came into contact with him throughout his lifetime. He had serious mental health issues and was in contact with a number of agencies as a result. He was also regarded by several agencies not as a vulnerable adult but as a perpetrator of anti-social behaviour and worse. He had been charged and convicted of assault, and was known to be verbally abusive when drunk. There were complaints from neighbours about noise emanating from his bedsit. He was experienced as being at the heart of many and repeated social and health problems where he lived (Flynn [for Cornwall Adult Protection Committee], 2007).

Case Study 1.3 provides us with an opportunity to reflect on the importance of safeguarding vulnerable adults. Everyone has the right to live as independently as possible, and being able to take risks is part of everyday living. Individuals are an active force in constructing and shaping their own life courses through the choices and action taken; this can be referred to as 'human agency'. But social workers have a significant role in ensuring that safeguarding processes are in place to prevent vulnerable individuals coming to harm. Grant (2012) reminds us that taking a life course perspective with vulnerable adults incorporates the key dimension of 'temporality' (timing in life course) into practitioner thinking, in which we need to take account of individual biographies in understanding their present experiences, as well as consideration of the past and its potential impact on the future. This means it is important to examine the factors that shape the evolving experience across the life course. As such we need to develop a capacity for *anticipatory thinking and intervention* (Grant, 2012, p. 230) when safeguarding individuals.

The research, case studies and examples shown in this chapter provide powerful lessons for us to reflect upon. Within our practice we need to ensure that we balance our personal beliefs and values about how we should live our lives – such as those based on religion and culture – with those of the service users and carers we work with. Further, we need to recognise how life course considerations may support an understanding of the context in which abuse takes place, the impact of time (past, present and future) on the life course, and the safeguarding practice that might then need to follow.

Ways of explaining human life course development

So far in this chapter you have considered how your own life course experiences may have influenced your growth and development; you have also explored the significance of personal beliefs and values in understanding the individual and the critical importance of developing skills in reflective practice.

Case study 1.4

Kayleigh is 14 years of age, living on a large inner city estate which has a reputation for anti-social behaviour from young people, with use of alcohol and other drugs. Kayleigh helps her mum as much as she can in caring for the home and looking after her younger brothers and sister. Kayleigh's teachers describe her as very able and, up until recently, she has been progressing well in her studies. Over the last few months her school attendance has

$\longrightarrow$

become sporadic; she complains about being bored and has begun to stay out late into the night. Sonia, her mother, is a regular user of alcohol and other drugs, supporting her habit by dealing in soft drugs. Sonia's mother died five years ago of causes linked to her alcohol dependency. Kayleigh's father, John, has been in and out of prison for most of Kayleigh's life, and is currently serving an eight-year jail sentence for drug offences. John's mother supports Kayleigh and her mother as much as she can, but she has poor physical health. John's stepfather has a history of violence towards his mother and now lives in another part of the country with a new family.

Activity 1.4

Think about the range of responses that Kayleigh's situation raises from you and answer the following questions:

- How do you feel about Kayleigh and her situation?
- What might Kayleigh feel about her life?
- What might Kayleigh's family feel about her?
- How might the public/society feel about Kayleigh/young people and alcohol and other drug use?

Comment

While you will have had to make judgements based on very limited information, it almost certainly will have raised a range of different views and dilemmas for you. Your response to this activity will not only be concerned with considering your professional response and values, it will also be influenced by your personal values and beliefs (for example, some people may feel that Kayleigh's behaviour is a 'cry for help'; others may feel that there are aspects of 'normal' behaviour for young adolescents, especially those with Kayleigh's background and circumstances; others may feel this is unacceptable behaviour that needs to be dealt with by public agencies such as the police). As a professional social worker you will need to think about how you can balance the support, care and rights of young people against your responsibility and accountabilities to the community and wider society.

Within Case Study 1.4 there seems to be some indication in Kayleigh's background that certain of her characteristics are part of her biological make-up. We also need to consider how individuals are influenced by their upbringing and surroundings.

Case study 1.4 continued

As a child Sonia attended a special unit for children with emotional and behavioural difficulties. Sonia and her younger brothers and sisters spent periods of time in care because of their parents' neglectful behaviour, linked to their mental health issues. John's own background was more stable until the death of his father in a car accident when he was three years old, and his mother's marriage to his stepfather when he was seven, who was physically and emotionally abusive towards his mother. At 14 years of age John spent increasing time away from home, with groups of other young people, including Sonia, becoming involved in drug use and dealing. At the age of 15 Sonia gave birth to Kayleigh.

Following this Sonia and John began to live together, living in a series of bed and breakfasts and a hostel for homeless people. In order to survive and have money for their increased drug use, John would steal and Sonia would work occasionally as a prostitute. Sonia suffered from serious postnatal depression after giving birth, which deepened into clinical depression when John was imprisoned for two years for a drug-related offence, when Kayleigh was six months old. Sonia's depression has been accompanied by binge drinking, leading to various periods of outpatient treatment and hospitalisation. Kayleigh was placed in the care of a series of relatives. Her parents finally obtained a council house when Kayleigh was three years old. By the age of 5 Kayleigh had two brothers and a sister. Although her parents are still together, they have a volatile relationship. The family continue to have an erratic lifestyle, largely due to her parents' drug and alcohol use. Since John was sent to prison, Sonia has been earning money to fund her drug and alcohol use through prostitution in her own home; one of the men recently tried to kiss Kayleigh and this has frightened her. Kayleigh has being attending school on a regular basis and is considered an 'able' student; lately her attendance has been giving cause for concern. She is a member of a local 'gang', a group of young people who are involved in shoplifting from local shops, using alcohol and experimenting with 'soft' drug use. They hang out at a local park, verbally abusing and bullying the children who come to play there.

Activity 1.5

Now you know more about Kayleigh's situation, list possible explanations for her behaviours.

Comment

You may have come up with a number of ideas. Your thoughts are likely to arise from two main perspectives. Perhaps you thought that Kayleigh's behaviour was caused by some natural, inborn predisposition for bad behaviour that was part of her individual make-up. Or perhaps you thought that her childhood, background and upbringing had led to some of these behaviours.

These two explanations are examples of opposing theories that attempt to account for individual behaviours and qualities. This is known as the 'nature or nurture' debate.

The 'nature' viewpoint argues that our genes predetermine who we are and our characteristics are inherited. We have inborn biological characteristics that are hereditary from our birth-parents at the point of conception. There is certainly significant evidence to suggest that some of our characteristics are inherited, such as intelligence and personality. However the danger in adopting this perspective is that it assumes change is not possible – we are the way we are and there is little we can do about this.

The 'nurture' viewpoint argues that fundamentally our environment, the influence of culture and social context, experiences and the way we are brought up influence our development – the complex forces of the physical and social world that influence our biological make-up and psychological experiences before and after birth. Evidence can be found of this in patterns of family behaviour (for example, whether family members are 'introvert' or 'extrovert', the way they demonstrate affection to one another and others). Yet does this argument stereotype individuals and families into certain 'types'? For example, in some 'extrovert families' there may be an individual who is extremely introverted.

Activity 1.6

You may wish to reflect on your own background and family and consider which aspects of your/your families' personality reflect 'nature' or 'nurture'. How might you account for 'differences' between family members? Can you identify ways in which your upbringing influences your values and beliefs?

Case study 1.4 continued

Jill is Kayleigh's aunt, her father John's sister. She is married to a software development consultant and they live in a pleasant home in the suburbs of the city. Jill and her husband have offered to care for Kayleigh. They have an active lifestyle and, although they have no children, appear committed to Kayleigh and supporting a change in her behaviour, believing that their lives and lifestyle can present a positive model for her.

Comment

This case example raises a number of fundamental questions: are people's behaviour and actions predetermined? How do we 'inherit' our behaviour? What effect does the environment we grow up in have on our behaviour and actions? Some people would argue that genes and the family we come from will determine the way we make choices and therefore the causes of our behaviour are predetermined, such as the way we live our lives. Others would argue that it is 'free will' – that we change by our own efforts.

The issues this case raises show that it is too simplistic to argue from one point of view. It is most likely that a complex interaction between a range of factors contributes to who we are, for example:

- the genes that we inherit;

- our physical appearance and characteristics, such as the way we look;

- our behaviour, which may attract a favourable or unfavourable response;

- the way we are brought up, such as by a range of carers;

- environmental factors, such as the area we live in, the food we eat;

- our cultural background and appearance;

- cultural stereotypes, such as those associated with age, the social class we are judged to come from;

- cultural values: each culture has certain values associated with different ages;

- role changes: attitudes towards different ages are greatly influenced by the roles that are played, such as for those who have retired, social attitudes are less sympathetic;

- our personal experiences;

- the choices we make;

- the opportunities that come our way;

- the impact of other people on and in our lives.

As you have been thinking about Kayleigh, her behaviours and her family, you have been examining different aspects of her situation and this shows how difficult it can be to understand people's life courses, the influences upon them and the complex events they may have been through.

The exploration of these 'nature' and 'nurture' theories in this chapter has introduced you to one of the fundamental broad debates on human development. Within Chapter 2 of this book we shall be looking in more detail at the key theoretical models used to help us understand development across the life course and consider how theory is applied to social work practice. One of the benefits of looking at different theoretical ideas is that it gives us a wider perspective, taking us beyond our own particular life experiences.

Interprofessional practice

We have seen, therefore, that social workers need to be open to a range of interpretations, critical approaches, theories and debates in relation to life course development in order to understand their use in practice. Social work practice within a human life course development context is no different. The logical consequence of taking this approach and developing an understanding of theories from a range of disciplines is that social work practitioners will take a holistic approach to their practice. This means taking account of every aspect of an individual's life – in other words, building up an understanding of the whole person. A truly holistic understanding of an individual's circumstances can only be achieved by working in partnership with other professional disciplines, with service users and their carers. Interprofessional practice will enable us to bring together a range of knowledge and understanding about all the different aspects of a service user's life, and thereby ensure a holistic approach to practice.

We have already highlighted the case of Stephen Hoskins (Flynn, 2007). The review into his death highlighted the complexity of the case and the various interventions by professionals. Professionals' systems failed to bring together this information into a coherent 'whole' that could be communicated between the different agencies to ensure a shared assessment and understanding of Stephen's needs.

The importance of taking all perspectives into account has been highlighted by a number of inquiries into the serious harm or death of children. This has been highlighted by the Victoria Climbié Inquiry that was referred to previously:

> It is deeply disturbing that during the days and months following her initial contact with Ealing Housing Department's Homeless Persons Unit, Victoria was known to no less than two further housing authorities, four social services departments, two child protection teams of the Metropolitan Police Service (MPS), a specialist centre managed by the NSPCC, and she was admitted to two different hospitals because of suspected deliberate harm. The dreadful reality was that these services knew little or nothing more about Victoria at the end of the process than they did when she was first referred to Ealing Social Services by the Homeless Persons Unit in April 1999.

> (Laming, 2003, p. 3, para. 1.16)

Davies and Ward (2011), in their review of research on identifying and responding to child maltreatment, highlighted studies which demonstrated that proactive social work can be very effective, with better outcomes for children where there is evidence of careful assessment, thoughtful planning and proactive case management. They highlight the importance of theories of child development as a central element, particularly in demonstrating the consequences of maltreatment on children's mental and physical health, learning and education, socialisation and life chances (ibid., p. 5).

We have provided this example to demonstrate one aspect of the significance of interprofessional working. It can be seen that there are many different professional perspectives and areas of knowledge which need to be brought together and co-ordinated. Within social work, therefore, if we are to ensure good practice, we need to work across disciplines, taking account of all aspects of an individual's life course in developing a holistic approach to social work practice.

Reflection point

- What do I know, or can I do now, that I did not know or could not do before I did this section of studying?
- Is there anything I do not understand or want to explore further?
- What else do I need to know to extend my professional development and learning in this area?

Chapter summary

Life course development is about each one of us and our life experiences from birth to death. It is important that social workers understand about human growth and development and the impact that this has on individuals, their experiences, and their own interpretations of their lives.

This chapter began by introducing you to some of the terms that are used in the study of human life course development. We also explained the importance of taking a life course perspective and supporting this with the application of a narrative approach to practice. These concepts are core features of the book and are revisited in its later chapters.

Social workers need to understand their own life course development and the significance that this has had on the values and beliefs that they have developed themselves. This will enable individual professionals to be aware of the significance of taking a non-judgemental approach to practice. Social work practice must take account of individual, social and cultural differences, otherwise it risks being oppressive and discriminatory. Therefore, social workers must also use their background knowledge and skills to enable service users to express their own interpretations of their life courses and their impact on the situations in which they find themselves.

As well as an awareness of the course your own life has taken, social work practitioners need to have a wide range of knowledge from a span of theoretical disciplines to ensure that all aspects of an individual's make-up are considered and appreciated when working with them. In this chapter, we have shown how a number of formal inquiries into health and care practices, following specific incidents of concern, have identified how knowledge and understanding of human development and growth can improve social work practice. By using appropriate skills, involving service users and working in partnership across professional disciplines, poor practice and resultant mistakes can be reduced and the overall understanding of individual service users' needs will be greatly enhanced.

(Continued)

(Continued)

In the next chapter we shall explore theoretical perspectives in more depth, outlining the models commonly used by social workers and other professionals when working with people in a variety of settings. We shall develop the concepts outlined in this chapter and begin to compare and contrast these models and apply them to familiar social work practice situations. This will form a link to the subsequent chapters which will deal with more specific areas of social work practice, with Chapters 3 and 4 focusing on social work practice with children, young people and their families, and Chapter 5 exploring social work practice with adolescents. Chapter 6 will develop your knowledge of life course development in early and middle adulthood, and the final chapter will concentrate on practice with older people and their families.

Further reading

Gaine, C (2010) *Equality and Diversity in Social Work Practice.* London: Sage.

This book acts as a guide for students in developing an understanding of different social and cultural groups, illustrating how the social work value base can be a central part of such understanding.

Horner, N (2016) *What is Social Work?* (5th edn). London: Sage.

This social work text explores the foundations of social care in the UK, how it evolved and why. It answers key questions on mental health, working with older people, working with families and children, directions for social care, and the implications of interprofessional working.

Howe, D (2008) *The Emotionally Intelligent Social Worker*. Basingstoke: Palgrave Macmillan.

David Howe explains the theory of emotional intelligence, its vital practical value and the importance of understanding and managing emotions for effective professional practice.

Parrott, L (2014) *Values and Ethics in Social Work Practice* (3rd edn). London: Sage.

This text identifies current issues in social work and applies an ethical dimension. These issues are then investigated further within an anti-discriminatory framework and against the background of the code of practice for social care workers and employers. Traditional value perspectives are clearly explained and current developments in virtue theory and the ethics of care for social work are also introduced.

Ruch, G, Turney, D and Ward, A (eds) (2010) *Relationship Based Social Work*: *Getting to the Heart of Practice.* London: Jessica Kingsley.

This book provides a thorough guide to relationship-based practice in social work. Relationship-based practice is founded on the idea that human relationships are of paramount importance and should be at the heart of all good social work practice.

The Social Care Institute for Excellence (SCIE) has excellent e-learning resources, allowing you to explore social work issues and the issues raised in this chapter in more depth. You can find them at www.scie.org.uk. The following are particularly relevant:

Adult Safeguarding Resource: A key theme of this resource is that safeguarding is everyone's responsibility. Safeguarding is also something that requires extremely sensitive handling.

Interprofessional and Inter-agency Collaboration (IPIAC): This resource explores the nature of interprofessional and inter-agency collaboration and improving collaborative practice.

The following journal articles examine life course perspectives and harm and abuse:

Bowes, A and Daniel, B (2010) Introduction: Interrogation harm and abuse: A life span approach. *Social Policy and Society*, 9 (2), 221–229.

Daniel, B and Bowes, A (2011) Re-thinking harm and abuse: Insights from a lifespan perspective. *British Journal of Social Work*, 41 (5), 820–836.

Johnson, F, Hogg, J and Daniel, B (2010) Abuse and protection across the lifespan: Reviewing the literature. *Social Policy and Society*, 9 (2), 291–304.

2: An introduction to theoretical models for understanding human life course development

Introduction

In this chapter theoretical approaches to understanding human life course development will be explored, particularly approaches commonly used by social workers and other professionals when working with people in a variety of settings, across their life course. You will develop an understanding of the importance of theories that are based on researched concepts and critical explanations of human development, and the contested nature of aspects of the knowledge claims.

The chapter will therefore start by explaining the importance of theory and research to social work practice; it will then provide you with an explanation of the perspectives that have been taken throughout this book, as the overall approach to human development. The chapter will then examine how a range of disciplines contribute to the knowledge base of social work, by examining the similarities and differences between approaches and applying these to a case study. It will also draw on the importance of listening to and understanding the individual service user's story and the meanings that they attach to the lives they have lived. This is known as a 'biographical' or 'narrative' approach. Over the course of the chapter the aim is to provide you with a background to the theories, models and tools that you can use in effective practice with service users.

What is theory?

Students and some professional workers often believe that theory is complex and unnecessary and that they need to take a more 'pragmatic' approach and learn or study information or facts alone. In reality though, facts alone cannot simply be understood – they need to be interpreted and explained. This interpretation will be influenced by theoretical approaches. Theories can be described as *'a generalised set of ideas that describes and explains people and how they can be understood'* (Payne, 2015, cited in Deacon and Macdonald, 2017, p. 6). They provide a framework to support understanding and so help us make sense of social relationships. Students and social workers need to understand the underpinning theoretical approaches in order to analyse and evaluate the information that is presented to them as 'fact'. For example, in Chapter 1 you looked at how theories of biological determinism (nature) and theories of environmental determinism (nurture) were the basis for different explanations of behaviour and development in the case study of Kayleigh and her family. We shall reconsider their situation in this chapter as we investigate how a different theoretical perspective influences the social work practice intervention chosen. People who receive social work services should expect that any decisions, and any services offered, are based on as sound and solid a basis as is feasible (Beckett and Horner, 2016).

Theories, and the research that accompanies them, can contribute towards our understanding of people and situations. Life course development theories help to explain and analyse the life course and may enable us to predict outcomes. In this way, theories and researched evidence are important tools in helping and guiding practice. However, different theoretical approaches can be seen to lead to different approaches to social work practices. Therefore, as a professional social worker you need to be prepared to assess and critically evaluate theories (for example, to be aware of their origins, underlying assumptions, their strengths and limitations). The relationships and oppositions between theories provide a context in which their values can be assessed against one another, and against the modern social context in which they must be used (Payne, 2014).

It is also important for professional workers to appreciate that theories themselves reflect the history, culture, assumptions and values of those who have developed them. In Chapter 1 we looked at how imposing your own values and beliefs on other people could infringe on their right as individuals to develop their own interpretations and understanding of their life. Similarly, when examining well-accepted theoretical concepts, social workers need to ensure that they question and explore the values and concerns that lie beneath these.

Taking a life course perspective on human development

Before you learn about specific theoretical ideas that explain how human beings develop, it is important that you understand the perspective that is being taken throughout this book. In Chapter 1 you read about the definitions of key terms and the concept of life course used in this text. The notion of life course has informed the approach that will be introduced to you throughout the chapters of this book.

Each of the chapters that follow will concentrate on age-related periods of life. The book has been put together in this way to assist you to develop your understanding of specific issues through the life course. However, a life course perspective has been adopted throughout, which means that it is maintained that human beings develop and grow across the whole of their lives, from conception to death. You may think that babies, children and young people go through the most noticeable growth and development and that there is little change in adulthood, with possible decline or degeneration in older age; however this view is disputed. Within the chapters of this book it is argued that growth and development, change and opportunity, are features of human development throughout the *whole* of life. Paul Baltes (1987) developed a number of theoretical propositions of life span developmental psychology. These propositions are the characteristics or assumptions that underpin the life course perspective that we adopt in this book.

You will find it helpful to refer back to this page as you study the rest of this chapter, which will explore how different disciplines have developed theoretical perspectives on life course development.

Research summary

Paul Baltes (1987): Theoretical propositions of life-span developmental psychology

- Human development is *multidimensional* – it is made up of biological, cognitive and social dimensions. Development is a lifelong process.
- Human development is *studied by a number of disciplines* – as mentioned previously, researchers and theorists from across the disciplines have investigated human development. Development needs to be seen in the interdisciplinary context offered by a range of disciplines (for example, biology, psychology, anthropology, sociology).
- Human development is *multidirectional* – it will be characterised by both growth and decrease or loss, but not with any single predetermined pathway that can be deemed as normal. The dimensions, noted above, will vary in terms of growth and decline throughout the life course.
- Human development is *plastic* – it is varied and may take many different paths dependent upon the person's life conditions.
- Human development is *embedded in history* – it will be influenced by the kind of conditions existing in a given historical period and the person's life history, as well as the sociocultural and socio-economic conditions they have lived through.
- Human development is *contextual* – it is dependent upon how an individual responds to the things that are going on around and within them, the context in which they live their lives. Thus development is influenced by the interaction between the person, their experiences, their history, their environment, and their biological make-up.

Theories of human life course development

There are a number of different perspectives that can be taken to form an understanding of how we develop into who we are. As you work through this book about life course development you will be looking at various ideas and theories that have been broadly taken from the disciplines of sociology, biology and psychology. Each of these disciplines has a different emphasis in its underpinning assumptions of what influences life course development.

Theories arising out of the sociological disciplines emphasise social and environmental factors. Sociologists attempt to explain situations in terms of the views and interpretations taken by society as a whole. Social relationships, and an individual's situation within the society in which they live and how that is understood or explained by members of society, are the main focus of this approach. Karl Marx (1818–1883) took a sociological perspective, emphasising the importance of social and economic structures in influencing our development.

Theories derived from the discipline of biology focus on the physical well-being of the individual. Thus physical development, genetic influences, human growth stages and instinct can be seen as key elements of any biologically-based theory. Charles Darwin (1809–1882) was one of the earliest theorists who argued that human behaviour is genetically determined.

Theories formed by taking a psychological perspective concentrate on what goes on in people's minds: their emotional development, the development of personality and related behaviours. Theories from this school of thought often describe human life course development in terms of stages or phases that individuals progress through. Sigmund Freud (1856–1939) explained human behaviours and psychological problems by exploring stages of early childhood experiences.

Figure 2.1 represents the different perspectives that will be explored further in this chapter and throughout the book.

As can be seen, each of these disciplines takes a different approach to explain what influences life course development. These explanations in turn would suggest different approaches to social work practices. In following sections of the chapter you will consider each of these disciplines in more detail and develop an understanding of how these perspectives impact upon social work practice. The case study introduced in Chapter 1 will be used as the example in each instance. A summary of the case study is given below.

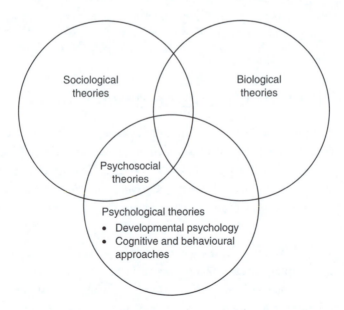

Figure 2.1   Theories of human life course development

Case study 2.1

Kayleigh is 14 years of age, living on a large inner city estate which has a reputation for anti-social behaviour from young people, with use of alcohol and other drugs. Over the last few months her school attendance has been sporadic. John, her father, is currently serving an eight-year jail sentence for drug offences. John's mother supports the family as much as she can, but has poor physical health. His father died in a car accident when he was three years old; his mother remarried when he was 7. John's stepfather has a history of violence towards his mother and now lives in a different part of the country with a new family. Sonia, her mother, is a regular user of alcohol and other drugs, supporting her habit by dealing in soft drugs. She suffers from severe depression, accompanied by binge drinking, leading to hospital outpatient treatment. As a child, she and her siblings spent time in care because of neglect by their mother. Her mother died five years ago of causes linked to alcohol dependency.

At the age of 15 Sonia gave birth to Kayleigh. Following this Sonia and John began to live together, living in a series of bed and breakfasts and a hostel for homeless people. In order to survive and have money for their increased drug use, John would steal and Sonia would work occasionally as a prostitute. Sonia suffered from serious postnatal depression after giving birth, which deepened into clinical depression when John was imprisoned for two years for a drug-related offence when Kayleigh was six months old. Sonia's depression has been accompanied by binge drinking, leading to various periods of outpatient treatment and hospitalisation.

Kayleigh was placed in the care of a series of relatives. Her parents finally obtained a council house when Kayleigh was three years old. By the age of 5, Kayleigh had two brothers and a sister. Although her parents are still together, they have a volatile relationship. The family continue to have an erratic lifestyle, largely due to her parents' drug and alcohol use. Since John was sent to prison, Sonia has been earning money to fund her drug and alcohol use through prostitution in her own home; one of the men recently tried to kiss Kayleigh; this frightened her. Kayleigh has been attending school on a regular basis and is considered an 'able' student; lately her attendance has been giving cause for concern. Kayleigh is a member of a local 'gang', a group of young people who are involved in shoplifting from local shops, using alcohol and experimenting with 'soft' drug use. They hang out at a local park, verbally abusing and bullying the children who come to play there.

Sociological approaches

The discipline of sociology and theoretical perspectives that can be categorised within this discipline explain human development by examining the interactions between people and the society in which they live. Sociological theories may start from this wide perspective, but then explain development and influences upon it by looking at different levels of that society. The work of Bronfenbrenner (1979) has been particularly influential to social work practice. He proposed a theory of human development that explores the different levels of society which may influence the individual's life course.

Research summary

Bronfenbrenner (1979a): Theory of ecological development

Bronfenbrenner described the influences of environmental factors on children. He used the terms 'microsystem', 'mesosystem', 'exosystem' and 'macrosystem'. He suggested that there is a reciprocal process of interaction, in that the child is both influenced by and influences its environment at each of the levels.

The *microsystem* refers to those factors that are located within the immediate environment of the child, such as people and events in the home. These factors have the greatest impact on the child, because they experience them directly and concretely. How people interact with the child will have an effect on how that child grows and develops: the more encouraging and nurturing those relationships are, the more positively they will be able to grow. Furthermore, how a child acts or reacts to those people in the microsystem will affect how they treat the child in return. Each child's genetic and biologically influenced personality traits, for example their temperament, may end up affecting how others treat them and how they in turn respond.

The *mesosystem* refers to the way in which the different parts of a child's microsystem work together for the sake of the child. For example, taking an active role in each child's life, such as playing with and engaging in positive activities with them, will support their overall positive growth and development. Conversely conflict and disagreement between caregivers has the potential to hinder a child's development.

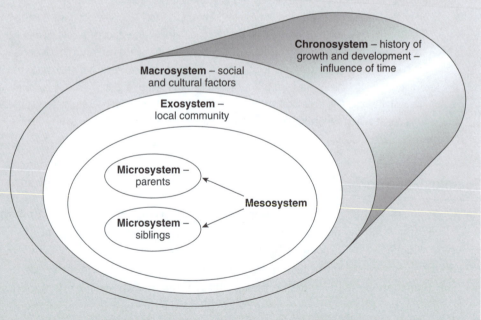

Figure 2.2   Diagram of Bronfenbrenner's theory of ecological development

The term *exosystem* is used to describe those factors that lie beyond the immediate environment of the child, such as the neighbourhood in which they live.

The *macrosystem* includes larger societal factors, such as overall economic conditions and cultural values, cultural values, the economy, government policy and so on.

Bronfenbrenner's theory (see Figure 2.2) also describes a further level of analysis, the chronosystem. This is used to account for the influence of time on development.

Each of these levels interacts with one another to make up the integrated and complex lives of people.

Activity 2.1

Look back at the case study on Kayleigh. What would be the influences in her life at the different levels described by Bronfenbrenner?

- At the microsystem level?
- At the mesosystem level?
- At the exosystem level?
- At the macrosystem level?
- How might Kayleigh's chronosystem affect her development?

Using Bronfenbrenner's model of development to explain Kayleigh's life course would enable us to break down the many influential factors we have found. When looking at her microsystem we would need to consider the influences of her parents, siblings and immediate family, while exploring her mesosystem would examine the way her parents and other caregivers work together to support her development. The exosystem would lead us to look at the local community in which she lives, her school and peer groups. At another level, the macrosystem in which Kayleigh lives would include social factors such as the economic, political and policy context in the country that may impact on both her and her family.

Looking at Kayleigh's behaviour through the chronosystem would enable us to account for changes and development as she has grown older and, for example, perhaps the influences of moving between different relatives when she was younger.

From this example, you can see how a sociological approach would concentrate on how wider factors and expectations of our society influence how Kayleigh's behaviour are construed and how they have developed. It would do this by considering the influence of her social class, her immediate environment and relationships on the behaviour that has been expected of her.

This explanation, understanding and assessment of Kayleigh's behaviour and her life course will influence the form and method of social work practice considered appropriate. Thus, this brief analysis would suggest that Kayleigh needs 'listening to', support and guidance to enable her to make safe choices and to explain and support her in understanding her own life course history. There are issues within the family that need to be explored, especially with her mother, in order to ensure that Kayleigh is 'safe' within the environment. Work would need to be undertaken with Sonia, her mother, to ensure that she has sufficient insight to understand the impact of her lifestyle choice on her daughter, and has the motivation and ability to ensure that Kayleigh's emotional and social needs are met and that she can be protected from harm. There are issues to do with her school attendance and support that would need to be given attention to help her return to school and achieve her academic potential. It may be that Kayleigh's aunt and uncle, Jill and Ian, can provide her with support and guidance.

This approach suggests that the social and environmental influences are significant contributing factors in Kayleigh's development. Social work interventions linked to community development work and improving education and employment opportunities through partnership working with key organisations are good examples. In Chapter 4 of this book you will further develop your understanding of Bronfenbrenner's theory of ecological systems and the importance of this approach to social work practice. Within that chapter you will be encouraged to consider how this approach to understanding human growth and development can contribute to the assessment of a child's needs. As Turney *et al.* (2011) highlight, '*Good assessment matters and should be underpinned by a clear focus on the child and careful attention to analysis. Without the solid foundation of an holistic and ecologically informed assessment, the edifice of professional interventions is unsafe*'. You should also look at Parker and Bradley's (2014) *Social Work Practice* to help inform your understanding.

Physiological approaches

The disciplines of physiology or biology explain human development by examining the physical development and genetic make-up of the individual. So within childhood, for example, biological theories explain a child's growth and development, focusing on characteristics that are inherent in their biological family. In Chapter 3 of this book patterns of children's growth and development are explored further. Biological explanations of later adulthood, on the other hand, concentrate on bodily changes and decreased physical and psychological functioning associated with increased age. In Chapter 7 of this book biological changes in later adulthood are discussed.

Activity 2.2

Think about Kayleigh again. Taking a biological perspective, write down the key factors that might influence her life.

Comment

The perspective from a biological-based discipline would consider Kayleigh's behaviour in relation to her age, looking at her physical development and how this relates to expected courses of growth and physical development. Additionally, theories taking this approach would consider Kayleigh's parents and grandparents, looking at how the genes she may have inherited could explain Kayleigh's development.

Psychological approaches

Psychology is about the study of people and how they are influenced by their thoughts, feelings and emotions. There are many specialist areas of psychological study and theory, so within this book we have chosen to explore two specific perspectives: developmental psychology and psychosocial approaches.

Developmental psychology

Theories that have been developed taking a developmental psychology approach consider how people develop across the life course by exploring their thoughts, ideas, feelings and behaviours. Theories of cognitive development, which are about how we learn, take a developmental psychology approach. In the next chapter you will develop your understanding of cognitive perspectives on children's development. One of the key theorists that you will read about there is Jean Piaget (1896–1990).

Research summary

Jean Piaget (1936): Theory of cognitive development

Piaget believed that the child seeks to understand and adapt to the environment. In doing so the child undertakes certain actions as it moves through progressive stages of development as shown in Table 2.1. (These are explored further in Chapters 3 and 4.)

Table 2.1   Piaget's stages of cognitive development

Stage	Age	
Sensorimotor	0–2 years	Using senses and movement to understand the environment.
Pre-operational	2–6 years	The child begins to be able to use basic logic, but is not able to understand how other people might perceive the environment.
Concrete operations	7–12 years	The child can now take account of different perspectives on the environment and is able to undertake more complex logical reasoning.
Formal operations	12 years +	The child has developed the ability to imagine and speculate. At this stage, the child can conceive new ideas underpinned by reasoning, without the need for prior experience.

Another approach to understanding the human life course from a developmental psychology perspective is presented through theories that focus on our behaviours and how behaviours and the consequences of our actions influence our learning. In Chapter 5, you will look in more depth at behavioural and social learning theories and how these influence social work practice with adolescents.

Research summary

B.F. Skinner (1904–1990): Behaviourism

Skinner explained development as the acquisition of behaviours, which are learned through responses to experiences. Skinner did not see the individual, their thoughts or conscious mind as influencing their behaviours, but rather behaviour being a response controlled by the rewards and punishments in the individual's environment.

Albert Bandura (1977): Social learning theory

Social learning theorist Albert Bandura also emphasised the importance of behaviour and the environment, but also saw cognition, or thought, as being a significant factor in the person's development. Therefore social learning theories consider the influence of values, beliefs, reasoning, self-determination, emotions and thought on the learning process.

Psychoanalytic perspectives

According to this perspective people move through a series of stages in which they confront conflicts between biological drives and social expectations. The ways in which these conflicts are resolved determine that individual's ability to learn, to get on with others, and deal with personal conflicts and anxieties.

Research summary

Freud (1856–1939): Personality theory

Freud believed there were three parts to a personality:

- *Id* – This is the largest part of the mind and is the source of basic biological needs and desires. It is largely 'unconscious'.
- *Ego* – This is the conscious, rational part of the personality, emerging in early infancy so that the id's impulses can be discharged on appropriate objects at the right time and place.
- *Superego* – Between the ages of three and six years the superego (or pre-conscience) develops from interactions with parents who mediate the child's conformity with society's values.

According to Freud the relations established between the id, ego and superego during the pre-school years determine an individual's basic personality.

In addition, Freud believed that during childhood sexual impulses developed and changed (see Table 2.2).

Table 2.2 Freud's theory of childhood development

Period of development	Psycho-sexual stage	Explanation
Birth–1 year	Oral	The dominant 'ego' directs the baby's behaviour to sucking activities towards the breast or bottle.
1–3 years	Anal	The focus of pleasure is holding or releasing urine or faeces. Holding it in and letting it go are greatly enjoyed.
3–6 years	Phallic	This relates to Freud's Oedipus conflict for boys and Electra complex for girls and to the sexual desire for the other sex partner. To avoid conflict they adopt the same-sex parents characteristic and values. The relations between the id, ego and superego established at this time determine an individual's basic personality.
6–11 years	Latency	As sexual instinct dies down, the superego develops further, and the child learns new social values from adults outside the family and from same-sex peers, for example, through play.
Adolescence	Genital	Puberty causes the sexual impulses of the phallic stage to reappear: if development has been successful in the earlier stages then it leads to mature sexuality and the continuation of the reproductive urges.

From these theories Freud, and his daughter Anna, developed a number of ideas and propositions based on these foundations, including: anxiety; denial; repression; displacement; projection; identification with aggressor; regression.

'Treatment' for Freud was through such areas as a relaxed atmosphere, in which the 'client' is free to express themself (the Freudian couch!), and free association, in which the client may talk about anything at all. However, in therapy there is the therapist, who is trained to recognise certain clues to problems and their solutions that the client would overlook, and dream analysis.

Whilst there are some significant critiques of Freud's theories and its limitations, his theories highlighted the importance of family relationships for children's development and his was the first theory to stress the role of early experience.

Psychosocial theories

Some of the theories we shall consider in later chapters in the book arise from a combination of perspectives from psychology and sociology disciplines and are seen as psychosocial theories. David Howe describes psychosocial as being:

created by the interplay between the individual's psychological condition and the social environment.

(Howe, 1998, p. 173)

Psychosocial theory can provide a foundation for social work in practice. It stresses an acknowledgment and assessment of the individual and their psychological processes, the relationships of the individual and the environment in which the person lives, and the resources available. As Coulshed and Orme (2006, p.109) state:

> *Understanding based on the psychosocial approach highlights that we should not be too precipitous in dismissing behaviour as just 'difficult' or 'non-compliant'. Trying to make intelligible how people behave and feel means there is a decreased likelihood of wasting time or dismissing someone as beyond help.*

Later in this book you will develop your knowledge of psychosocial theories by looking at theories that explain the human life course as a series of stages. One of the important models that will be examined in Chapters 6 and 7 is that of Erik Erikson. Erikson's (1995) 'eight stages of man' is a model of development which states that individuals move through each of eight life stages.

Research summary

Erik Erikson (1995): Model of life stage development

Erikson saw people developing their identity as they move through stages or 'crisis' points in their lives. He held that individuals move through the stages by virtue of increasing age; the successful progression through each stage, by the negotiation of the particular 'crisis' to a positive outcome, ensures healthy development.

Erikson's eight stages of development

- *Birth to one year* – Trust versus mistrust, in which the child learns to trust others based upon the consistency of their caregiver(s). If trust develops successfully, the child gains confidence and security in the world around them and is able to feel secure even when threatened. Unsuccessful completion of this stage can result in an inability to trust, and therefore a sense of fear about the inconsistent world. It may result in anxiety, heightened insecurities, and an overt feeling of mistrust in the world around them.
- *One to three years* – Autonomy vs shame and doubt, in which children begin to assert their independence. If children in this stage are encouraged and supported in their increased independence, they become more confident and

secure in their own ability to survive in the world. If children are criticised, overly controlled or not given the opportunity to assert themselves, they begin to feel inadequate in their ability to survive and may then become overly dependent upon others, lack self-esteem, and feel a sense of shame or doubt in their own abilities.

- *Three to six years* – Initiative vs guilt, in which children assert themselves more frequently. They begin to plan activities, make up games, and initiate activities with others. If given this opportunity, children develop a sense of initiative and feel secure in their ability to lead others and make decisions. If children experience either criticism or over-control, they develop a sense of guilt and they may develop a lack of self-initiative.

- *Six to eleven years* – Industry vs inferiority, in which children begin to develop a sense of pride in their accomplishments. They initiate projects, see them through to completion, and feel good about what they have achieved. If children are encouraged and reinforced for their initiative, they begin to feel industrious and feel confident in their ability to achieve goals. If this initiative is not encouraged, then children begin to feel inferior, doubting their own abilities, and therefore may not reach their potential.

- *Adolescence* – Identity vs role confusion, in which children are becoming more independent, and begin to look at the future in terms of career, relationships, families and so on. During this period, they explore possibilities and begin to form their own identity based upon the outcome of their explorations. This sense of who they are can be hindered, which results in a sense of confusion about themselves and their role in the world.

- *Young adulthood (20–30s)* – Intimacy vs isolation, in which the person begins to share themselves more intimately with others, exploring relationships leading toward longer-term commitments with someone other than a family member. Successful completion can lead to comfortable relationships and a sense of commitment, safety, and care within a relationship. Avoiding intimacy, fearing commitment and relationships can lead to isolation, loneliness, and sometimes depression.

- *Middle adulthood (40–60s)* – Generativity vs stagnation. Careers are established, relationships are 'confirmed' and families are established. A feeling of contributing to society is achieved. By failing to achieve these objectives, the person may feel stagnant and unproductive.

- *Late adulthood (ego integrity vs despair)* – There is a tendency to slow down productivity and explore life as a retired person. Life and its accomplishments are explored and a person develops integrity if they are leading a successful life. If life is seen as unproductive, the person may feel guilt about their past, or feel that they did not accomplish their life goals. They may become dissatisfied with life and develop despair, often leading to depression and hopelessness.

As you can see, explanations of human life course development that take a psychological perspective explore human behaviour from a number of different positions. In order to understand how people develop, psychologists investigate thoughts, feelings, emotions and behaviours, looking at how these interact with the person's social environment.

Activity 2.3

Think about Kayleigh again. She is 14 years of age and has developed a number of behaviours that are labelled 'anti-social', such as theft, misusing substances and non-attendance of school. List some of the aspects of her life that would be particularly relevant if using a psychologically-based theory.

Comment

If we take a general overview of the theories adopting a psychological approach, we can see that they would look at Kayleigh's own perspective on the behaviours. This approach would also consider her development in respect of her life stage, with a focus on her learning, analysing her reasoning and motives. Developmental psychology might emphasise the importance of her relationship with her mother during the early stages of her life and how this has led to certain behaviours. A social learning or behaviourist approach would consider the influence of how she has been responded to by others, including her parents, the school and her peers, looking at, for example, how she has been rewarded or punished for her actions as she has developed in her childhood.

As stated earlier in the chapter, the theoretical perspective chosen will affect and influence the approach the social worker takes to intervention and practice. Practice interventions that arise from behavioural perspectives usually take the form of cognitive-behavioural therapy (CBT), which aims to enable the service user to reconsider the meanings they attach to their behaviours and thereby change those behaviours (Ronen, 2002).

Comparing and contrasting the theoretical approaches

In this chapter you have been presented with a brief overview of the theoretical perspectives that will be developed throughout the rest of the book. You have looked at some competing theoretical approaches and considered how each might explore the situation presented in the case study of Kayleigh and her family.

You have seen how these theories attempt to explain and develop our understanding of people and how they have developed. You have also considered how the different underpinning theoretical approaches can be seen to give rise to different forms of social work intervention.

Therefore, when considering even the most acclaimed theoretical concepts, you should not think of these as 'fact'; social workers should question and explore the assumptions, values and ideas that are evident. As you develop your knowledge and experience as a professional social worker, it is important therefore not only to understand the different perspectives being offered, but also to be able to analyse and evaluate the theories and subsequent intervention in respect of its appropriateness in any given situation.

Each of the disciplines that have been described in this chapter reflects a specific focus and certain assumptions. For example, a biological approach concentrates on the physical being and takes, as its focal point, the individual person. In contrast, theories from a sociological base explore the issues by starting to examine the society in which individuals grow and develop. These theories explain human development as being largely dependent upon the impact of the environment as well as social and cultural influences. Theories can also be critiqued for their strengths and weaknesses in how they explain and describe certain aspects of development. For example, Jean Piaget's theory of cognitive development could be considered one of the most comprehensive and coherent theories in helping us understand children's mental development. However, Piaget's theory is not as useful if you want to understand how life events and challenges influence growth and development in adulthood. For this area of life course development, Erik Erikson's model of life stage development is likely to be more relevant.

At this point, it would be useful to refer back to the work of Paul Baltes (1987) described earlier in this chapter. In defining the features of a life course perspective, Baltes states that human development is *multi-dimensional*. This is a view that we support, seeing human development across the life course as complex and, in reality, a concept that can be seen to be influenced by the interaction of biological, social, psychological and environmental factors. It is, therefore, important to appreciate that in social work practice a range of theories from across the disciplines needs to be considered. It is not possible for any one theory to explain all aspects of human life course development: taking any one approach in isolation would lead to other aspects of the person's life being ignored. Each of the models and theories introduced within this book has made a valuable contribution to our understanding of human development through the life course. Thus, as described in Chapter 1, social workers need to develop an understanding of theories from a range of disciplines in order to take a holistic approach to their practice.

Research summary

The concept of well-being makes a very important contribution to understanding the life course. 'Well-being' is an umbrella term that seeks to cover the multi-dimensional objective and subjective dimensions of everything a person needs to lead a good life, from friends and family to school and physical fitness. *It is best thought of as a dynamic process, emerging from the way in which people interact with*

(Continued)

(Continued)

the world around them (Michaelson *et al.*, 2009). The foundation of well-being is to have the support, strengths and opportunities to experience full lives. This means such things as purposefulness, developing satisfying relationships, social responsibility, optimising health, and supporting lifelong learning abilities. Dodge *et al.* (2012) propose a definition of well-being as the balance point between an individual's resource pool (psychological, social and physical) and the challenges (psychological, social and physical) faced: '*Each time an individual meets a challenge, the system of challenges and resources comes into a state of imbalance, as the individual is forced to adapt his resources to meet this particular challenge*' (Kloep *et al.*, 2009, p. 337). When an individual has the psychological, social and physical resources to meet a particular psychological, social and/or physical challenge, this leads to stable well-being. When individuals have more challenges than resources, their well-being is challenged.

The Office for National Statistics (www.ons.gov.uk/ons/)

Measuring National Well-Being (The Office for National Statistics) aims to provide a fuller picture of progress by using wider measures of economic and social progress, including the impact of the environment. The commitment is to develop wider measures of well-being so that government polices can be tailored to a wider and systematic consideration of well-being to support better outcomes.

The Organisation for Economic Co-operation and Development (OECD) Better Life Initiative: Measuring Well-Being and Progress (www.oecd.org)

This initiative aims to further understanding of what drives the well-being of people and nations and what needs to be done to achieve greater progress for all.

The 'Better Life Index' (www.oecdbetterlifeindex.org)

This allows you to compare well-being across countries based on 11 topics the OECD has identified as essential (housing; income; jobs; community; education; environment; civic engagement; health; life satisfaction; safety; work–life balance), in the areas of material living conditions and quality of life.

The biographical approach

The most important skill in taking a holistic approach is to understand each individual's life course, as they describe it. Listening to and taking account of an individual's description of their life, the events they consider to be important or influential, and the high and low points of their development, means you are listening to their biographical narrative, or taking a narrative approach.

Activity 2.4

You have considered the case study of Kayleigh throughout this chapter. Note down your thoughts on what her own story, her narrative account, might consist of.

Comment

This is a highly speculative activity, as you cannot know how Kayleigh might describe her life and her environment. However, we do know that through listening to Kayleigh you would, for example, be able to develop an understanding of what is important to her, how she views the relationships she has with her parents and family, what she enjoys about her life, what upsets her, and what have been the high and low points of her life so far.

The narrative or biographical approach, by definition, will enable you to understand that person's life from the life course perspective we described earlier – in other words, taking account of the whole of their life and the growth (or high) and decline (or low) points as they see them. The appreciation of social and cultural diversity is integral to this approach, as it negates stereotypical assumptions or discriminatory attitudes, enabling the individual to take control of the life they portray. Chamberlayne *et al*. state that:

> *working with the 'whole person' calls for knowledge of that person's past as well as their current needs and preferences.*

> (2000, p. 10)

They also suggest that biographical approaches provide:

> *an opportunity for the development of appropriate and sensitive care practice and interventions and the promotion of more socialised and empowering perceptions of the self in circumstances when stigma, segregation and disempowerment may have been a more common experience.*

> (ibid.)

More specifically in relation to social work practice, Cree and Davis (2007, p. 8) reinforce the central idea that personal stories are a legitimate way of exploring and understanding the world, and furthermore that such narrative approaches that build upon the stones of individuals have the capacity to recognise people's strengths and engage people in active, meaning-making dialogues (Fraser, cited in Cree and Davis, 2007, p. 8).

In their book on *Social Work Practice* (3rd edn, 2014), Parker and Bradley describe a number of aids and activities which social workers use when they are gathering and analysing information as they make assessments with service users.

Reflection point

- What do I know, or can I do now, that I did not know or could not do before I did this section of studying?
- Is there anything I do not understand or want to explore further?
- What else do I need to know to extend my professional development and learning in this area?

Chapter summary

This chapter has introduced you to theoretical approaches to understanding human life course development. As required by the social work academic standard subject benchmark statement, you will have developed your knowledge of research-based concepts and critical explanations from social work theory and other disciplines that contribute to the knowledge base of social work, including their distinctive epistemological status and application to practice.

You have looked at the significance of theory and research and how they can support your knowledge, understanding and skills as a social worker.

We introduced the concept of taking a life course perspective, which sees human development as a lifelong process and is an underpinning value throughout this book. You have then looked at three broad disciplines or schools of thought, from which some key theoretical perspectives on life course development have arisen. Using the case study that was initially introduced in Chapter 1 (Kayleigh and her family), you have had the opportunity to think about how these theories explain a life situation and how this explanation might impact upon social work practices.

Having looked separately at some approaches and key theories from sociological, biological, developmental psychological and psychosocial perspectives, you considered how these might be compared, contrasted and analysed in order to develop effective social work practice, based upon robust theoretical and research-based knowledge.

In the final section of this chapter, you have learnt about taking a biographical or narrative approach. We have stated that understanding the person's life experiences and the 'meaning' that they give to those experiences is fundamental to developing holistic social work practice.

Further reading

Baltes, PB (1987) Theoretical propositions of life-span developmental psychology: On the dynamics between growth and decline. *Developmental Psychology, 23,* 611–626.

In this journal article Paul Baltes describes the characteristics of taking a life course perspective.

Berryman, J, Smythe, P, Taylor, A, Lamont, A and Joiner, R (2002) *Developmental Psychology and You* (2nd edn). Oxford: BPD Blackwell.

This second edition of Berryman *et al.*'s book is a comprehensive, introductory text to developmental psychology across the life course. The theories of cognitive development are particularly clearly explained.

Cree, V (ed.) (2013) *Becoming a Social Worker: Global Narratives.* London: Routledge.

This book extends narrative, biographical approaches through the voices of social work professionals from all over the world.

Cree, V and Davis, M (2007) *Social Work: Voices from the Inside.* London: Routledge.

This book provides a vivid example of how the narrative, biographical approach enables social work practitioners to see people within the context of their whole lives.

Ingelby, E (2010) *Applied Psychology for Social Work* (2nd edn). London: Sage/Learning Matters.

This book shows that, for social workers, it is important for psychology to be studied in the contexts of social care, as it offers potential explanations of complex aspects of human behaviour and development.

Nicolson, P (2014) *A Critical Approach to Human Growth and Development.* Basingstoke: Palgrave Macmillan.

This book, aimed at students and social workers, provides an understanding of the psychological, biological and social aspects of human development.

Slater, A and Bremner, G (eds) (2011) *An Introduction to Developmental Psychology* (2nd edn). Oxford: Blackwell.

An introduction to developmental psychology, written at an understandable level by an international team of respected researchers.

3: Using life course development knowledge in social work practice with infants, young children and their families

---

Achieving a social work degree

This chapter will help you begin to meet the following capabilities, to the appropriate level, from the Professional Capabilities Framework:

- **Knowledge**
  - Apply knowledge of social sciences, law and social work practice theory.
- **Critical reflection and analysis**
  - Apply critical reflection and analysis to inform and provide a rationale for professional decision making.
- **Diversity**
  - Recognise diversity and apply anti-discriminatory and anti-oppressive principles in practice.

It will also introduce you to the following academic standards as set out in the social work subject benchmark statement:

3.1.1   Social work services and service users.
3.1.4   Social work theory.
3.2.2   Problem solving skills.
3.2.2.3 Analysis and synthesis.

Introduction

The following three chapters focus on infant, child and adolescent development. Whilst the following chapters will consider specific age-related issues, these three in particular are interrelated in developing themes and issues in relation to child growth and development.

This chapter will set out knowledge in respect of early child development. It begins by outlining themes in relation to social work and child development. The section sets out the importance of an understanding of infant, child and adolescent development for social workers. It will then explore the contexts of development – the 'social construction' of childhood – considering the relative importance of historical, hereditary, environmental and cultural factors in determining an individual's development. This chapter will specifically develop your understanding and ability to critique theories that explain human development taking a cognitive approach and theories taking a biological and physical perspective. In particular it will explore social and emotional development, developing themes in relation to the critical issues of attachment, vulnerability and resilience. It will also introduce issues in relation to child protection and related issues of legal intervention.

Social work practice and child development

Why an understanding of infant, child and adolescent development is important for social workers

This book is set within the context of contemporary social work practice and related policy and legislation. Whilst the intention is not to set out in detail the content of relevant legislation in England, the following are key legislation:

- The Children Act 1989 is the central piece of legislation guiding children's social care. It sets out the duties, powers and responsibilities local authorities hold in respect of their looked after children and care leavers.

- The Children Act 2004 provides the legal basis for how social services and other agencies should deal with issues relating to children, to make arrangements to promote co-operation between agencies in order to improve children's well-being. It extends the existing framework of children in care to make sure that they receive care that is well supported, of a high quality, and tailored to need.

- The Children and Young Persons Act 2008 encourages 'fostering for adoption', allowing adopters to foster children prior to court approval to adopt; introduces a 26-week time limit for the court to decide whether or not a child should be taken into care; and also introduces 'staying put' arrangements, allowing children to stay in their foster family until the age of 21.

- Other legislation includes: Children (Leaving Care) 2000, which sets out the duties of the local authorities towards children leaving care from 16–21 years; the Adoption and Children Act 2002, which places a duty on local authorities to maintain an adoption service; and the Children and Adoption Act 2006, which gives courts more flexibility to facilitate child contact and enforce contact orders when separated parents are in dispute.

Peter Connelly (1 March 2006–3 August 2007) was a 17-month-old boy who died in London after suffering more than 50 injuries over an eight-month period, during which he was repeatedly seen by social and other services. Peter's mother, Tracey Connelly, her boyfriend, Steven Barker, and Jason Owen were all convicted of causing or allowing the death of a child, the mother having pleaded guilty to the charge. The child protection services of Haringey Council and other agencies were widely criticised. Following the conviction, three inquiries and a nationwide review of social service care were launched.

The case of Victoria Climbié (see Chapter 1, p. 21) and the consequences following her death have already been highlighted. Following the tragic case of 'Baby Peter', Lord Laming was invited to undertake an update on the progress of implementation arrangements for safeguarding children (Laming, 2009). The second Laming Report highlighted the complexity of the systems in place that seek to protect children:

> *It is clear that most staff in social work, youth work, education, police, health and other frontline services are committed to the principle of interagency working, and recognise that children can only be protected effectively when all agencies pool information, expertise and resources so that a full picture of the child's life is better understood … Yet it is evident that the challenges of working across organisational boundaries continue to pose barriers in practice, and that cooperative efforts are often the first to suffer when services and individuals are under pressure.*

(2009, paragraphs 4.1 and 4.3)

He made further recommendations, including the need for in-depth understanding of child development (2009, paragraph 5.17).

More specifically for social work practice with children, their families and carers, the policy document *Every Child Matters* (ECM) (DfES, 2003), the national strategic development programme *Every Child Matters: Change for Children* (DfES, 2004b) and the *Children Act 2004* (the legislative spine on which reforms will be built; DfES, 2004a, p. 5) continue to have widespread implications and are relevant to your reading of this chapter and Chapters 4 and 5. Although it is no longer official government policy, there is no obvious equivalent policy and there have been changes to terminology (see Introduction); however the focus remains the same. The publication of the latest version of *Working Together to Safeguard Children* (DoE, 2015) is an updated version of the key statutory guidance for anyone working with children. It sets out how organisations and individuals should work together and how practitioners should conduct assessments of children. The guidance sets out the responsibilities of professionals towards safeguarding children, with the focus shifting away from processes and onto the needs of the child. For example, Local Safeguarding Children's Boards (LSCBs) (established for every local authority area, with a range of roles and statutory functions, including local safeguarding policy and procedures and scrutinising local arrangements; see Section 13 Children Act 2004), local authorities and their partners should be commissioning and providing services for children at risk of sexual exploitation, female genital mutilation and radicalisation (Chapter 1, Section 17). The guidance reminds us of the need for a child-centred approach: for services to be effective they should be based on a clear understanding of the needs and views of children.

The Munro Review

The first report in October 2010 (Munro, 2010) suggested that a defensive system had developed in relation to children and young people, with an emphasis on procedures and recording. Insufficient attention was being given to developing and supporting expertise to work effectively with children, young people and their families. The review's second report in February 2011 (Munro, 2011) considered the child's journey through the child protection system to show how the system could be improved. It stated that instead of 'doing things right' (i.e. following procedures), the system needed to be focused on doing the right thing (i.e. checking whether or not children and young people are being helped). As part of a number of recommendations it stated the importance of *'knowledge of child development and attachment and how to use this knowledge to assess a child's current developmental state'* (2011, p. 96).

Further reviews undertaken by Sir Martin Narey (in 2014 – initial education of children's social workers – and 2016 – report into children's residential care) and David Croisdale-Appleby (2014) acknowledge the challenge faced by children's (and adults) social care, for example stating that services are not always being designed around vulnerable children, and innovation has insufficient space to thrive.

Children's Social Care Reform: A Vision For Change (DoE, 2016a) outlines the government's reform programme for children social care services in England over the next five years. By 2020 the ambition is that all vulnerable children, no matter where they live, will receive the same high quality of care and support, and the best outcome for every child will be at the heart of every decision made. This is under three fundamental pillars of reform: *people and leadership*, bringing the best people into the profession and developing leaders to nurture practice excellence (2016a, p. 14); *governance and accountability*, supporting the emergence of innovative organisational models for children's social care, including Trusts, and as a strategic priority within devolution deals, ensuring sharper and more focused accountability, and intervening decisively in cases of failure (ibid., p. 43); and *practice and systems*, covering what the children's social care workforce does when working with children and families – namely making sure that they are intervening in a way that will make a genuine, long lasting difference to children and families (ibid., p. 27). *Putting Children First* (DoE, 2016b) sets out the government strategy to make these transformations a reality.

Khyra Ishaq (01 January 2001–17 May 2008) was a seven-year-old girl who starved to death at her home in Birmingham in May 2008. Khyra's weight at death was so low it could not be plotted on a body mass index chart. All of her surviving siblings were malnourished to a greater or lesser extent and all had specific nutrient deficiencies. Khyra's mother, Angela Gordon, and her mother's partner, Junaid Abuhanza, were charged with causing or allowing Khyra's death between 9–17 May 2008. The serious case review concluded that although the scale of the abuse inflicted would have been hard to predict, Khyra's death was preventable.

Daniel Pelka (15 July 2007–03 March 2012) died in March 2012 aged 4 years and 8 months. He died from a blow to the head but had suffered months of serious neglect and abuse prior to his death. He had been systematically deprived of food, fed salt, locked in a room and physically abused. He had numerous injuries at the time of his death. Daniel's mother and her partner were convicted of his murder. Daniel had an older and a younger sibling. The family were Polish. A serious case review found Daniel Pelka was 'invisible' at times and 'no professional tried sufficiently hard enough' to talk to him.

The death of any child because of neglect or abuse is tragic. Lessons from serious case reviews allow lessons to be learned. There is no single 'answer' to preventing tragedies, however it is clear that professionals working together in the best interests of the child, with the child at the centre of concerns, is critical. The review into Daniel's death stated, '*It could be argued that had a much more enquiring mind been employed by professionals about Daniel's care, and they were more focussed and determined in their intentions to address those concerns, this would likely have offered greater protection for Daniel. There needed to have been a greater focus on his day to day experiences, with concerns about his injuries responded to in accordance with procedures, as well as more holistic and probing assessments undertaken at earlier stages*' (Coventry Safeguarding Board, 2013, p. 36).

Development occurs across a number of dimensions: biologically, socially, emotionally and cognitively. As children develop physically, they also learn about the social and emotional skills that will support them in relationships within the family, with friends, within their community and culture, and within the larger society. They show changes in their thought processes. Whilst theorists often appear to compartmentalise these changes, the reality is that development progresses in many different directions at the same time.

Understanding the stages and processes of development can help us identify the achievement of developmental milestones – important developmental events in a child's life, such as the age at which they take their first step or say their first word. It also helps us to understand developmental norms – the age at which they achieve skills and understanding compared with other children and 'normal' expectations. Understanding the achievement of milestones and what is 'normal' in relation to development is important for social workers so that they can judge and make sense of each child's progress and experience. However, whilst development is concerned with how people change over time, these changes are not always predictable. Some children may demonstrate steady, predictable changes whilst others may not.

Development is influenced by a number of different and interrelated processes or systems. Change in one part of a system may have a direct or indirect influence on the development of a child. An example of this is the impact of ethnicity, race and culture on the individual child and the family and community in which they live. This can often have a positive influence, providing a sense of belonging and identity and helping us to understand who we are and where we came from. However it can also play a much more negative role in creating and/or sustaining divisions between groups of people that can result in prejudice and discrimination and also, at times, conflicts and wars. Competent cultural sensitivity and care provide children with a sense of security, belonging and personal history (Obegi and Natan Ritblatt, 2005).

As a social worker you will need to gain an understanding of the 'whole' child, their development and their life course. It is important to take a range of theories and perspectives into account that can support us in understanding each child's growth and development and individual experience, the role and impact of their families and the influence of processes and systems on their lives. Through this you should be able to see beyond the description of the child, to give meaning to their lives and experiences. You will also be recognising the individuality of that child:

> *It is important to keep in mind that even a tiny baby is a person. Holistic development sees the child in the round, as a whole person – physically, emotionally, intellectually, socially, morally, culturally and spiritually.*

> (Meggitt, 2006, p. 1)

We also need to acknowledge that there are children with unique and specific needs that may impact on their individual development and behaviour, and certainly on their experiences and how others view and respond to them (DfES, 2007a, p. 6). An example here would be the experience of children with a disability. Priestley (2003, p. 4) suggests that '*adopting a life course approach to disability means examining the ways in which disabled lives are understood, organised and governed within societies – from regulation of birth and reproduction to the social organisation of death and dying (and all points in-between)*'.

The social construction of childhood

We begin by posing some questions. Do we have a shared understanding of what constitutes 'childhood'? In what way does the experience of childhood change – across history, as the result of different personal understanding from the experience, in relation to the community in which you were raised and as a result of different cultures?

We probably have a clear idea of what we mean by 'childhood' as we have all experienced childhood. Generally, it is assumed to be a distinct phase in our lives, which should be 'protected', free from worries and responsibilities, a time in which we play and learn, and are nurtured and supported along our path towards adulthood. As a social worker a critical part of your role will be to work with children and families in empowering them to be involved in processes and decisions that affect their lives. Social workers need to develop skills in communicating and working with children and with their families to support this. The right of children to have their voices heard has been enshrined in an international treaty, the Convention on the Rights of Children 1991.

The Convention on the Rights of Children 1991 is a universally agreed set of standards and obligations in relation to the basic human rights that all children have – without discrimination. Children are defined as persons up to the age of 18. It incorporates the full range of human rights (civil and political rights, economic, social and cultural rights):

- The right to survival.
- The right to develop to the fullest.
- The right to protection from harmful influences, abuse and exploitation.
- The right to participate fully in family, cultural and social life.

In addition there are two optional protocols in relation to the involvement of children in armed conflict and the sale of children, child prostitution and child pornography. The Convention has been signed up to by the United Kingdom.

Within England and Wales the legislative and policy context of social work practice with children, young people, their families and carers was framed by the national strategic vision within *Every Child Matters: Change for Children* (DfES, 2004b). This overarching strategy underpins the Children Act 2004. The Children Act 2004 does not replace or even amend the basic principles of the Children Act 1989, but supersedes some of them (Johns, 2007), whilst the Children Act 2004 sets out the process for integrating services to children so that every child can achieve the five outcomes laid out in *Every Child Matters*. The *Framework for Assessment of Children in Need and Their Families* (DH, 2000) provides a systematic way of gathering, analysing and recording the experience of children within their families and communities. This was supplemented through the *Every Child Matters: Change for Children* programme with a Common Assessment Framework (CAF)(DfES, 2006). The Common

Assessment Framework process was developed for practitioners from a range of backgrounds to use in order to gather and assess information in relation to a child's needs in development, parenting and the family environment.

As stated earlier, the Children and Young Persons Act 2008 is intended to 'speed up' opportunities for adoption where it is deemed in a child's best interest. The paper *Adoption: A Vision for Change* (DoE, 2016c) sets out the government's plans for a radical redesign of the adoption system. It reiterates the government's pledge to avoid unnecessary delay in the adoption process and increases the support available to adopted children and their families. More recent developments by government have included the Innovation Programme (2014), intended to develop an understanding of the conditions required to create excellent practice in children's social care. 'Partners in practice' local authorities will provide evidence about new structural models and innovations, trial the new social work workforce reforms, explore greater freedoms in how they design and deliver their services, and support work looking at how best to measure performance and outcomes (DoE, 2016c).

In many ways this legislative and policy context can be seen to inform the views, perceptions and meanings that are attached to childhood in contemporary society. However, this view of childhood has not always been so. Ariès (1962), studying the concept of childhood from the Middle Ages to the end of the eighteenth century, found that children were viewed as small-scale adults; childhood as a distinct age grouping did not exist – rather, he suggests, it was a later historical creation. Therefore, based on Ariès' views, childhood could be seen as a 'new' concept.

Activity 3.1

Think about your experience of childhood. Think about such things as those listed below:

- Family structure – What sort of family were you brought up in, for example in a two-parent or single-parent family? How many children were in your family? Were you the only child, the middle child or the youngest child? Can you identify any impact you feel that this may have had on you?
- Roles within the family – What role did your mother have in the family? Did she work outside the home? What role did your father have in the family? Did he work? Did you have an extended family? What impact did these relatives have on your family's life? How did these arrangements impact on your experience of childhood?
- Social circumstances – Where did you live? What kind of neighbourhood was it? Did you have any hobbies and pastimes? At what age did you go to school? What was your first experience that you remember at school?

(Continued)

(Continued)

- Economic circumstances – How would you describe the economic circumstances of your family? What impact did this have on the way you lived, for example the toys that you had, the holidays you took, going on outings and excursions?
- Culture – What kind of cultural group would you describe yourself as coming from? What impact did this have on the way you were raised? What, if any, impact did this have on the way others viewed you? What impact did religion have on your childhood? Can you identify any specific values and beliefs that your family held as important?

Compare your experience to that of people older or younger than you, for example your parents and grandparents.

Comment

Your experience and those of your children, or your parents and grandparents, will be unique and will have been shaped by specific circumstances and events. Different generations of the family will be influenced by personal circumstances, historical, cultural and societal contexts. You may have found similarities. However, it is more likely that your experience of your childhood is different from your parents', and almost certainly from that of your grandparents. One of the principal reasons for this is simply because of the era in which you were raised – your life course will differ from those of your parents and grandparents because of the historical age in which you and they were brought up.

Across history as society has progressed, we can see the emergence of 'childhood' due to the influence of a number of factors. Improving medical and health care has increased survival rates both for babies and their mothers; additionally, there is the opportunity to plan for families through improved birth control methods. With increasing industrialisation, there was campaigning to protect the rights of children. Education within Britain has made a major impact in prolonging childhood with the gradual raising of the school leaving age.

Consequently, children spend distinct and prolonged periods of their lives in education, in being socialised and prepared for adulthood. This can be seen in the emergence of 'adolescence' as a further distinct period before adulthood is reached.

Generations of families are also influenced by significant political, social and personal events. Some events may be experienced as having an intense effect on the family, such as economic depression or war. The impact may be experienced differently because of age; for example, war may have no direct impact on the experience of a baby compared to that of a young person of fighting age. However other events could have a profound effect on their families, and consequently the way in which they have to care for their children; for example, being displaced from their home, the lack of water and food.

Other impacts on the experiences of different generations of families will be linked to changing social and economic circumstances. An example of this would be the changing role of women in relation to work. The number of women in work today is 69.1 per cent, the highest level since comparable records began in 1971 (Office for National Statistics, 2016). Previous generations of women were 'normally' expected to give up their jobs in order to stay at home to bring up children and take care of the home. This changing role for 'mothers' could be attributed to women campaigning for rights and equality, especially as compared to men. There are also economic reasons. These may be personal to the individual woman, such as to increase the available resources, and therefore the potential opportunities available, for that family. There is also a 'political' dimension in recognising the powerful 'voice' and experiences of women, requiring more people to be available within the labour market. Further, there is evidence that with the raising of the age for women to receive a state pension, more women are remaining in the labour market.

We need to recognise that communities raise children in diverse ways, with each culture encouraging the kinds of habits and traits that will help them to integrate and function within that culture. All families exist within a larger cultural context – a way of life shared by members consisting of a system of meanings and customs, including values, attitudes, beliefs, morals and laws. This includes physical symbols such as the kind of houses we live in and so on (Bee, 1995). It is shared by identifiable groups and is transmitted through the group from one generation to another. Recognising the importance of culture on children's development is important for a number of reasons. First, we need to identify and understand those aspects of development that impact on all children, not just through theories and studies based on the stereotype of white, middle-class children living within a western culture. Second, we need to have an understanding of the culture as it impacts on that child. We need to understand the impact of cultural beliefs as part of that environment. We need to consider how different cultural beliefs impact on how people experience their lives.

Paludi (2002) provides a range of examples of difference across cultures: for example, in the role of the father and how it is perceived; in children's sleeping arrangements; in the importance attached to 'play'; and in physical development. Services provided for families should be culturally sensitive. However it is important that a common culture or religion does not override other considerations, especially child safety. A lack of understanding of the religions and cultural context of families can result in professionals overlooking situations that may put family members at risk, whilst the desire to be culturally-sensitive can result in professionals accepting lower standards of care. The NSPCC (2014) have identified that where there are child protection concerns, some parents claim that their parenting practices are part of their cultural or religious beliefs. Parents may refuse to co-operate with services on cultural or religious grounds. They may accuse professionals of discriminating against them in an attempt to prevent intervention.

The impact of where a child lives, the family income and the educational attainment of the parents further define the child's perceived position and status within society, in particular their experience of social exclusion. Particularly for families in low socio-economic groups, children will experience disadvantage in real and crucial ways, including potential disadvantages in relation to health and education.

A research report by UNICEF (2016), the United Nations Children's Educational Fund, titled *The State of the World's Children 2016: A Fair Chance for Every Child*, provides stark evidence of the numbers of children living in poverty in the world. The last three decades have seen unprecedented progress in reducing extreme poverty, with the number of people living in extreme poverty worldwide almost half of what it had been at the end of the 1990. Nevertheless, in 2012 almost 90 million people lived below the international poverty line set by the World Bank at US$1.90 per day. Because poorer families tend to be larger, children are disproportionately represented among the extreme poor. While children aged 17 and under account for about one third (34 per cent) of the total population in low- and middle-income countries, they make up nearly half (46 per cent) of the population living on less than US$1.90 per day. Millions of children living above this line still live in poverty, are vulnerable to it or experience deprivations in other dimensions of their lives. Relative poverty, which is of particular relevance in richer countries, can also affect the lives of children. Having fewer opportunities to be educated, healthy or nourished compared to their peers puts children at a disadvantage and limits their life chances. In addition, race, ethnicity and social exclusion often play a role in determining a child's life chances, even in some of the world's richest countries:

> *Being deprived, by any measure, is damaging to a child's development, particularly when deprivations are experienced in early childhood. A child rarely has a second chance at a good start in life. Deprivations of health, nutrition or stimulation in the earliest months and years of life when the brain is developing at a rapid pace, can lead to damage that is difficult or even impossible to overcome later.*

(UNICEF, 2016, p. 70)

In the introduction to the report Anthony Lake, Executive Director of UNICEF, states that:

> *Before they draw their first breath, the life chances of poor and excluded children are often being shaped by inequities. Disadvantage and discrimination against their communities and families will help determine whether they live or die, whether they have a chance to learn and later earn a decent living. Conflicts, crises and climate-related disasters deepen their deprivation and diminish their potential ... For the most part, the constraints on reaching these children are not technical. They are a matter of political commitment. They are a matter of resources and they are a matter of collective will – joining forces to tackle inequity and inequality head-on by focusing greater investment and effort on reaching the children who are being left behind.*

(ibid., p. vi)

The State of the World's Children: Children with a Disability (2013b) highlights the importance of promoting the rights of children with a disability, at the heart of which is the inclusion of all children:

> *The Convention on the Rights of the Child (CRC) and the Convention on the Rights of Persons with Disabilities (CRPD) challenge charitable approaches that regard children with disabilities as passive recipients of care and protection. Instead, the Conventions demand recognition of each child as a full member of her or his family, community and society. This entails a focus not on traditional notions of 'rescuing' the child, but on investment in removing the physical, cultural, economic, communication, mobility and attitudinal barriers that impede the realisation of the child's rights – including the right to active involvement in the making of decisions that affect children's daily lives.*

(UNICEF, 2013b, p. 11)

When talking about social issues the term 'well-being' is used to refer to the quality of people's lives, and covers both objective well-being – external verifiable indicators such as health and educational outcomes – and subjective well-being – how people are feeling.

Child Well-being in Rich Countries: A Comparative Overview (UNICEF Innocenti Research Centre, 2013) focuses on the well-being of children and young people in 29 of the world's most advanced economies. The five dimensions taken to measure the well-being of children (material well-being, health and safety, education, behaviours and risks, and housing and environment) offer a picture of the lives of children, and no single dimension can stand as a reliable proxy for child well-being as a whole. The Netherlands retains its position as the clear leader and is the only country ranked among the top five countries in all dimensions of child well-being. Four Nordic countries (Finland, Iceland, Norway and Sweden) sit just below the Netherlands at the top of the child well-being table. The bottom four places in the table are occupied by three of the poorest countries in the survey, Latvia, Lithuania and Romania, and by one of the richest, the United States. The United Kingdom has risen up the rankings from bottom place (21st out of 21 countries) in 2000/2001 to a mid-table position today.

The Children's Society (2016) has examined subjective well-being, children's assessment of how their lives are going, of children in the UK in a series of research reports over the last decade. They have identified subjective well-being as consisting of two key elements:

1. Life satisfaction – the evaluation that children make about their own lives at a cognitive level and is comprised of judgements about their life as a whole, as well as judgements about different aspects of their lives, for example happiness with family relationships.
2. The experience of positive and negative emotions at a particular point in time.

(Continued)

(Continued)

A related approach is psychological well-being, which is concerned with children's sense of meaning, purpose and engagement. Children can be considered to be flourishing if they score highly on subjective and psychological well-being (p. 5). The Good Childhood Index is a measure of children's well-being and happiness on 10 aspects of children's lives – family, health, home, friends, time use, money and things, future, choice, appearance and school. Some of the themes the research identified were:

- A gender gap, with girls becoming increasingly unhappy with their lives and appearance.
- Although more than 8 out of 10 children (82 per cent) are 'flourishing', 10 per cent are 'languishing', having low scores for both subjective well-being and psychological well-being.
- Boys are more likely to have mental health problems at age 10 – but by age 14 girls are more likely to experience emotional problems such as anxiety and depression.
- Children's perception of their local area, including the quality of local facilities, how safe they feel, how much freedom they perceive they have and their experience of local problems, are clearly linked to their well-being.

In summary, what is being suggested is that childhood is a 'social construction'; that is to say that childhood has been formed from a shared perception of what constitutes social order within society. Each individual develops within three contexts: historical, cultural and socio-economic. Whilst each person is unique, these contexts will have an influence and effect on that person's experience and therefore their development.

The developing child

Activity 3.2

Julie (15) and Shaun (16) have known each other for six months. Both use drugs, particularly heroin and alcohol. Julie is three months pregnant with her first child. Shaun, the father of the child, has recently received a six-month sentence for drug-related offences to be served in a Young Offenders Institute. Julie is unhappy and depressed, saying that she does not want to have a baby.

- Consider the issues that may impact on the development and give rise to concerns for the unborn child.

The development of the unborn child

We know that even before a child is born the environment will influence them indirectly through the impact and effects on the mother. As a social worker you will need to have an understanding of the relationship and interdependence of a number of inequalities that impact on a person's capacity to parent a child, (for example, those linked to structural inequalities such as poverty and the consequent impact on other aspects of life). O'Loughlin and O'Loughlin (2008) identify a range of such factors, including family history, the wider family, housing, employment, income, the family's social integration, and community resources. You will have been able to identify some of the factors that raise concern for Julie's baby (the mother's own mental health, for example). Julie's depression, and feelings and attitude towards the unborn child, are linked to that child's well-being. Children born to mothers who do not want them or are under stress can give rise to concerns about their development.

A mother's general health and nutritional intake will have an influence on the growing foetus. Julie's drug and alcohol use could be linked to increased risk for the unborn child (for example, premature birth, low birth weight, vulnerability to illness, and potential disability). Drinking substantial amounts of alcohol while pregnant can lead to impairment of development, potential behavioural difficulties, and in severe cases for the baby, foetal alcohol syndrome – a set of symptoms that cause learning disabilities.

Babies of mothers who are addicted to heroin are born addicted themselves and will need help in being weaned off the drug. Jowitt and O'Loughlin (2005, pp. 61–63) offer a brief review of the possible impact that parental mental health, problem drug and alcohol use or domestic violence may have on children's development. This review is helpfully structured by childhood age-groups. However, in any assessment you will need to balance the concerns for the ability of the parents to meet the child's needs with an assessment of strengths (for example, the likely impact of problems on their parenting capacity, their family history, their relationship, and the range of support networks available to them). For social workers working with a parent where there are concerns for the unborn child, the critical issue is to focus on an assessment of that child's needs (Parker and Bradley, 2014). The primary aim of any plan for the child must be to maximise the opportunities and chances for the parent to care for their child. However the focus must always be on the best interests of the child.

The growing child: a physical perspective

During the first two years of life the rate and range of development is enormous. Whilst babies are born with a small number of innate reflexes, all other physical movements and skills are learned and improved through practice and interaction with their environment.

Children generally show patterns in their development – they grow taller, gain weight, and their head circumference increases. Brain growth reflects the expected experiences of the child (for example, the stimulation that they are given through emotional, sensual and linguistic experiences).

All the senses operate at birth, with hearing as the most developed and sight the least developed, although developing quickly, with binocular vision developing at about 14 weeks. Children use all of their senses to strengthen their early interactions with others, especially their main carers.

As they develop, babies acquire a relatively predictable range of sensory and motor skills. Motor skills at birth are largely limited to the reflexes linked to survival – sucking and breathing. Gross motor skills, such as sitting up and walking, develop from about six months onwards.

Fine motor skills, such as picking up small objects, take longer to develop and acquire, but over time the ability to reach, grab and hold is developed. Whilst babies and children may share many patterns in their growth and the skills they develop, there are still many individual differences – you will need to get to know, observe and assess each child. Variations in the development of skills could be attributed to a child's genes, the culture in which they grow up, or may relate to development delay linked to disability.

Between the ages of two and six years significant development occurs in children's growth and in their ability in relation to gross and fine motor skills – from a toddler to a five-year-old who can run, skip and jump. Children continue to gain weight and height, generally becoming longer, thinner and more active. However, there are significant height and weight variations caused primarily by genes as well as cultural variations due to nutrition when compared with children in other parts of the world. Gross motor skills continue to develop so that an uncoordinated two-year-old develops into an able five-year-old, using their body in a way that will reflect the ways in which their cultural values have influenced them. Greater control is gained over fine motor skills, with confidence and competence emerging as children acquire greater skills.

The intention here is to illustrate the different influences on children's development. These may be attributed to a child's own genes, their temperament, their emotional and social development, the impact of the family, the context in which the family lives, and the culture in which that child grows up. Each of these cases carries limited information and to make an informed social work judgement you would need to gather further information. The critical issue is not to make assumptions. Additionally, you will need to avoid stereotyping – attributing to, or interpreting traits in, children and adults because of such things as social background, gender, race and culture. However, you should be aware of the importance and impact of 'difference' (for example culture) as well as the impact on your practice of your own values and assumptions.

One way to monitor and judge growth, related to height and weight, is the use of percentile charts – UK Growth Charts. Centile charts are based on mapping the individual physical growth of weight and height against a set of average standards or 'norms'. Medical professionals, particularly health visitors, use these extensively. Children need to be compared not only to the 'norms' of other children but also to their parents, their siblings and their own pattern of growth. Additionally, physical development should not be separated from other developments – everything else they are learning.

The centile chart is used to record weight, length and head size. Boys and girls have different charts because their growth pattern is slightly different. The chart has a thick vertical line a quarter of the way along the page. The baby's birth weight is plotted on this line with a dot marking the birth weight. (This may vary if the baby came more than three weeks early.) As the baby grows older the dot marks the place where their weight and age come together.

The thick line that goes across the page in a curve denotes the average line; this means that children plotted above the line are above average and those below the line are below average for weight or growth. Babies generally double their birth weight by four or five months.

Most babies treble their birth weight by one year. If a parent is of Asian origin, their baby will on average be lighter and shorter. If they are of African-Caribbean origin, the baby will on average be heavier and longer. The baby should have a fairly steady growth, which will show as a roughly curving line usually within the centile lines on the chart. However, as reinforced in the Early Years Foundation Stage theme 'Learning and Development' (DfES, 2007a, p. 17) different children will do different things at different times.

Activity 3.3

For each of these examples identify the factors that may have influenced the young child and led to the behaviours:

- Deanne, a three-year-old girl, was born prematurely to her young single mother. Deanne is developmentally delayed and has frequent episodes of ill-health, resulting in periods in hospital. When she is unhappy she bangs her head repeatedly on the floor. Deanne's mother finds her behaviour increasingly difficult to cope with and is depressed.
- Khalid, aged three, and his family are refugees who arrived six months ago from Afghanistan, following the death of his father. He is small and underweight for his age. The two older boys have settled well into their school lives. However, his mother is very concerned about Khalid as he is shy and withdrawn, clinging to his mother or two older brothers.
- Kieran and Patrick, twin boys aged 4, are described as the 'terrors' of the local nursery school. They are slightly underweight for their age with poor diets, only wanting to eat 'chips'. They are energetic and lively boys who have poor concentration skills, rarely sitting still; as a consequence they often have bruises or scrapes. Their hand–eye co-ordination is poor. They 'pick' on the other children; for example, punching and kicking the smaller children to obtain a toy or any food. Their mother appears timid and shy, finding it difficult to control their boys; their father, who appears quite dominant, says 'Boys will be boys'.

(Continued)

(Continued)

Comment

Each of these children is demonstrating behaviours that their parents may need advice and support with from professionals; all of them have a number of apparent needs. Deanne's mother needs support with Deanne's care and in supporting her development. It may be that she would benefit from support from Early Years Services such as Portage, a home-visiting educational service for preschool children with support needs and their families (www.portage.org.uk).

It could be that they would both benefit from a short/respite care break. Khalid appears to be suffering from the consequences of his past life and difficulties in 'making sense' of his current situation. Such things as support for his mother in identifying techniques and resources to help her with Khalid may help, particularly with the support of a person from a similar cultural background. In addition, Khalid may benefit from extra support to develop his confidence and integration with other children, through Early Years provision such as nursery school and family centres.

Kieran and Patrick appear to be influenced by their parents' behaviour and approaches to their behaviour; the focus may need to be on parental advice and guidance. For example, they may benefit from the use of behaviour modification techniques.

The growing child: biological perspectives

The focus of biological theories is that individual patterns and those shared with others are based on inherent patterns laid down in our genes, the control of hormones within our bodies and patterns of growth and development triggered through our brains. Gesell (1928), through studies of twins, advocated that our genes dictate the sequence of our growth, a process he called 'maturation'. Whilst there is no doubt that our genes impact on our growth and development, it is now recognised that a range of other interactions with the environment influence this. Through studies on animal behaviours, for example, the work of Konrad Lorenz (1970) established that some patterns of behaviour were innate – that is to say inborn – and therefore not learned. Additionally, there were crucial periods in the early days of animals and mammals when attachment took place between the child and the mother.

The study of attachment was developed in relation to human behaviour by the work of John Bowlby (1953), who believed that the development of attachment between a mother and a child was innately-driven behaviour. We shall return to the crucial issue of attachment shortly. Biological theories offer explanations for some sets of behaviour. You may be able to recognise instinctive behaviours (something done without thinking) in babies, such as physical reflexes. However, although biological explanations offer answers for some aspects of human behaviour, it is a more complex process.

The growing child: cognitive perspectives

Cognitive development is concerned with thinking – the mental activities by which we acquire and process knowledge. It involves a range of processes that we develop: intelligence and learning; memory and language; beliefs and assumptions; facts and concepts; teaching and education. Consequently, in any studies of human behaviour an understanding of the development and application of cognitive skills has a critical part to play in developing an understanding of that child or person.

One of the most influential people on the development of cognitive skills was Jean Piaget (1896–1980). His central assumption was that children are active participants in the development of knowledge, adapting to the environment through actively seeking to understand their environment. (You will notice that this contrasts with learning theory, which argues that the environment shapes the child.) The process of adaptation has several important sub-stages: schema, assimilation, accommodation and equilibration.

- *Schemas* are the basic building blocks and are the internal representation of a physical or mental action. Babies have limited schema such as touch, tasting and hearing. By the time they are adolescents they will show evidence of complex mental schema, such as analysis and reasoning. This ability to change is accounted for by Piaget by the three basic processes below:

  o *Assimilation* is the process of taking in the new elements of new experiences and information in terms of the schema that the child already possesses.

  o *Accommodation* is the process of modifying existing schema to fit new experiences or to create new schemas.

  o *Equilibration* refers to the process of balance in which accommodation is consolidated via assimilation.

Piaget identified distinct sets of age-related stages. The first of these stages was identified from birth to two years – the sensorimotor stage. In this stage exploration and learning occur primarily through immediate perception and physical experiences, being largely dominated by their immediate experiences. As they develop objects and acquire such concepts as thinking, memory and language, they will move into the next stage.

Between the ages of two and six years is the stage of pre-operational thought, in which the child shows interest and increasing understanding of how the world works and sophistication in their thinking, giving meaning to their experiences. There are several features of this stage:

- Egocentric – they have difficulty seeing things from a point of view other than their own.
- Centration – they focus their attention on one aspect of the situation due to having difficulty seeing that a situation may have a number of dimensions.
- Lack of reversibility – they fail to understand that working backwards can restore whatever existed before or that carrying out a second transformation can negate the first.

There have been critiques of Piaget's theory. One criticism is that his central concept of deductive reasoning is a typical characteristic of modern western society. This focus also denies other aspects of thinking, such as intuition and creativity. Additionally, Piaget appeared not to be interested in an examination and explanation of individual differences between children. The process is more complex than he would have us believe. In Chapter 4 we introduce the work of Lev Vygotsky (1896–1934), who places a different, but important, emphasis on the development of children's cognitive capacity and skills.

What are the implications of cognitive theories for social workers?

Activity 3.4

Michael is 5. He has been fostered with the Smith family for the last two years. He no longer has contact with his birth family. He is aware that the plan is to find him a 'new family' and you have been asked to talk to him about meeting a family who potentially wish to adopt him. Consider how you might do this, taking into account the level of cognitive understanding of a child of his age.

Comment

Social workers need to be sensitive to all aspects and levels of development and a child's ability to deal with concepts of varying kinds. Working with any child involves building up a relationship – one in which there is trust and commitment. In Michael's case, from a cognitive perspective you will be aware that he is able to use language and symbols as well as actual objects. However, he will be 'egocentric' in his views. Children need to be actively involved through discovery. They need concrete representations, gradually building up to more abstract reasoning. New ideas must be built on what children already know. Consequently, you will have to view this meeting from Michael's perspective – a focus on him as the key person. You could use paper, pencils and toys to explain the process, to say what is going to happen. A family album from the potential adoptive family will help Michael in mentally representing this family. Additionally, he will need to know what he will have to do before the meeting and what will happen after the meeting from his perspective.

Child development overview

The summaries below are taken from *The Early Years Foundation Stage (EYFS): Setting the Standards for Learning, Development and Care for Children from Birth to Five* (DfES, 2007b). They relate to the key themes and principles of the EYFS and broad phases of development. The summaries include areas of physical, cognitive, emotional and social development.

The EYFS recognises that all children are different, and to reflect this age ranges have been overlapped in it to create broad developmental phases. This emphasises that each child's progress is individual to them and that different children develop at different rates. Children do not suddenly move from one phase to another, and they do not make progress in all areas at the same time. However, there are some important 'steps' for each child to take along their own developmental pathway. There are six broad developmental phases.

Birth to 11 months

During this period, young children's physical development is very rapid and they gain increasing control of their muscles. They also develop skills in moving their hands, feet, limbs and head, quickly becoming mobile and able to handle and manipulate objects. They are learning from the moment of their birth. Even before their first words they will have discovered a lot about language by hearing people talking, and will be especially interested when this involves them and their daily lives. Sensitive care giving, which responds to children's growing understanding and emotional needs, helps to build secure attachments to special people such as parents, family members or carers. Regular, though flexible, routines help young children to gain a sense of order in the world and to anticipate events. A wide variety of experience, which involves all the senses, encourages learning and an interest in the environment.

8–20 months

As children become mobile, new opportunities for exploration and exercise open up. A safe and interesting environment, with age-appropriate resources, helps children to develop curiosity, co-ordination and physical abilities. This is a time when children can start to learn the beginnings of self-control and how to relate to other people. In this period they can be encouraged to develop their social and mental skills by people to whom they have a positive attachment. Building on their communication skills, they now begin to develop a sense of self and are more able to express their needs and feelings. Alongside non-verbal communication children learn a few simple words for everyday things and people. With encouragement and plenty of interaction with carers, their communication skills grow and their vocabulary expands very rapidly during this period.

16–26 months

Children in this phase are usually full of energy and need careful support to use it well. Growing physical strengths and skills mean that children need active times for exercise, and quiet times for calmer activities. Playing with other children

(Continued)

(Continued)

is an important new area for learning. This helps children to better understand other people's thoughts and feelings, and to learn how to co-operate with others. Exploration and simple self-help build a sense of self-confidence. They are also learning about boundaries and how to handle frustration. Play with toys that come apart and fit together encourages problem solving and simple planning. Pretend play helps them learn about a range of possibilities. Adults are an important source of security and comfort.

22–36 months

Children's fine motor skills continue to develop and they enjoy making marks, using a variety of materials, looking at picture books and listening to stories, all of which are important steps in literacy. Self-help and independence soon emerge if adults support and encourage children in areas such as eating, dressing and toileting. Praise for new achievements helps to build their self-esteem. In this phase, children's language is developing rapidly and many are beginning to put sentences together. Joining in conversations with children is an important way for children to learn new things and begin to think about past, present and future. Developing physical skills mean that they can now usually walk, climb and run, and join in active play with other children. This is an important time for learning about dangers and safe limits.

30–50 months

An increased interest in joint play such as make-believe, construction and games helps children to learn the important social skills of sharing and co-operating. Children also learn more about helping adults in everyday activities and finding a balance between independence and complying with the wishes of others. Children still need the comfort and security of special people. Close, warm relationships with carers form the basis for much learning, such as encouraging children to make healthy choices in food and exercise. At this stage they are becoming more aware of their place in a community. Literacy and numeracy can develop rapidly with the support of a wide range of interesting materials and activities. Their language is now much more complex, as many become adept at using longer sentences. Conversations with adults become a more important source of information, guidance and reassurance.

40–60+ months

During this period children are building a stronger sense of their own identity and their place in a wider world. They are beginning to recognise the importance of social rules and customs, to show understanding and tolerance of others, and to learn how to be more controlled in their own behaviour. Learning and playing in small groups helps to foster the development of social skills. Children now become better able to plan and undertake more challenging activities with a wider range of materials for making and doing. In this phase they learn effectively in shared activities with more able peers and adults. Literacy and problem solving, reasoning and numeracy skills, continue to develop. Children's developing understanding of cause and effect is encouraged by the introduction of a wider variety of equipment, media and technologies.

(Adapted from DfES, 2007b)

The social and emotional development of infants and children: developing attachments

The relationships that we develop and form with others, especially caregivers, are central to our emotional and social security. Child development takes place, to a large degree, through social relationships.

Communication

A necessary start to socialisation is the existence of communication between children and others, particularly adults. Facial expressions, particularly smiling, are usually the beginning of communication. Although voluntary smiling may begin at around four to six weeks, it begins to be reserved for a social context from around two to three months, with particular smiling for those who are recognised. As babies pay attention to human faces and voices, they learn to distinguish between familiar people and voices, such as a parent. They also learn the social consequence of their actions, such as crying and smiling, through the response and importance that is given to them by their carer. Therefore the child is able to give meaning to their behaviour through noting the effect and response on their carers. Babies learn to respond to the parent through learning about their response. For example, a baby smiling initiates a positive response in the parent, the parent interacts with the child and the baby responds with further smiling. Finally, children learn to use their carer for 'social referencing' – gauging a parent's emotional response to a situation before deciding how to interact themselves (Smith *et al.*, 2015).

Research has shown that even before birth babies can identify familiar voices (Karmiloff and Karmiloff-Smith, 2002) and it is to those familiar sounds that the newborn child will initially develop attachments.

Attachment

Children need to feel secure in their relationships. An adult, for example a parent, needs to form a positive, emotional attachment to the child to care for them. Early relationships are seen as important as they are viewed by theorists as having a critical role in the person's emotional well-being throughout their life. Therefore, attachment is central to infants' and children's social and emotional development.

> *How we are depends on how we experience* [these] *early relationships. Warmth, mutuality, support and security are qualities of relationships that tend to produce coherent, well-organised later selves.*

(Payne, 2014, p. 81)

Attachment theory involves the study of relationships, in particular the critical early relationships of infants and children.

Children use the people to whom they are attached as:

- a safe base from which to explore;
- a source of comfort;
- a source of encouragement and guidance.

Attachment behaviours are patterns of action that keep them in touch with the other person: smiling, crying, laughing, talking and so on.

Traditionally, research into attachment was heavily influenced by psychoanalytic theory, in particular Freud's, who emphasised the importance of the infant–mother relationship. Learning theory explained attachment as operating to satisfy innate needs or drives: the primary drive was the need for satisfaction of basic needs (e.g. the need for food); the secondary drive was the attachment to the mother in order to meet these needs. Further studies would suggest that the development of attachment is a more complex process.

There are two parts to the development of attachment between a baby and their parents: an initial first part immediately after birth, referred to as 'bonding' (usually with the mother); and a second, more important part that develops during the early years of a baby's life.

Bonding

The process of bonding was thought to critically take place usually within hours of birth between the mother and the child. 'Bonding' primarily signifies a bond between the mother and baby, which has been linked to a profound effect on their future relationships with each other. However, it may be more useful to some to view this process as 'claiming' behaviour: 'checking out' the baby and beginning to make physical and emotional links with the child.

Whilst immediate and close contact is helpful in the beginning of the development of a relationship, studies (Svejda *et al.*, 1980; Eyer, 1993) have shown that it is not essential in the establishment of a long-term positive relationship. It is more helpful to see the process of attachment as a process that could begin during these early days but which then continues.

Supporting mother–baby contact in the early days can help those mothers who are most at risk of providing poor parenting, but only if this support continues in later months. The failure to bond is not by itself an indication of difficulties in parenting or an explanation of later abuse. Though the baby seems to prefer the mother, this does not mean that they have formed a relationship. Early relationships do not have to be with the mother; babies can equally form relationships with their fathers and others.

Attachment during the early years of life

Whilst the early days are not irrelevant, the first few months appear to be more crucial in developing a sense of attachment, particularly between parents and children. The original concept of 'attachment' has been attributed to the studies developed by John Bowlby (1953, 1969, 1973, 1988). He was highly influential from the mid-1940s to the mid-1970s, shaping research, policies and practice over several decades. Like Freud, Bowlby believed that the root of the development of personality lay in early childhood and that any trauma or failure in these early relationships would permanently shape the development of the child's personality. Drawing on ethological theory, the study of animals and humans within an evolutionary context, he suggested that human evolution resulted in babies having a biological need or *instinct* to form an attachment. Mothers, whom Bowlby believed were the critical relationship in a child's early life, also had a biological need to be near and protect their children. Therefore 'attachment' is a primary motivational need. The impact of prolonged separation on children was viewed as 'maternal deprivation' – the temporary or permanent loss to a child of their mother's care and attention. He believed that prolonged separation of the child from their mother, especially during the first five years of their life, was a major cause of 'delinquent' behaviour and mental health issues. Additionally, this loss of their mother's love appeared to make them incapable of normal emotions, a condition he described as 'affectionless psychopathy', which in turn led to problems in their own ability to parent.

Bowlby's research has had a major impact on the study of attachment. However, as research has developed there have been criticisms of some of the early thinking on attachment theory.

Children can make attachment relationships to other people, not just their mother. They can also form several attachments. Developing relationships with others is equally important, for example with fathers, siblings and other relatives. The key factor is that the person spends time with them building a relationship. Reliance on one 'exclusive' relationship can itself be damaging, as it does not allow for supportive, healthy relationships with others. Children need to experience stable, reliable relationships. Whilst early experience is important, the idea that this is the pattern for the rest of their lives denies the opportunity to potentially reverse the effect of negative early experiences. A child's outlook on the world depends on how distressing events are handled by others. Children's experiences and development also depend on what happens after the early years. Equally, positive experiences in early life do not make a child safe from later emotional damage. Attributing problems in behaviour and in later life to maternal deprivation (loss) denies the impact of other factors, especially the impact of privation, that is to say a chronic lack of, for example, basic needs, stimulation such as play, the role of others rather than just emotional warmth (Rutter, 1981). The multi-cultural dimensions of relationships need to be taken into account: for example, the different patterns of child rearing and the role of the wider family network.

Bowlby did recognise that the quality and strengths of attachments do vary. Mary Ainsworth, a colleague of Bowlby's, designed an experimental situation, the 'Strange Situation' procedure, which sought to evaluate the relationship that a child has with attachment figures. Ainsworth's (1973) classification demonstrates that infant behaviour can be attributed to secure or insecure attachments (see Table 3.1).

Patterns of attachment can be affected by a variety of factors. The best predictor of a child's secure attachment is the attention and sensitivity of the carer. Howe (1995) notes that observation of children (for example when tired, frightened or unwell) can support the assessment of the attachment relationship with the main carer (see Table 3.2).

Other factors include the impact of family stressors such as low socio-economic status and marital discord. The child's own characteristics may contribute towards the quality of the attachment relationship: for example, children who get upset easily.

Table 3.1 Patterns and characteristics of attachment (adapted from Ainsworth, 1973)

Patterns of attachment	Characteristics
Secure (Type B)	Explores freely when their caregiver is present using the caregiver as a secure base. May be distressed at separation. Always greets the caregiver on reunion. If distressed during separation, seeks contact and comfort during reunion, then settles down to continue play.
Insecure-avoidant (Type A)	Explores freely, seems uninterested in the caregiver's presence or departure. On reunion, ignores or actively avoids caregiver.
Insecure-resistant/ ambivalent (Type C)	Resists active exploration. Preoccupied with caregiver. Upset at separation. On reunion both resists and seeks contact, showing anger, passivity or clinging. Does not easily return to play.
Disorganised (Type D)	Neither plays freely nor responds to the caregiver in any one coherent mode. May cry and then hit; may 'freeze', trance-like; may move in slow motion or other stereotyped manner; may show fear of parent.
Not classified	Some children fit into none of the four categories.

Table 3.2 Carer response to attachment (adapted from Howe, 1995)

Patterns of attachment	Response of carer
Secure	Usually knows the best way to give comfort and care. Caregiver is available and accessible during times of distress and able to contain and regulate distressed state. Inclined to hold and cuddle child as a regular part of their behaviour. Acknowledges their child with smiles and conversation, with a tender-warm voice. Responds to their child's vocalisation. Emotional availability and sensitivity supports the child in the development of sense of self-esteem and self-worth.
Insecure-avoidant	Caregiver uses more controlling co-operative tactics. Rebuffs or is indifferent towards the child. Child is insecure but compulsively self-reliant.
Insecure-resistant/ambivalent	Caregiver is not hostile or rejecting but inconsistent, insensitive and lacking in accurate empathy. Child views self as dependent and poorly valued.
Disorganised	Carer shows little or no sensitivity to the child's emotional needs. Frightening or frightened.
Not classified	Child views self as helpless, angry or unworthy.

Research summary

Disorganised attachment in children

Disorganised attachment is claimed most frequently to happen in abusive relationships by a parent to a child. Attachment disorganisation has been very closely linked to a history of parental maltreatment, maternal depression and drug abuse.

Attachment to an adult or primary carer provides a child with a secure base from which the child can explore independently but always have a safe place to return to. When a child experiences safety and support and/or abuse from a parent or carer, they may experience this behaviour as life threatening. Unreliability and mistrust of adults and chronic uncertainty of being kept safe dominate the child's experience. Survival instincts may tell the child to flee; however, their secure base is in the very person who is frightening them, their attachment figure. Main and Hesse (1990) call this 'fear without solution'. This can lead to confused and disorganised behaviours:

- As an attempt to take control the child demonstrates controlling behaviours, including role reversal: the child might act towards others as the parent acts towards the child, for example, compulsively caregiving or compulsively self-reliant.

(Continued)

(Continued)

- Rejection is feared so approaching the carer for support and help is avoided. In this case the child may psychologically by disassociate from themselves, detaching themselves from what is happening to them. Because they do not have a reliable enough secure base, coping with challenge and fear is minimal, with feelings of helplessness and shame; consequently, the child may find tolerating not knowing as a severe challenge. The defence to cope with their feelings of helplessness is overwhelming anxiety, which can be accompanied with aggression.

Shemmings and Shemmings (2011) have undertaken a review of contemporary research into disorganised attachment. For example, they have examined the correlation between 'being an abuser' and having been abused as a child:

- Although strongly correlated with abuse, caregiver characteristics – such as parental mental ill-health, serious drug or alcohol use, or having been abused as a child – are unreliable predictors of maltreatment.
- Disorganised attachment is a more reliable indicator of maltreatment.
- Children who are abused are likely to show disorganised attachment behaviour, which manifests itself differently depending on the age of the child.
- Certain caregiver behaviours have also been shown to be more reliably predictive of maltreatment. These are: unresolved loss and trauma; disconnected or extremely insensitive parenting; and low reflective function.

Crittenden (2008) has developed the dynamic-maturational model of attachment and adaptation (DMM). This model emphasises the dynamic interaction of the maturing person across the life course with the context in which maturing possibilities are used to protect the self, reproduce, and protect their children.

In developing attachment it is important to be sensitive to a child's needs. Vera Fahlberg (1991) developed two models to understand the development of attachment: the 'arousal and relaxation' cycle and the 'positive interaction' cycle:

- The arousal and relaxation cycle – The child experiences a need leading to displeasure (arousal). The caregiver responds to the need and the child is calm (relaxation). The child initiates this cycle and their experience of the response leads to trust, security and attachment by the child.

- Positive interaction cycle – The caregiver initiates positive interaction with the child, which produces a positive response from the child. This response leads to further positive interaction from the carer and so on. The carer initiates the cycle and the child's experience of this cycle leads to the development of self-worth and self-esteem.

Fahlberg has produced a clear, detailed observation checklist to support the assessment of attachment in her book *A Child's Journey Through Placement* (1991).

The case of Denny (see Case Study 3.1) demonstrates concerns in relation to his attachment. Whilst his behaviour may signify distress at the loss of his main attachment figure, his apparent inability and/or lack of desire to respond to any overtures on the part of his foster carers gives rise to concerns. He appears to have become self-sufficient, relying on his own strategies to care for himself. This is further reinforced when his mother visits. She makes no attempt to initiate contact or comfort him. As Howe (1995) suggests, different attachment styles and care-seeking behaviours represent different psychological and behavioural strategies developed by children to maximise the care and protection available under particular care-giving regimes. Children actively seek ways of adapting to their world rather than becoming victims of it.

Case study 3.1

Denny, aged 14 months, has been fostered with the Greys for four weeks. He came into care because of concerns about his mother's ability to care for him. He is very independent. Denny feeds himself, refusing to take food from his carers when offered directly – they have to put it in a place where he can reach it himself. The same happens with toys – he will only take toys that are placed where he can reach him. He prefers solitary play. Denny rarely responds to the carers and when attempts are made to cuddle him he goes rigid. When his mother visits he goes to her and offers her a toy. She looks at the toy and gives it back to him. He sits near her. Denny's mother spends a lot of time talking to the foster carers about her problems – with her boyfriend, with friends, with money. Denny does not cry when she leaves but sits quietly staring out of the window.

Why is attachment theory important for social workers?

The nature, form and development of relationships are crucial to social work practice. The assessment of these relationships will play a critical part in your practice. When assessing and planning for the needs of children you are seeking to identify strengths within the family and their relationship, areas of existing strengths and safety, to build on to address issues and move forward:

> *There can be no doubt that the child protection worker must gather information about past and potential harm and family deficiencies, but to balance the picture it is also vital to obtain information regarding past, existing, and potential safety, competencies, and strengths. This balance of information regarding family functioning allows the worker to achieve a comprehensive assessment of risk in child protection cases.*

> (Turnell and Edwards, 1999, p. 101)

Attachment theory provides part of a model of analysis in judging the quality of a relationship. This can be essential in knowing any risks or complicating factors in the case, when to intervene, or even remove a child, where there are concerns in relation to attachment. Examining issues in relation to attachment supports the critical importance of keeping the child 'in view', at the centre of practice, as fundamental to good assessment. Additionally, we need to understand the impact of the loss of their attachment figure on the child, for example in order to understand their subsequent behaviour. You will need to support carers in developing behaviours which will promote attachment in the child, such as within an adoptive family. Your skills in communication and observation will be essential in assessing and supporting the development of attachment behaviour.

Resilience and vulnerability

In this case study, and Case Study 3.2 below, we can identify factors that could impact on the children's development. In respect of Rachel we are able to identify factors such as the parents' substance use and dad's mental ill health, and she could be said to be demonstrating secure attachment patterns. Likewise Sarah has experienced the impact of her parents' break-up and moving to a new area, and may be demonstrating ambivalent or avoidant patterns of attachment.

However, each of these children appear to respond differently to the apparent adversity in their lives. How can we explain these different responses? We could say that the teachers' perception of the children may be because of their response to liking or disliking school. Certainly in your role as a social worker it is important that you undertake an assessment of each child, to obtain as full a picture as possible from all those involved, to help you understand that child and their response in a range of situations (see Parker and Bradley, 2nd edn, 2010). However, the teachers' perceptions of the children lead us to ask a number of broader questions:

- What are the adversities – life events or circumstances – that pose a threat to healthy development?

- Are there factors within the environment that provide children with support to safeguard them against adverse experiences?

- Are there factors that may make some children more vulnerable than others to coping with adversity?

- What are the factors that promote resilience – the ability in an individual to overcome stressful and difficult situations and function competently and confidently? (Daniel et al., 1999/2010)

Case study 3.2

Rachel, the youngest of four children, is 5 and has just started school. Her teacher is aware that her parents are long-term substance users. Rachel's father suffers from mental ill-health, which results in his having in-hospital treatment on occasions. The family lifestyle is described as 'chaotic' and Rachel's maternal grandmother provides a lot of support to the family. Her teacher describes Rachel as a happy, outgoing child, who is bright and responsive and mixes well with the other children.

Sarah, the older of two children, is 5 and has just started school. Sarah, her mum and brother have recently moved to the area. Her mother describes this as a 'fresh start' after a difficult marital break-up. She has infrequent contact with her dad. Her teacher describes her as a shy, unhappy little girl who does not mix with the other children.

Adversities that impact on a child

The family environment into which children are born will have the most profound and significant impact on the child. Factors within the family that may influence their ability to respond to the child's developmental needs include the parents' own experience of childhood and parenting style, adverse circumstances within the family and the socio-economic status of the family. Additionally, there are children who suffer abuse and neglect, which pose a threat to their healthy development.

Protective environments

Protective environments refer to the immediate network of relationships between the individual, their immediate family and their local community. For children this includes one enduring supportive relationship. Additionally, a good school experience can support children in overcoming adversities. For the parent, protective environments may be in the form of community support and networks, particularly those that offer emotional support and practical help and advice.

Vulnerability

Factors which promote vulnerability for children include: disability, racism, children who appear to have an 'unusual' or 'difficult' temperament. Parental issues which may lead to vulnerability for the child include experiences of their own childhood lacking in affectionate contact with key adults, mental health issues and when parental needs are focused elsewhere, for example through frequent drug and alcohol use.

Resilience

Despite adversities some children are able to develop reasonably well-adjusted personalities, demonstrating resilience and normal development under difficult circumstances. Resilience can be described as a phenomenon or process reflecting relatively positive adaptation despite experience of adversity or trauma (Luthar, 2015, p. 742).

Research summary

Tony Newman and Sarah Blackburn's report describes effective strategies for helping children cope with periods of transition and change through the promotion of resilience. They suggest resilient children are better equipped to resist stress and adversity, cope with change and uncertainty, and recover from traumatic events and episodes. They have identified a number of resilience factors, as shown in Table 3.3.

Table 3.3 Strategies for helping children cope with transition (adapted from Newman and Blackburn, 2002)

The child	The family	The environment
Temperament (active, good-natured)	Warm, supportive parents	Supportive extended family
Female bonding prior to and male during adolescence	Good parent-child relationships	Successful school experiences
Age (being younger)	Parental harmony	Friendship networks
Higher IQ	Valued social role (e.g. care of siblings, helping neighbours)	Valued social role (e.g. a job, volunteering)
Social skills	Close relationship with one parent	Close relationship with unrelated mentor
Personal awareness		Member of religious or faith community
Feelings of empathy		
Internal locus of control		
Humour		
Attractiveness		

Newman and Blackburn (2002) outline the current evidence in relation to research:

- Evidence from longitudinal studies indicates that a large proportion of children recover from short-lived childhood adversities with little detectable impact in adult life.
- An excessive preoccupation with the identification and elimination of risk factors may weaken children's capacity to overcome adversities.

- All interventions in health, education and social care may do harm as well as good.
- Resilience may be weakened by unnecessary or harmful interventions.
- Where adversities are continuous and severe, and protective factors are absent, resilience in children is a rare phenomenon.
- The most common sources of anxiety for children are chronic and transitional events.
- Chronic problems will usually have more lasting effects than acute adversities.
- While self-esteem is a crucial factor in the promotion of resilience, it is more likely to grow and be sustained through developing valued skills in real-life situations, rather than just through praise and positive affirmation.
- It is necessary to promote children's ability to resist adversities as well as moderating risk factors.
- Resilience can only develop through exposure to stressors. Resistance develops through gradual exposure to difficulties at a manageable level of intensity.
- A supportive family is the most powerful resilience-promoting factor.
- The acquisition of valued social roles, the ability to contribute to the general household economy and educational success are resilience-promoting factors.
- Experiences that promote resilience may not always be pleasant or socially acceptable.
- Poor early experiences do not necessarily 'fix' a child's future trajectory. Compensatory interventions in later life can trigger resilient responses.

They suggest that the factors that promote resilience are:

- strong social support networks;
- the presence of at least one unconditionally supportive parent or parent substitute;
- a committed mentor or other person from outside the family;
- positive school experiences;
- a sense of mastery and a belief that one's own efforts can make a difference;
- a range of extra-curricular activities that promote the learning of competencies and emotional maturity;
- the capacity to re-frame adversities so that the beneficial as well as the damaging effects are recognised;
- the ability, or opportunity, to 'make a difference' by, for example, helping others through volunteering, or undertaking part-time work; and
- exposure to challenging situations which provide opportunities to develop both problem-solving abilities and emotional coping skills.

(Newman and Blackburn, 2002)

Safeguarding children: children in need and children in need of protection

As a social worker you will deal with vulnerable people. Under Section 17 of the Children Act 1989, local authorities are required:

> *to safeguard and promote the welfare of children in their area who are in need by*
> *providing a range and level of services appropriate to those needs.*

This means that you will be working with families in supporting them in responding to the development needs of their children. Inevitably, you will be working with children who are the victims of abuse – physical, sexual, emotional, and through neglect.

The government defines 'safeguarding' as the action we take to promote the welfare of children and that to protect them from harm is everyone's responsibility. Everyone who comes into contact with children and families has a role to play.

Safeguarding and promoting the welfare of children is defined as:

- protecting children from maltreatment;

- preventing impairment of children's health or development;

- ensuring that children grow up in circumstances consistent with the provision of safe and effective care;

- taking action to enable all children to have the best outcomes.

(DH, 2015, p. 5)

A concern will be whether the child is experiencing significant harm or impairment. Your intervention will be based on an assessment that is timely, transparent and proportionate to the child's needs and that of their family. *Working Together to Safeguard Children* (DH, 2015: 20) sets out an Assessment Framework. This framework is intended to support a systematic approach to enquiries using a conceptual model that is the best way to deliver a comprehensive assessment for all children. It identifies three systems, which need to interact together to promote a child's long-term well-being: their developmental needs; parenting capacity; and family and environmental factors. You will be assessing the child's needs and the family's previous and current ability to respond to those needs and sustain this throughout their childhood. Incorporated into your assessment should be an assessment of the developmental needs of the child. The framework identifies seven dimensions of developmental need which children require to progress towards achieving a healthy adulthood: health, education, identity, family and social relations, social presentation, emotional and behavioural development and self-care skills (see Parker and Bradley, 2014).

An understanding of child growth and development will be an essential skill in your work with children who have been abused and in an assessment of their needs. For example, in assessing a child's identity, the sense of themselves as a separate and valued being, you will need to be aware of their experience within their family and within the wider community in which they live: do they receive praise and encouragement within their family? Do they feel 'accepted' by their community? It would be helpful to draw on the work of Erikson in assessing this. Assessment of the child's emotional and behavioural development will be supported by considering issues in relation to attachment. For example, is there evidence of a warm and positive relationship in which the child is given consistent boundaries?

> *Child development theories are essential underpinning knowledge for social work practice but in the area of child protection are crucial.*

> (Jowitt and O'Loughlin, 2005, p. 59)

Reflection point

- What do I know, or can I do now, that I did not know or could not do before I did this section of studying?
- Is there anything I do not understand or want to explore further?
- What else do I need to know to extend my professional development and learning in this area?

Chapter summary

Growth and development within early childhood are rapid and involve a complex interaction of 'internal' process supported by 'external' support and stimulation. Understanding the nature of development supports social workers in their practice – in assessment, intervention and review in children's and families' lives. The concept of 'childhood' has undergone a historical process of change. We now recognise the changing nature of childhood and its importance in creating happy, healthy adults, for example through their legitimised rights. However, we also need to recognise that many children continue to live in adverse circumstances. We acknowledge that children from different cultures and children with disabilities may experience their development in a different way from other children. Within Britain today we can see the continuing impact of poverty and the potential adverse result this may have on children both during childhood and subsequently as they grow into adults. Whilst physical and biological changes impact on children, the area of the development of cognitive skills offers many challenges. The development and sustaining of attachment for babies and children is of critical importance, and social work practice has a key role in assessing and supporting its development. We recognise that there are children who may be particularly vulnerable to adversity.

(Continued)

(Continued)

However, we have also been able to identify factors which promote resilience in children. Finally, we have introduced the topic of abuse and highlighted that an assessment of a child's development needs will support a wider assessment process. In the next chapter we build on these foundations and examine themes and issues in relation to the middle years of childhood.

Further reading

Boyd, DG and Bee, HL (2014) *The Developing Child* (13th edn). Harlow: Pearson.

This book provides a readable account of child development.

Cleaver, H, Nicholson, D, Tarr, S and Cleaver, D (2008) *Child Protection, Domestic Violence and Parental Substance Misuse.* London: Jessica Kingsley.

The focus of the research is children referred to children's social care where there are safeguarding concerns and evidence of domestic violence and/or parental substance misuse. An Executive Summary can be found at: http://dera.ioe.ac.uk/8820/7/child-protection-domesticviolence-parentalsubstance-misuse-2_Redacted.pdf

Daniel, B, Wassell, S and Gilligan, R (2010) *Child Development for Child Care and Protection Workers* (2nd edn). London: Jessica Kingsley.

This book summarises important current thinking on child development and applies it directly to practice. It covers key issues such as resilience and vulnerability and the impact of protective or adverse environments. Different stages of development (infancy, school age and adolescence) are discussed and attachment theory is used to offer insights into the impact of abuse and neglect on development. A key feature is the inclusion of case studies and activities to allow the reader to improve their understanding and reflect on good practice.

Fahlberg, V (1991) *A Child's Journey Through Placement*. London: BAAF.

This book takes readers through the stages of development and attachment, providing examples and frameworks to assess children's needs, particularly for those in the looked after system.

Meggitt, C (2012) *Child Development: An Illustrated Guide* (3rd edn). Harlow: Pearson Education.

Although this book offers a guide to child development from birth to 16 years, the first 12 parts of Section One are devoted to birth to five years old. This is a very readable text which develops a holistic approach to understanding child development.

Prior, V and Glaser, D (2006) *Understanding Attachment and Attachment Disorders: Theory, Evidence and Practice.* London: Jessica Kingsley.

This book is structured into five parts, which include discussion about theoretical perspectives as well as a critical appraisal of attachment theory-based interventions.

Robinson, M (2011) *Understanding Behaviour and Development in Early Childhood: A Guide to Theory and Practice.* Abingdon: Routledge.

This book examines the behaviour of babies and young children in a developmental context, and takes into account the shifts and changes over time as young children grow and mature.

www.rip.org.uk – Research in Practice is a network of more than 112 Partner Agencies from local authorities and voluntary agencies. They aim to bridge the gaps between research, practice and service users' lived experiences to improve practice and ultimately outcomes for children and families. They produce a range of learning resources aimed at building knowledge and skills to support confident decision making.

www.scie.org.uk – The Social Care Institute for Excellence (SCIE) has a number of resources and publications that examine issues in relation to the development of children.

4: Using life course development knowledge in social work practice with older children and their families

Introduction

In this chapter you will consider life course development knowledge in respect of older children, children in their 'middle years', with particular consideration given to social work practice in the context of contemporary policy and legislation. The chaper will start by providing an overview of middle childhood and outlining the context of development. You will explore theories and explanations of development in middle childhood that examine psychosocial processes, biological processes and cognitive processes in particular aspects of learning. You will also examine the role of the family and adults, especially parents and carers, in supporting the development of children. The final section in this chapter will demonstrate how an understanding of development needs to be placed in the context of patterns of interactions – the ecological approach.

As discussed in Chapter 3, this book is set within the context of contemporary social work practice and related policy and legislation. Of particular relevance to your learning in this chapter about older children's development and social work practice are better outcomes for children. Whilst *Every Child Matters: Change for Children* is no longer official government policy and terminology, the DfE state there is no lack of focus on *Every Child Matters* nor on positive outcomes for children. *Every Child Matters* identified five key outcomes that are considered to be the most important to children and young people:

1. Be healthy.
2. Stay stafe.
3. Enjoy and achieve.
4. Make a positive contribution.
5. Achieve economic well-being.

Figure 4.1 illustrates how the outcomes and their underlying aims come together in the Every Child Matters programme.

The Children and Families Act 2014 became law in March 2014. The act is wide-ranging, tackling a number of issues, including school meals and smoking in cars. At its core, however, it is intended to improve services for vulnerable children (described as children in the adoption and care systems), those affected by decisions of the family courts and those with special educational needs, and to provide greater supporting to families. It contains measures intended to:

- remove barriers to adoption (as responses to *An Action Plan for Adoption: Tackling Delay* (DfE, 2011a) and *Further Action on Adoption: Finding More Loving Homes* (2013b)). The overall aim is to get children placed with adoptive families more quickly, and to increase the number of adopters and reduce the delays that adopters and children face in matching. The act requires local authorities to consider placing children with families or friend carers in the first instance and, where this is not appropriate, to place children in foster-to-adopt with their prospective adopters. It repeals the requirement for councils to give 'due consideration' to children's racial, religious, cultural or linguistic background when matching them with adopters.

- introduce 'staying put arrangements' that will allow young people to remain in foster care until their 21st birthday. Local authorities are able to reject these arrangements if they believe they are not in the best interest of the young person, but when those arrangements are approved councils must provide advice, assistance and support, including financial help. The new law also requires local authorities to appoint at least virtual school heads to promote the educational achievement of looked after children.

- reform the family justice system as a response to the *Family Justice Review* (Ministry of Justice and DfE, 2011) and introduce changes in the system for the benefit of children and families. For example, it makes it a requirement to attend a family mediation, information and assessment meeting to find out about and consider mediation before applying for certain types of court order; introduces a maximum 26-week time limit for completing care and supervision proceedings, with the possibility of extending the time limit in a particular case for up to eight weeks at a time, should that be necessary to resolve the proceedings justly.

- reform the special educational needs system as a response to the Green Paper *Support and Aspiration: A New Approach to Special Educational Needs and Disability* (DfE, 2011b). The act introduces changes to support for children and young people with special educational needs (SEN), creating education, health and care (EHC) plans to replace SEN statements. EHC plans will need to reviewed regularly and cover people up to the age of twenty-five years old. The basic goals are to give families a greater involvement in decisions about their support, and to encourage social care, education and health services to work together more closely in supporting those with special needs or disabilities. As part of the changes local authorities are required to publish a 'local offer' setting out what support is available to families with children who have disabilities or SEN. The local offer should also explain how families can request personal budgets, make complaints, and access more specialist help. The act says families with EHC plans will be offered personal budgets and also places a duty on local authorities to identify all children in their area who have SEN or disabilities.

- in conjunction with the adult-focused Care Act, make sure that young carers get the support they need. Under the act, local authorities are expected to try and identify young carers so they can be offered support, and both adult and children's social services will need to work together on helping young carers.

- strengthen the role of the Children's Commissioner as a result of *Review of the Office of the Children's Commissioner (England)* (DfE, 2010), by amending the Commissioner's primary function to one of independence, promoting and protecting children's rights, and ensuring that services place children and young people at the centre of decision making and support.

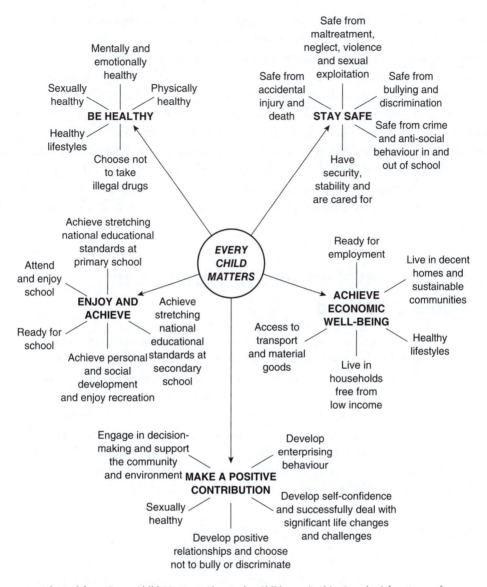

Figure 4.1 Adapted from *Every Child Matters: Change for Children*, cited in Crawford (2006, p. 14)

Defining middle childhood

The transition into middle childhood is defined as the period of growth and development between the ages of approximately 5–12 years of age. It is suggested that it is qualitatively different from that of young childhood. This is evident through shifts in the child's social world with increased understanding of self and the development of complex thinking. There are greater opportunities for independence, highly influenced by the transition to formal education.

The period of middle childhood is one of relative stability. It is marked on one side by the rapid growth and development of infancy and young childhood, and on the other by the beginning of adolescence and puberty. However, there are important features of middle childhood. Physical developments allow children to master a range of new skills. Children make advances in cognitive skills and patterns. Features of personality develop that will support and affect development in adolescence and adulthood. They begin to see the world from others' perspectives. Whilst the family is still important, they learn more about the world and their role within it as they have increased autonomy and independence. Children's social networks expand; they establish relationships with a wider range of others. Friendships become important, particularly same-sex friendships. Adults outside the family have a greater influence on the child, for example teachers. Children may become part of wider society, such as clubs and groups.

Theories and explanations of development in middle childhood

In this section we shall explore in greater depth theories and explanations of middle childhood. Whilst theorists and researchers appear to give less emphasis to this area, this is an important phase of development in consolidating and developing the abilities and skills acquired in early childhood and in preparation for adolescence. In middle childhood, children become more independent, exploring and gaining an understanding of the wider world of their community. Their lives continue to be shaped and guided by their family and cultural values. Social development is an essential part of the skills that develop in middle childhood, being a unique configuration of social, biological and cognitive characteristics. In all cultures, middle childhood appears to be a universal stage of human development.

Physical development in middle childhood

In relative terms, children in middle childhood grow more slowly as compared to early years. However, they continue to grow gradually and steadily throughout this period. Growth varies depending on genes, gender and nutrition. Typically, the majority of school-age children become stronger and are healthier.

One of the five outcomes identified in the Every Child Matters programme (www. everychildmatters.gov.uk) is 'being healthy': enjoying good physical and mental health and living a healthy lifestyle. As you will have seen, however, in the previous chapter, children's development is very individual.

Generally in the middle years of childhood both gross and fine motor skills continue to develop, especially in relation to expertise, for example sporting abilities and abilities in penmanship. Boys and girls are almost equal in their physical abilities. However, cultural influences have a significant impact on differences between sexes. Boys tend to play with other boys in large groups in organised games that involve 'conflict'. Girls form smaller, more intimate groups where fine motor skills are practised (Maccoby, 2002).

For some children their specific needs will only become apparent when they begin school. Some children with specific needs will have benefited from identification in early childhood. However, other children, for example those with behavioural or specific learning issues, may not be identified until they begin school.

Activity 4.1

Jake, aged 5, has Down's Syndrome. As a consequence he has a moderate hearing impairment, speech problems and slow motor development. His mother feels he would benefit from more specialised help in a specialised school. She feels this would give Jake better access to expert help and appropriate resources and treatment that would support him in developing his physical and cognitive skills. However, his father would like him to attend the local primary school; he feels that this would offer Jake the chance to integrate with other children and develop his social and emotional skills.

Consider both of these responses. What are the advantages and disadvantages of each approach? Which approach would you favour? Why?

Comment

Certainly both approaches have advantages. It is important that Jake has the kind of specialist support to support his specific needs. It could be suggested that in this approach the focus is on the 'disability'. The other approach focuses on an opportunity for Jake to integrate with the other children, the school community and his local community. It could be suggested that this approach has more of a focus on social integration.

Two theoretical models that represent these approaches are the medical (or individual) model of disability and the social model of disability. In the medical model, the disability is seen as the primary focus with a particular 'pathology' – a scientific approach to the cause and treatment of the 'disease'. The social model of disability considers disability in the context of society, in particular the impact of society's values and attitudes in relation to disability and the physical and social barriers faced by people with a disability. A major problem for children with a disability is that they live in a society that views this as a 'problem'. In thinking about your approach to the viewpoints in relation to Jake you will have had to think about your own understanding of disability – your attitude and values. Are you able to acknowledge any prejudices and fears that you may hold in relation to disability? Do you recognise the way in which you or others may stereotype disability, for example considering that people with a disability are vulnerable and helpless? In any work with children, young people and adults you will need to take responsibility for understanding the impairment and the impact of that impairment from the individual's perspective. What does the disability mean to that person; what impact does it have on their stage of development? Listening to the child is essential and you will have to take responsibility for ensuring that communication is facilitated, particularly if the child may have specific needs in relation to communication.

Supporting children in education with special educational needs or a disability

The Children and Families Act 2014 states that councils must make sure that education, health and social care services all work together, if doing so helps them do better for children and young people with special educational needs or a disability. Every local council in England must write down what help there is in their area for children and young people with special educational needs or a disability. This is called the 'Local Offer', and everyone can read it. If a child has significant/complex support needs, there is one new plan for how different professionals will give the child or young person the help they need with their education, health and social care (an 'Education, health and care plan', or 'EHCP' for short). This is instead of the 'Statement' of special educational needs or the 'Learning Difficulty Assessment' which children and young people used to receive. The EHCP must include parents, carers, children and young people. The aim is to make it more individually focused, and to state clearly the goals the child wants to achieve and what support is in place to reach those goals. As well as saying what help the child or young person needs with their education, the plan will say what they should be able to achieve if they get that help. The assessment must be co-ordinated across education, health and care services. The EHCP can run from birth until age 25.

Where an EHCP is not required an SEN support plan sets out the help a child will get at their pre-school, school or college if they have special educational needs, to ensure that individual's needs are met. This can include: for children under 5 for example, a written progress check when the child is two-years-old, a written assessment in the summer term of the child's first year of primary school; for children aged between 5 and 15, for example, a special learning programme, extra help from a teacher or assistant; and support for young people aged 16 or over in further education.

All the potential problems identified in middle childhood benefit from prevention, early recognition, assessment and appropriate intervention. Each child has unique skills and abilities to cope; all children need support, advice and guidance both at school and at home.

Psychological development in middle childhood

The transition to school coincides with greater independence and capabilities in the child. The interplay of self-understanding and social perception is increasingly evident as they develop throughout the middle years.

Whilst psychoanalytical theorists have emphasised the development of personality, there is recognition that in middle childhood this is influenced by increasing competency. Freud refers to this period as the 'latency' period – a period of relative calm with a focus on ego development, particularly social and intellectual skills.

Erikson refers to the stage between 6 and 12 years as a period of industry (competence) versus inferiority. This is a period when the child seeks approval through the mastering of new intellectual and social skills, such as reading, writing and the formation of friendships. These tasks represent the development of the expected skills of their culture and of society. This has to be balanced with a realistic sense of their limitation to avoid a negative sense of inferiority. If a child is unable to develop these skills then they will develop a sense of inferiority and incompetence; this may be particularly reinforced through the response of others.

Activity 4.2

Paul, aged 8, is described by his mother Sandra as 'useless'. She says that he cannot be bothered to learn and spends all his time out of the house, usually on his own at the local park. When confronted he is verbally abusive.

Sadie, aged 7, is described by her mother Jackie as 'useless'. She says that she cannot be bothered to learn and has no friends. Sadie is timid and anxious. She spends all her time on her own, usually in her bedroom.

Think about the responses of these children. Write a few sentences that answer the questions below.

- Using Erikson's model, briefly explain Paul's and Sadie's situations.
- Having formed an opinion of Paul's and Sadie's situations using Erikson's approach, what are the implications for the way in which you would work with each of these children as a social worker?

From the information you have it is impossible to understand everything influencing these situations (for example, previous influences on the child and family; the context of the child's behaviour). However, whilst both children demonstrate different behaviour, their response could be seen as the result of a potential 'failure' to develop their intellectual and social skills. Their individual action, whilst representing two potential examples of 'extremes', could be seen as the response to and the reinforcement of feelings of inferiority. As a social worker you will need to gather further information in order to reach a clearer assessment of each child's needs and feelings. For example, you will want to talk to both children's teachers to gain an understanding of each child's educational ability (for example if they have specific learning needs). You will need to listen to each child – their perception of themselves, their friendships, and their feelings about their family. The parent will need support in listening to and understanding their child and the reasons for their behaviour. The parent may also need support and guidance in developing strategies and responses that will help to build their child's self-esteem and self-worth. Standard 2 of the *National Service Framework* (DH, 2004) sets out a range of measures for supporting parents to increase the life chances of children.

Cognitive development in middle childhood

Children in middle childhood are ready to learn. Piaget (1936) referred to this stage as that of 'concrete operations' (approximately 7–11 years). Children become less egocentric, being able to take into account other people's ideas, and more logical in thinking through ideas and reaching a conclusion. It is distinguished by the development of an understanding of *conservation* (the realisation that weight, mass and volume remain the same despite changes in their shape or physical arrangement); by *decentration* (the ability to focus on more than one dimension of the object at the same time); and *seriation* (the ability to order objects according to some identified 'property', such as size). Children acquire the ability to reverse their thinking as they are able to take into account a number of features.

Case study 4.1

Carly, aged 8, has been in foster care with a plan for adoption by the foster family for three months, following concerns about her emotional and physical neglect. Carly appears to accept this without question. Her social worker, Bill, having undertaken a full assessment of her needs, knows that Carly's early childhood has been marked by frequent moves, inconsistent care and care by a number of people. He recognises that for Carly, from her point of view, this may be 'just another occurrence'. Her understanding of the concept of family and family relationships is limited because of her early experiences. Bill and her foster-adoptive family work with Carly in developing a life story book about her past. In addition, Bill uses drawings – timelines to help Carly understand her previous life, and family trees and network diagrams to help her to 'cognitively' locate herself in her past and future family. He also uses play with dolls and models as an aid to developing Carly's understanding.

Piaget's (1936) views were based on the individual – the structures within children's minds and how they gradually become more sophisticated with age. However, some developmental psychologists have also explored the social influences on children's development, notably Lev Vygotsky (1896–1934). Like Piaget, Vygotsky (1962, 1978) saw the child as an active participant in their own development. He differed from Piaget, who focused on the content of children's thought, in concentrating on functional (practical) aspects. His view was based on the importance of the role of other, more knowledgeable, people. Vygotsky believed that children acquired the means of learning and thinking from the social interaction between themselves and the adults around them. These adults provided the scaffolding (framework) within which a child could acquire greater understanding. Vygotsky also placed greater emphasis on language development, and that this should be seen in the context of the child's culture and the help and support available within that culture. A central idea of his theory was the 'zone of proximal development'. This refers to the distance between the child's actual development and the level of potential development that they can acquire with support and guidance. Unlike Piaget, who believed that children needed to be ready before they were able to learn, Vygotsky argued that adults could and should provide activities for children that were beyond those expected of them – far enough to provide challenge but not so far as to demoralise them.

Activity 4.3

Consider the case of Carly. Can you identify ways in which Bill is using Vygotskian principles to support her development?

One way in which this is occurring is in the relationship that Bill has developed with Carly – a social interactive relationship that is based on such things as mutual trust, understanding, taking an interest and so on. Rather than assuming that Carly will be able to 'work things out for herself', Bill recognises the need to work together, engaging in mutual activities to develop understanding, with sensitive stimulation by Bill in developing the 'scaffolding' that is required to support Carly's cognitive understanding of her past and future.

Vygotsky places great emphasis on the social interaction of a child's understanding. Consequently, as a social worker you will need to have an understanding of the child's race, culture and language, and their understanding of what this means to them. You will have to reflect on the past, present and future role and relationships of the adult in the child's life: the role of parents; other adults in the child's life; those of other professionals; and in particular your role and relationship with the child.

Social development in middle childhood

In this section we will seek to develop an understanding of how children develop a sense of 'themselves' and how others may view them. In particular we will examine explanations of why children may behave in the ways that they do.

The development of self

Young children tend to define themselves through physical characteristics (e.g. 'tall', 'short', 'big', 'little'). Children in the middle years increasingly define themselves through social characteristics (e.g. 'funny', 'happy', 'sad' and by social comparisons), the expectations and reactions of others, and what kind of response they generate. This may come as no surprise as children are mixing more with other children and adults, especially within the school environment. A critical part of the development of self is concerned with feelings of self-esteem. Self-esteem is the degree to which children feel accepted and valued by adults and children who are important to them. The development of self-esteem is complex. It is shaped within the child and also by the people around that child.

Activity 4.4

Think about the following and try to identify areas in which Richard demonstrates he has low self-esteem.

Richard, aged 7, has had a troubled and turbulent childhood, involving physical and sexual abuse. He has experienced numerous moves in his life. Richard is short and thin for his age. He has been placed with the Jones family for the last three months; plans are in place for the Joneses to adopt Richard. They have found his behaviour difficult and demanding, describing him as 'aggressive' and 'sulky'. At school Richard struggles to read and write as he has missed so much schooling. Although he has additional support he is rude and often aggressive towards his support worker. The other children are scared of Richard so tend to stay away. He says that this is okay with him as they are all 'stupid'. He is good at football but is aggressive when he plays. His teacher says that if he can learn to control his temper on the football pitch he could play for the school team.

According to Susan Harter (1999), self-esteem is based on a balance between what the child would like to be and what they actually think they are. She identified six domains of competence that were important to the child:

1. Scholastic competence.
2. Athletic competence.

3. Physical appearance.

4. Peer acceptance.

5. Behavioural conduct.

6. General feelings of self-worth.

In the case of Richard you will have been able to identify issues in every area. What matters here is to identify the area that is most important to him. In this instance we could assume that this may be initially his competency as a footballer. Your role as a social worker and the work of other people who are important in his life would be to help and encourage him in his task; provide emotional support and approval in his achievement; and support in learning that mistakes and failures are acceptable and an inevitable part of learning and can lead to success. The 'behaviours' that Richard exhibits are clear signs of low self-esteem. Children with low self-esteem expect to fail and often show self-defeating behaviour, seeing any success as the result of chance, rather than a result of their own skills and effort. The Joneses will need support and advice in dealing with Richard's behaviour and developing his self-esteem and self-worth. The development of behaviours that promote attachments in the relationship will be crucial (see Chapter 3).

In an extensive study of parent–child relationships and self-esteem, Coopersmith (1967) identified a number of parenting attributes that were associated with boys' high self-esteem. Although his study was based on boys, it is also highly relevant to girls:

- expression of acceptance and affection;

- concern about the child's life and any problems;

- harmony in the home;

- participation in joint family activities;

- availability to give competent, organised help when they need it;

- setting clear and fair rules.

Developing a sense of gender identity

By the time children enter middle childhood they will have developed an understanding of their gender identity and the behaviours associated with this. Differences between boys and girls are sometimes explained by inborn biological differences. Another explanation is that the differences that can be observed between girls and boys can be explained through the process of socialisation within their social and cultural settings.

There is no doubt that there is a sex difference determined at birth between boys and girls. They are biologically and physiologically different. This is especially emphasised during puberty. However, it would be more realistic to suggest that there is a great deal of variation between children – within sexes and between girls and boys. Studies have suggested some variation between the sexes (for example, girls tend to talk more and in longer sentences in early childhood; boys seem to be better at solving intellectual problems based on numerical reasoning). However, these studies are often based on 'averages' and are certainly not applicable to all boys and girls. An alternative view is that differences between the sexes are learned through the roles that are ascribed to them by society.

Once they start school, children acquire a sense of being a 'boy' or 'girl'. Most children will have been encouraged in activities that are usually ascribed to gender roles – boys involved in physical activities and girls in a more interpersonal world that encourages caring and closeness. During the middle years they learn about more complex ideas of gender roles. While children recognise that individuals can vary in relation to their personal preference, a number of studies identify the 'different' way that girls and boys behave and are socialised into their stereotypical roles.

Activity 4.5

Denise is 10 and is described as a 'typical girl'. Liam is 10 and is described as a 'typical boy'.

- What kind of behaviours and actions would you expect to see in these children?

Comment

It is acknowledged that in this exercise we are asking you to stereotype these children and also that it does not account for the individual variations for individual children. However, it may be that you have been able to identify gender differences. For Denise this would be closer, more intimate friendships and games that would be more 'passive'; she would be neater, more obedient, receiving praise for this kind of behaviour. Liam would tend to be involved in more boisterous games, express himself more aggressively, and dominate in games, pastimes and in the classroom. He probably has more freedom in what he is able to do and in relation to travel outside the home.

There are important issues for social workers in gender-stereotyping: limiting behaviour to gender roles can restrict the development of individual identity, skills and competency. Viewing behaviour in terms of gender may result in 'labelling' (e.g. 'he's a sissy', 'she's aggressive'). Boys in particular may demonstrate aggressive, dominating behaviour, finding it hard to express emotions and demonstrate caring actions and skills. Girls may find it difficult to express their individuality and independence. You will recall from Chapter 3 that these are important in developing resilience. As a social worker you will need to support children in expressing their feelings and in developing a positive independent view of themselves. In your work with families, for example through the assessment process, you should be aware of the ways in which the family develops and assigns gender roles (for example, through a boy 'modelling' the aggressive behaviour of his father; through language and actions which encourage certain behaviours, such as boys to be 'dominant' and girls to be 'passive'). You will need to recognise the impact of gender identity on this as being potentially restrictive and stereotypical. Families may require support in identifying the impact that this has on the behaviour of children and roles within the family. You can actively support children through being a positive role model yourself – modelling behaviours and roles that are non-stereotypical; by promoting positive images of gender roles through books and play, and by encouraging non-stereotypical behaviours and activities. You will need to recognise the influence of others, (for example foster carers, adoptive families, residential childcare workers) and ensure that you work together in promoting positive role models and images for children.

The influence of the family

It will be clear by now that family actions and reactions (in terms of what they do and do not do), particularly of the main caregivers, have a critical influence on children's growth and development. In 2016 there were 18.9 million families in the UK (Office for National Statistics, 2016). There were 12.7 million married or civil partners, the most common type of family, although cohabiting couple families were the fastest growing type of families over the last twenty years (from 1.1 million in 1996 to 3.3 million in 2016). It is important to recognise that the concept of the 'family' is increasingly being challenged from a stereotypical view of a mother, father and their children. Children are more often being raised in different family forms, for example in lone parent families and reconstituted families. Nearly half the children in England and Wales are not being brought up in traditional families, with the majority being brought up in lone parent families, mostly headed up by the mother. The Office for National Statistics (2016) identified that in 2016 there were 2.9 million lone parent families in the UK, with 86% headed by a female lone parent, 24 per cent of all dependent children lived in a single parent family (that is nearly one in every four children), and 44 per cent of children in single parent families live in relative poverty, which is around twice the risk of relative poverty faced by children in couple families (24 per cent) (DWP, 2016). However, it is also known that the situation of families is dynamic and diverse.

As a social worker you will play a critical part in assessing, planning and providing appropriate interventions to support families who may be experiencing difficulties. Consequently, it is important for you to have an understanding of the role, expectations and values that influence them in supporting the growth and development of their child.

Research summary

The Signs of Safety (SoS)® approach, is based on the use of strengths-based interview techniques and draws upon techniques from solution-focused brief therapy. It aims to work collaboratively and in partnership with families and children to conduct risk assessments and produce action plans for increasing safety and reducing risk and danger by focusing on the strengths, resources and networks that a family have. It was created by Andrew Turnell and Steve Edwards in the 1990s in Western Australia and is being used in 12 different countries across Australasia, North America and Europe. It is also being used in a significant number of local authorities in England. There are six key practice elements: 1. Understand the position of each family member; 2. Find exceptions to the maltreatment; 3. Discover family strengths and resources; 4. Focus on goals; 5. Scale safety and progress; and 6. Assess willingness, confidence and capacity (Turnell and Edwards, 1999).

The SoS assessment and planning tools form/protocol, which is intended to map harm, danger, complicating factors, strengths, existing and required safety and a safety judgement where children have been maltreated or are vulnerable, is intended to be the action plan and central case record for organising interventions right from the beginning of a case through to closure. The framework aims to address four questions:

1   What are we worried about? (past harm, future danger and complicating factors)
2   What's working well? (existing strengths and safety)
3   What needs to happen? (future safety and next steps)
4   Where we are on a scale of 0 to 10? (where 10 means there is enough safety for the child protection authorities to close the case, and 0 means it is certain the child will be re-abused – 0 often indicates the situation is so dangerous the child will be rehoused)

To involve children in the assessment and processes SoS uses a number of different tools. These are intended to give children an understanding of what is happening to them and why child protection services are involved in the case. They also provide a way to help different family members communicate with each other and create an opportunity to to ensure the child's voice is heard. These include:

- Three houses tool: A diagram of three houses in a row: one labelled House of Worries (What are we worried about?); one labelled House of Good Things (What's working well?) and one labelled House of Dreams (What needs to happen/how would things look if they were as wanted?)
- Wizard and Fairies: The same three questions are explored with a fairy and magic wand (for girls) and a Wizard figure (for boys). Problems and worries from the child's perspectives are written down on the clothes and represent

what needs to be changed. The good things in the child's life are written on the wings or cape, being symbolic of flying away or escaping or protecting/problems becoming invisible for a while. The child's wishes are written at the end of the wands and represent hopes for the future and 'wishes coming true'.

- The Safety House: This helps to represent and communicate how safe a child feels in their own home and what would be involved to improve this. A picture of a house with a roof, path and garden is drawn for this tool. Usually the house and garden are divided into sections and the child will describe who they would like to be living with, who can visit and stay over, and who is not allowed to come into the house. Safety rules are devised and put into the roof of the house and details of what happens in the house and what people do will be discussed. The house can also introduce scales to the child by using the path as an indicator of how ready they are to return home.

(Bunn, 2013; www.signsofsafety.net)

Activity 4.6

Ian is 6 and lives with his mother and father. He has begun attending the local school, having recently moved into the area with his parents. His teacher has expressed concern about his care and behaviour. Ian is very boisterous and his concentration is poor, finding it difficult to concentrate on any activity for any length of time. The other children avoid him as he is so boisterous and will often punch and kick to get his own way. His physical care has been poor; for example, his hygiene is poor and he has had no dental care. He appears to have no sense of danger; for example, being unaware of the dangers on the road. You have been asked to assess the parents' parenting capacity. What are the kind of questions you would wish to address?

Comment

'Parenting capacity' is a phrase deriving from the Children Act 1989 (s.1.3), that refers to the question of whether or not parents are capable of meeting their children's needs (Department of Health, 1989). Parenting capacity can be defined as *the ability to parent in a 'good enough' manner long term* (Conley, 2003, p. 16). Parenting capacity therefore is concerned with the parents' ability to nurture their children, protect them from risk, and enhance their developmental experiences. Parenting capacity varies at different points in time depending on the circumstances facing parents and their children. 'Good enough' parenting, on the other hand, is a term generally used to describe the minimum amount of care needed so as not to cause harm to a child. In other words, if a parent is

(Continued)

(Continued)

faced by adversity (such as being single, poor or depressed) but the quality of parenting behaviour is still adequate, the outcome for the child should not be compromised. It is the quality of the immediate moment-to-moment behaviour of the parent towards the child that is the major influence on that child's well-being (Scott, 1998).

In a study by Kellett and Apps (2009) it is suggested that 'good enough' parenting involves four elements:

- Meeting children's health and developmental needs.
- Putting children's needs first.
- Providing routine and consistent care.
- Acknowledging problems and engaging with support services.

Risky parenting was associated with the following:

- Neglecting basic needs.
- Putting adults' needs first.
- Chaos and a lack of routine.
- An unwillingness to engage with support services.

The concerns of Ian's teacher raise a number of questions and would suggest that his mother may need some support; for example, you need to understand Ian's history and background and his mother's ability to meet his basic needs. Table 4.1 may help you in thinking through areas of concern and thinking about the range of questions this raises.

Table 4.1   Parenting capacity and thresholds of intervention (adapted from DH, 2000)

Area of assessment	Expectations	May require intervention if …	Complex needs	Immediate concerns
Basic care	Provision of child's physical, medical, optical, and dental care; provision of food and drink, warmth, shelter, clean and appropriate clothing; adequate personal hygiene.	Basic care is not provided consistently; food, warmth and other basics not always available; parent struggling without support and/or adequate resources; young inexperienced parent(s).	Basic care is frequently inconsistent; food, warmth and other basics not often available; large family with poor coping skills; very young inexperienced parent(s); parent's mental health problems or substance misuse significantly affect care of child/young person; parents have struggled to care for previous child/young persons.	Basic care is rarely consistent; parents have seriously abused/ neglected the child/young person; food, warmth and other basics frequently not available; supervision is haphazard; previous child/young persons have been removed from parent's home; parent's own needs mean they cannot keep child/young person safe.

Area of assessment	Expectations	May require intervention if …	Complex needs	Immediate concerns
Ensuring safety	Protection from harm and danger; protection from unsafe adults/other children; protection from self-harm; recognising hazards.	Haphazard supervision, unaware of child/young person's whereabouts; haphazard use of safety equipment, e.g. fireguards; insufficient awareness of dangers to the child/young person; inappropriate childcare arrangements and/ or too many different carers; inappropriate frequent visits to doctor/casualty.	Instability and domestic violence in the home; absence of appropriate supervision; inappropriate care arrangements such as succession of carers.	Level of supervision is inadequate given child/ young person's age; parent unable to restrict access to home by dangerous adults; chronic and serious domestic violence involving the child/young person.
Emotional warmth	Child's positive sense of being valued and own racial and cultural identity; secure stable and affectionate relationship with adults; adults providing sensitive appropriate response; demonstration of warmth, praise and encouragement.	Inconsistent responses to child/ young person by parent(s); child/young person not able to develop other positive relationships; parents struggling to have their own emotional needs met.	Child/young person receives erratic or inconsistent care; parental instability affects capacity to nurture; parents own emotional needs starting to compromise those of the child/young person; some relationship difficulties.	Low warmth, high criticism; parents inconsistent, highly critical or apathetic towards child/young person; parents' own emotional experiences impacting on their ability to meet the child/young person's needs; relationships characterised by rejection.
Stimulation	Provision of encouragement and cognitive stimulation; responding appropriately to a child's language and questions; encouraging play and promoting educational opportunities; encouraging success and ensuring school attendance or equivalent opportunity.	Child/young person spends considerable time alone; child/ young person is not often exposed to new experiences; limited access to leisure facilities.	Child/young person receiving little positive stimulation, with lack of new experiences or activities; restricted access, if any, to leisure facilities; child/young person under undue parental pressure to achieve/aspire.	No constructive leisure time activities; no access to leisure facilities; no relevant stimulation or inappropriate for age.

(Continued)

(Continued)

Area of assessment	Expectations	May require intervention if ...	Complex needs	Immediate concerns
Guidance and boundaries	Demonstrating and modelling appropriate behaviour towards the child; control of emotions and interactions with others; developing in the child an internal model of moral values and conscience; develop appropriate social behaviour; not being over-protective regarding exploratory and learning experiences; boundaries to include social problem solving, anger management, consideration for others, effective discipline and shaping of behaviour.	No constructive leisure time activities; no access to leisure facilities; no relevant stimulation or inappropriate for age.	Child/young person has multiple carers, but no significant relationships with any of them.	Child/young person beyond parental control; family life may be chaotic; child/young person has no one to care for him/her; multiple carers, with no consistency.
Stability	Providing a stable family environment to ensure secure attachments and optimal development; ensuring consistency of emotional warmth to prevent disruption; adaptation by parent to child's developmental progress; maintaining child's contact with significant others.	Child/young person behaves in an anti-social way in the neighbourhood, e.g. petty crime; parent/carer offers inconsistent boundaries.	Erratic or inadequate guidance provided; parents struggle/refuse to set effective boundaries; parent does not offer a good role model, e.g. by behaving in an anti-social way; child/young person regularly behaves in an anti-social way in the neighbourhood.	No effective boundaries; child/young person out of control in the community.

Families serve a number of essential functions:

- Meeting physical need by providing such things as food, clothes, shelter.

- Encouraging cognitive development through supporting the mastering of skills (for example academic skills) by motivating and guiding their learning.

- Supporting the development of self-esteem through praise and encouragement, particularly because, children become more cognitively aware, they become more self-critical. Families need to help children feel loved, competent and assertive in what they do.

- Nurturing relationships with others through encouraging relationships with people such as other relatives, adults and children. They need to provide the time, space and opportunities to achieve this.

- Giving harmony and stability by providing a safe, secure routine, with appropriate guidance and boundaries, that is protective and predictable.

Research summary

You may find the following documents helpful in further developing your understanding of issues in relation to parenting capacity, as well as wider issues in relation to assessment and planning for children in need:

Brandon, M, Bailey, S, Belderson, P and Larsson, B (2013) *Neglect and Serious Case Reviews.* London: NSPCC.

This study provides a new contribution to our learning about neglect by exploring the circumstances in which neglect can be catastrophic and have a fatal or seriously harmful outcome for a child. It provides a systematic analysis of neglect in serious case reviews (local multi-agency reviews of child deaths or serious injury where abuse or neglect is known or suspected) in England between 2003–2011. Available from: www.nspcc.org.uk

Cleaver, H, Unell, I and Aldgate, J (2011*) Children's Needs – Parenting Capacity. Child Abuse, Parental Mental Illness, Learning Disability, Substance Misuse, and Domestic Violence* (2nd edn). London: The Stationery Office.

This edition provides an update on the impact of parental problems, such as substance misuse, domestic violence, learning disability and mental illness, on children's welfare.

Forrester, D and Harwin, J (2011) *Parents Who Misuse Drugs and Alcohol: Effective Interventions in Social Work and Child Protection.* Chichester: Wiley-Blackwell.

(Continued)

(Continued)

This book is about children affected by parental substance misuse, reviewing the latest literature and studies.

Turney, D, Platt, D, Selwyn, J and Farmer, E (2012) *Improving Child and Family Assessments: Turning Research into Practice.* London: Jessica Kingsley.

The book draws together evidence from research to provide an understanding of the relationship between the quality of assessment and outcomes for children in contact with children's social care services.

Ward, H, Brown, R and Hyde-Dryden, G (2014) *Assessing Parental Capacity to Change when Children are on the Edge of Care: An Overview of Current Research Evidence.* London: Department of Education.

This document is an overview of current research evidence, bringing together some of the key research messages concerning factors which promote or inhibit parental capacity to change in families where there are significant child protection concerns.

As a social worker, you will be assessing the negative and positive parenting capacity of the caregiver and the impact on their child. You will need to take into account the ability of the parent to meet the development needs of the child in the past, currently and in the future; the development perspective will therefore be key. In addition, you will need to put the parent's behaviour and competence in the context of broader issues within the child's world – the ecological perspective.

Research summary

Diane Baumrind (1971) studied patterns of childrearing through a combination of four dimensions:

1   Expressions of warmth, ranging from very affectionate to quite cold.
2   Strategies for discipline, which may involve explanation, criticism, persuasion and/or physical punishment.
3   Communications, which ranged from extensive listening to demands for silence.
4   Expectations of maturity; how much responsibility and self-control were demanded.

She identified three specific combinations:

i. The authoritarian parent is high in control and maturity demands, but low in nurturance and communication. They think it is important for the child to learn how to behave properly.
ii. The permissive parent is high in nurturance but is low in maturity demands, control and communication. Learning happens best through conversation.
iii. The authoritative parent is high in nurturance, maturity demands, control and communication.

Maccoby and Martin (1983) have identified fourth and fifth types: iv) the neglecting, uninvolved parent, who does not seem to care at all; and v) indulgent parents, who accommodate the child's every whim. Baumrind's studies have come to the basic conclusion that:

*   children raised by authoritarian parents are likely to be quiet, conscientious and obedient, however, they can feel guilty or depressed;
*   children raised by permissive parents lack self-control, especially within friendships, and are the least happy;
*   children raised by authoritative parents are likely to be successful, happy, intelligent, articulate and generous.

The ecological approach

The focus in the last two chapters has been on identifying the different theories and processes as they apply to individual children. Most textbooks written thirty years ago would have emphasised the individual child and, in particular, the role of the parent in shaping that child. Whilst these are still important, we recognise that the development of the child involves and is influenced by more complex interactions with the 'social' world. This section will focus on bringing together the themes and issues from our study of childhood into a framework that seeks to recognise the influence and interactions between all of the different systems involved in a child's growth and development – the ecological approach. This is particularly important in supporting your practice in assessment. This is the model that underpins the *Framework for the Assessment of Children in Need and Their Families* (DH, 2000).

You will recall that we introduced the ecological approach, specifically the work of Urie Bronfenbrenner (1979a), in Chapters 1 and 2. The ecological approach is based on the principle that the development and behaviour of individuals can only be fully understood in the context of the environment in which they live. This context is made up of a series of interrelated systems that mutually influence and are influenced by each other. You should re-read this section to remind yourself of the different systems within his model.

Activity 4.7

Having re-read the explanation of Bronfenbrenner's ecological model, use the model to outline your own systems. Think about how these influence and impact on your own life and how the systems interact.

You may have found this challenging and complex. Thinking about each of the individual systems and their influence on your life is in itself difficult. This becomes even more complex when you have to consider how they interact with each other, requiring you to consider and interpret a range of information, facts and personal experiences and opinions. For example, you will have recognised and considered the direct and indirect influence of parts of the system, such as those in the macrosystem. These may not have a day-to-day influence on your life, as the microsystem does, but will strongly influence the direction and choices within it; for example, the political issue in relation to student grants and loans may impact on you. Hopefully it will show you that there is a strong interrelationship between each of the parts that make up 'the system'. 'System' refers to the mutual influences that the different parts (the child, the family, friends, neighbours, community and wider society) have upon one another. The ecological model is based on a systems framework. It can be described as a 'holistic model': it focuses on the assessment of the ways in which the different parts interact on and with each other (for example, the child's developmental needs, the capacity of the parents to respond and the wider environmental context in which this occurs). The other important aspect of the system is the 'chronosystem' – the aspect of time and how this impacts on development.

We are now going to consider the application of Bronfenbrenner's ecological model and how an understanding of child growth and development can contribute to the assessment of the child's needs.

Case study 4.2

Kenny, aged 11, is described by his mother Christine, aged 29, as 'difficult, demanding and out of control'. Christine asks for your support in managing Kenny's behaviour, as she fears that as he approaches adolescence she will no longer be able to manage him. Kenny lives with his mother, her partner Ray and their children, Steven, aged 6, and Bethany, aged 4. Christine and Ray have been together for seven years.

Christine describes Kenny as an 'accident'. At the time she was dependent on drugs, earning money as a prostitute to support her addiction. All of her money was spent on drugs. She was living with Greg, Kenny's father, who was dealing in drugs. Kenny was born eight weeks prematurely and was drug-dependent. He spent three months in hospital. Christine visited him infrequently, continuing with her drug use and earning money through prostitution. Kenny was

→

a difficult baby. He cried a lot and was difficult to settle. He was slow to walk and talk. Kenny would be left with a number of different carers, often placed in his playpen for hours. Greg has a history of violence and would frequently beat and punch Christine. When Kenny was 2, Christine's mother, Judy, was increasingly concerned about him, particularly as Greg was being increasingly abusive towards Kenny, striking him on the face, pushing and shoving him, shouting and calling him names. Judy was concerned with the conditions in the home – the lack of furniture, toys and food in the house. With Christine's agreement, she took Kenny to live with her. He lived with his grandmother for a year, during which time he appeared to benefit from the stability and routine. Kenny gained in height and weight, developing his language and play skills, and attended the local playgroup where he enjoyed playing with the other children.

After a year and having left Greg, Christine took Kenny to live with her in a flat close to her mother. Christine describes this as a difficult time as she sought to withdraw from the drugs on which she had become so dependent. She was often depressed, resulting in Kenny spending lots of time in his room playing with his toys. Greg would visit on occasions. However, their relationship remained volatile. Christine describes her mother as a great support, continuing to help her with Kenny's care. Kenny started school at 4. However, he found it difficult to settle; he was slow to learn and was unpopular with the other children. With support from the teaching staff, though, Kenny quickly learned to read and write and developed skills as a good footballer. Christine describes meeting Ray as 'the turning point' in her life. Ray, a butcher, and Christine began to live together in his house in another part of the city. Kenny missed his grandmother and did not settle in his new school. However, with support from his teachers he began to make progress, showing himself to be an able student. Christine tells you that despite all the problems they have with him he continues to attend school and is in the school football team. Now she is concerned that when he moves to senior school this may change. She admits that she does not have much contact with the school and does not bother to ask Kenny anything about how he is getting on.

Kenny dislikes Ray, frequently ignoring him. His mother is caught between the two relationships and admits that she often sides with Ray to attempt to 'keep the peace'. Kenny refuses to join in with family activities and now, Christine tells you, they just leave him behind as it 'is easier than getting into a fight'. She says that Ray's job means that they have a nice house in a 'good area' and they have made lots of friends. Christine has a part-time job in the local supermarket and tells you that she has made many friends as a result of this job. She does not want Kenny to spoil this, particularly considering the life she used to have. With the birth of Steven and Bethany, Kenny spent more and more time out of the house. By the age of 10, Kenny was mixing with older boys, hanging around the local park. They frequently 'dared him' to do things – smoking, annoying the neighbours by shouting abuse at them, hitting other children.

Local residents often call the police complaining about the young people hanging around the park and the vandalism that they believe they cause. However, one of the local residents has approached the council for support in setting up a football team and skateboard area within the park. The local council are 'sympathetic'. Recently the other boys have been encouraging Kenny to shoplift small items for them. One of the boys stole a car and when Kenny refused to get in the car, they called him 'chicken'.

Activity 4.8

Using Case Study 4.3 of Kenny and his family, and also the ecological model, apply the theories of development we have covered so far. A good starting point would be for you to begin with Kenny's life course line, noting the key events in his life. (You will recall you completed your own life course line in Chapter 1.)

Comment

Clearly, with only limited information, it is difficult to identify all of the issues and you may have had to make assumptions based on this limited information. You will need to talk to a range of people in forming a judgement – Kenny, his grandmother, the school and others. Hopefully you will have identified a number of themes and issues.

Within the wider macrosystem you may have considered the response of wider society to children and young people and the issue of resources available. You may have considered your role as a social worker in working with children and families and the systems that underpin this. For example, the legal aspects: in this case the duties placed on local authorities and others under the Children Act 1989, in particular your duties as a social worker in relation to the *Framework for the Assessment of Children in Need and Their Families* (DH, 2000) and the *Common Assessment Framework for Children and Young People* (DfES, 2006). Additionally, you may consider the attitudes of the public to children in trouble with the law, the legal and political response (e.g. the setting up of the Youth Justice Boards and Youth Offender panels) and the response of agencies to children (e.g. the work of the Youth Offending Teams (YOT): www.yjb.gov.uk).

Within the exosystem you may have considered the impact of Christine's and Ray's social support, for example, friendships and work. Whilst not directly involved, the child may still be strongly affected. In this case you may have recognised the social position that Christine now feels that she has achieved and the network and friends that she has established. When you explored Kenny's life from a chronological perspective you should have noted the potential impact of the different exosystems in which he lived: for example, the impact in early life of the chaotic lifestyle of Christine's (and Greg's) drug use. Within the mesosystem you will have been able to draw on a range of theories and issues in relation to child development. Some are listed below:

- The development of the unborn child – impact of drug use and mother's lifestyle.

- The feeling in relation to the pregnancy and the impact this had following the birth – issues of bonding and attachment, including the impact of these throughout Kenny's life and currently.

- Developmental issues, particularly concerns when under 5, for example the development of fine and gross motor skills.

- Cognitive perspectives – how confident and competent is Kenny in his learning?

- The impact of early life in meeting the different stages.

- Six to 12 years – concerns for ability to grasp the logic of classification and conservation.

- Social and emotional development – communication was poor up to age 2; influence of grandmother on Kenny's life; issues of resilience and vulnerability.

- Issues in relation to child protection – impact on Kenny's emotional, social and physical development.

- Psychoanalytical theory.

- Impact of early life in meeting the different stages.

- Industry versus inferiority: for example, mother's lack of interest and contact with school.

- Styles of parenting, for example Baumrind's (1971) study.

- Gender issues – exploring Christine's perception that 'boys will be boys'.

- Behaviour and aspects of social learning theory – issues of 'learned' behaviour, for example early modelling by Greg.

- Exploration of issues in relation to moral development.

You may also wish to consider what other issues you might need to think about if Kenny's family was from a different culture, for example African-Caribbean. What other issues would you need to consider if Kenny had a disability, for example Down's Syndrome?

Reflection point

- What do I know, or can I do now, that I did not know or could not do before I did this section of studying?
- Is there anything I do not understand or want to explore further?
- What else do I need to know to extend my professional development and learning in this area?

Chapter summary

The period of middle childhood in developmental terms is one of relative stability, growing gradually and steadily and consolidating and developing the skills acquired in early childhood. Children develop a wider view of the world, associated with independence outside of the home, particularly school and the development of friendships. The transition from

(Continued)

(Continued)

home to school coincides with the mastering of new intellectual and social skills, taking in new ideas and dimensions of the world. Through social interaction children draw on and build on their feelings of self-esteem and self-worth. They experience the socialisation and social behaviour that are linked to their gender roles. Individual behaviour can be attributed not only to individual temperament, but also to patterns of learned behaviour and how the world is represented to them. This can be linked to moral development. The family continue to exert important influences on the continuing growth and development of the child. Finally, there is an attempt to draw together some of the themes and issues from the last two chapters into the ecological model, representing the different interfaces and influences between all of the systems in which the child exists. In the next chapter we explore the world of the adolescent as the transition from childhood to adulthood.

Further reading

Aldgate, J, Jones, D, Rose, W and Jeffery, C (2006) *The Developing World of the Child*. London: Jessica Kingsley.

This book has been written to support an understanding of successful outcomes for children. The text is structured in three parts, with the first offering chapters that explore a range of theoretical perspectives on child development, the second part being dedicated to particular age-related phases of childhood, and the third part being related to direct work with children.

Howarth, J (ed.) (2009) *The Child's World: The Comprehensive Guide to Assessing Children in Need* (2nd edn). London: Jessica Kingsley.

This book focuses on assessing children in need and their families, and integrates practice, policy and theory to produce a comprehensive and multi-disciplinary guide to all aspects of assessment.

Lindon, J and Webb, J (2016) *Safeguarding Children and Young People: Linking Theory and Practice*. (5th edn). London: Hodder Arnold.

This book covers recent developments in legislation and guidance. It examines the approach to daily practice for professionals taking responsibility for children and young people in early years provision, schools, out-of-school settings, play and leisure facilities.

Websites

National Society for the Prevention of Cruelty of Children (NSPCC): www.nscpcc.org.uk

The 'Inform' section of this website provides some excellent and up-to-date information and resources in relation to children in need and children who have been abused and their families.

5: Using life course development knowledge in social work practice with adolescents

Introduction

In this chapter you will consider human life course development in respect of young people in their teenage years – adolescence.

It will enable you to develop your understanding and ability to critique theories that explain human development, as you will explore a range of approaches for explaining the period of adolescence. It will start by considering how adolescence is defined and experienced in the context of our society. The construction of adolescence in our society can be seen to be partially influenced by political, legislative and policy rhetoric.

Through consideration of the transition into adulthood, changing roles and the growth of independence and maturity, you will learn about social development in adolescence. Issues related to physical changes, including puberty, sexuality and growth, will be explored as examples of biological development. The chapter will then look at how behavioural and social learning theories explain human development through the teenage years. There will be a specific section that focuses on theoretical perspectives in relation to the development of behaviour. You will explore moral development. You will also briefly consider individual issues in relation to adolescence.

Throughout the chapter you will have opportunities to consider your own thoughts about being a teenager and the importance of each individual's life story within a life course perspective. You will look at how some examples of individual difference, such as gender, race, culture and disability, can impact on an individual's experience of adolescence. Therefore, having developed your understanding of life course development in adolescence from a range of perspectives, the chapter reinforces the view that although there are trends and expected changes within this period of life, there are no pre-determined pathways that lay out predictable ways in which the transition to adulthood will affect all people. The only way of understanding an individual's development and the issues that adolescence may hold for them is to listen to their life story, as they perceive it and tell it. It is important for social workers to value an individual's own narrative and biographical account.

Defining adolescence

Adolescent development starts with the physical changes associated with puberty, which begin the physical changes to the body. Whilst these are important, it is the critical processes of development of 'self', the search for identity and the development of relationships (e.g. with friends) and the changing nature of relationships (e.g. with families) that are a central feature of this period of an individual's life.

The context of adolescence

Activity 5.1

Let us begin by looking at your experience of adolescence. When would you perceive yourself as having begun adolescence? When would you consider that your adolescence ended? What were you like as an adolescent? Did you perceive it as a happy time? A difficult time? What were the good things about being an adolescent? What were the things that were difficult? Did you have lots of friends? Did you have one particular friend? Did you have a group of friends? Did you have a particular group 'identity'? How did the adults around you help you? What did they get right? What did they get wrong? Do you consider your experience of adolescence was the same/different as compared to adolescents growing up in contemporary society? Why? How does your experience compare with that of other generations, for example your parents' and grandparents'?

Obviously everyone's experience is unique and a wide range of family and social circumstances can influence the experience of adolescence. However, almost certainly, you will have perceived it as a period of immense change. You may have been able to recognise that, as adolescence covers a span of some years, there was a significant difference between your experiences and feelings at the onset of adolescence and those that you had as you neared the end of adolescence. If you had an opportunity to compare your experiences with those of previous generations, you may have been able to identify similar themes, for example around friendships and relationships. You might have been able to acknowledge the challenges and opportunities for young people growing up into today's society. Deciding when your adolescence ended will have been very individual (for example, it may have been associated with leaving home, getting a job, the start of a relationship).

You have considered changes in terms of transitions or phases within a person's life course development in previous chapters. Adolescence as a period of life is often seen as a whole period of transition, the transition from childhood to adulthood, probably the most challenging and difficult period of life in terms of development. Important biological, psychological and social changes take place. All adolescents confront the same development tasks – adjusting to changes in their bodies and the challenge of their developing sexuality and new ways of thinking – as they strive for their own identity, emotional maturity and independence. Consequently relationships, particularly with the family, will be subject to adaptation and change. However, the timing of these changes varies between individuals, influenced by such things as gender, genes and culture. For some young people the challenges of adolescence result in choices, which lead to a number of problems, and some problems peak at this time.

We recognise that the social context of adolescence is considerably different from those of previous generations. In a traditional society where social change may be slow and the same values are held (e.g. moral, political and religious values), there may be greater acceptance and integration of these views and values for adolescence. In some cultures the transition from childhood to adolescence is marked by a rite of passage, a ceremony marking this transition, based on strong cultural cohesion in relation to roles and responsibilities. However, we recognise that contemporary society holds many challenges (for example rapid social change, broader values and goals, and the expansion of choice in our society). Consequently, we need to be familiar with a number of perspectives on adolescence. We need to view it as a series of passages: biological, psychological, social and cultural.

UNICEF's *The State of the World's Children 2011: Adolescence, An Age of Opportunity* describes adolescence as 'an age of opportunity for children, and a pivotal time for us to build on their development in the first decade of life, to help them navigate risks and vulnerabilities, and to set them on the path to fulfilling their potential' (2011, p. 2). The Association for Young People's Health's (AYPH) *Key Data on Adolescence 2015* suggested that the developmental stage of adolescence is the period from 10 to 19 years of age, acknowledging that characteristics of this stage may extend up to age 24, and that adolescent well-being is also determined by early child development before age 10.

They identified the following:

- There are 11.7 million 10 to 24-year-olds currently living in the UK, which is one in five of the population.

- More than 20 per cent are from an ethnic minority.

- More than one tenth of those under 19 are living in situations of low income and material deprivation. One in eight young people under 15 live in workless households in the UK, and 14.6 per cent of secondary school children are eligible for free school meals. Nearly two million young people aged 10 to 19 live in the most deprived areas of England. Nearly one in five of the 19 to 24 age group is not in education, employment or training. Deprivation is linked to a range of health outcomes, including obesity.

- Many life-long health behaviours are set in place during the second decade of life. Physical activity declines across adolescence, particularly for young women, and nutrition often falls short of national recommendations.

- The average age of first heterosexual intercourse is 16. In 2013, rates of conceptions in the under-18 age group were at their lowest level since 1969, but the UK still has a relatively high rate of births among 15 to 19-year-olds compared with other countries.

- Half of all lifetime cases of psychiatric disorders start by age 14 and three quarters by age 24. Some estimates suggest the majority start before age 18.

Theories and explanations of development in adolescence

In the first section of this chapter you thought about how you might define your adolescence in terms of the main characteristics or features that it encompassed, and how it may be the same and/or different for today's adolescents. Adolescence as a period of development may be considered from a range of different perspectives that focus on biological, psychological and social aspects of development. We shall now explore each of these approaches in more depth, using models from key theorists and case examples. You should note, however, that whilst you will look at each approach separately here, it is important for social workers to take a holistic approach to understanding life course development in adolescence. Therefore, in developing your understanding of this period of life, you should be mindful that an individual's life course development and life experiences are affected by a range of factors, which include their experience of development so far, as well as social and economic aspects, and cultural, historical, psychological, cognitive and physiological influences. Additionally, it is important to consider the unique experience of the individual; it is common for adolescence to be 'stereotyped', for example as rebellious and difficult, and defined by its problems.

Biological development in adolescence

Activity 5.2

Think about young people in their teenage years, perhaps reflecting on your own teenage years or those of members of your family or friends. List the physical/biological changes that may happen throughout this period of life.

You may have associated a whole range of physical changes here that occur during adolescence. Puberty is the period of rapid changes that occur as the person moves from childhood and begins adolescence. Hormones affect every aspect of growth and development and the level of certain hormones rises naturally during adolescence, primarily causing increased sexual interest and mood swings. A number of physical changes take place. There is a rapid acceleration in growth in height and weight: a growth spurt – a sudden, uneven and unpredictable surge in size of almost every part of the body. This is initially experienced as an increase in weight, followed by an increase in height and strength. There are changes in the body in relation to the distribution of fat and muscle. During puberty proportions of fat rise among girls and decline among boys, while the proportion of weight that is muscle rises in boys and declines in girls. It is important to remember that these are generalisations (for example females who are 'athletic' may not show such variations). The consequence of this may be that adolescents appear 'out of proportion' and look clumsy and awkward as their bodies change and they come to terms with these changes.

The hormonal changes associated with puberty result in the important changes that are associated with sexual maturity. Adolescents develop sexual characteristics, the gonads (sexual organs), testes in males and the ovaries in females, and there are changes in the genitals and breasts, and the growth of genital, facial and body hair. For girls, menarche, the beginning of menstruation, is a relatively late development, with a great deal of development taking place before a girl begins to menstruate, with the full reproductive capacity not being achieved for several years. It is difficult to predict the age at which individuals may experience the changes associated with puberty. The beginning of puberty can start as early as 8 for girls and for boys about two years later. Some individuals will have completed their cycle of changes before others have begun. This is due to individual differences relating to genetic factors and also environmental influences. There are also variations in the onset of menarche across different countries (for example, girls are likely to start menarche earlier in Western Europe than in the African continent). This is influenced by differences in affluence and, consequently, the impact of economic disadvantage, such as poor nutrition and health-related issues.

Increases in hormone levels, especially testosterone, cause rapid arousal of emotions – from feelings of 'high' to 'low'. Hormones increase interest in sex and sexual activity. Whilst the erratic, powerful impact of hormones has a significant impact on adolescents, the social context of their development will also have a significant impact as they are influenced by the cultural context in which they are raised.

Activity 5.3

Think about your reaction to the following. How would you advise these young people?

Jed, aged 15, says, 'I am frightened. I like girls but just as friends. I find that I am sexually attracted to boys. I really fancy Paul but I don't know how to tell him. What if he does not feel the same way? I would be so ashamed.'

Dale, aged 14, has Down's Syndrome. His mother has expressed concern about discussing sex, in particular masturbation, with him.

Jessie, aged 13, tells you about her boyfriend, Brad, aged 17. 'I really love him and he loves me. We want to be together forever.' She tells you that she wants advice about contraception.

Ali and Sara, both aged 15, have unprotected sex. Ali 'prefers it' and Sara thinks that having a baby would be 'cool' and bring them closer together.

> Clare, aged 15, has been with her foster carers for a year. Prior to that she was in a children's home for two years. Clare goes out every evening and, despite rules about the time she should return, ignores these and comes in when she 'feels like it'. The foster carers express concern about her promiscuity. Recently they heard her talking on her mobile, arranging to meet a man and agreeing a price of £25.

Naturally, individual reactions will vary – you may consider sharing your thoughts with someone else. As a social worker you will need to be prepared to respond to a range of issues and concerns. The critical issue is to be open to the experience and concerns of the young person, listening and respecting their issues, being non-judgemental. There may be conflicts with your personal beliefs, for example a religious belief. You need to acknowledge this and consider how it may conflict with and influence your professional values and practice. Seeking advice, for example from colleagues and other professionals, and discussion in professional supervision, should be used to explore the conflicts and difficulties you have and feel.

There may be a number of other physical changes that you have thought of. However, it is important that you appreciate that whilst many of these biological changes appear to be commonplace, this does not mean that, as we age, these changes can be predicted or considered inevitable.

Social development in adolescence

All societies distinguish between children and adults. The period of transition between these periods associated with adolescence requires an individual to reconsider and redefine themself and their capabilities and make choices as they encounter their new social status.

The process of development allows for greater autonomy, the development of more mature and independent relationships from their carers, and adolescents will spend increasing time with their peers, providing an opportunity to make independent decisions with fewer adults present. A peer group plays an important part in the development of an individual's identity, the changes in their self-concepts and self-image. As adolescents have a broader intellectual capacity providing new ways of thinking about problems, values and relationships, this gives them a chance to think about themselves and the persona they are taking on. Erikson (1995) recognised this as the critical crisis of adolescence in his eight stages of development – identity versus role confusion. He believed that a successful resolution of this depended on how an individual resolved the previous crisis of childhood. This period is thus critical in making sense of the future. Erikson believed the key to this lay in the interactions an adolescent had with others – peers, families, institutions, especially school, and society. Forging an identity is a social as well as a mental process.

Erikson suggested that the search for identity is ongoing during adolescence and adolescents may experience more than one stage:

- *Foreclosure* – premature identity formation in which the adolescent adopts parents' or societies' roles and values without questioning them.

- *Negative identity* – the opposite of that which is expected, which is taken on as rebellious defiance. Ogbu (1993) identified one version, oppositional identity, in which the adolescent adopts and exaggerates a negative stereotype.

- *Identity diffusion* – a situation in which the adolescent does not seem to know or care what their identity is. Almost every adolescent will experience diffusion at some stage.

- *Identity moratorium* – a pause in identity formation that allows the young person to explore alternatives without making a choice.

- *Identity achievement* – the achievement of identity and/or the stage at which the person feels that they are 'unique', through the assimilation of past experiences and future plans.

(Steinberg, 1993)

You may recognise these stages in adolescents you know, friends that you knew as adolescents, or even yourself. Let us consider the potential implications for your practice.

Activity 5.4

Think back to the case study on Clare in Activity 5.3. What stage would you describe Clare as being in? Consider how you might support her in making alternative choices.

It could be suggested that Clare is undergoing negative identity or identity diffusion. What is clear is that her behaviour is generating significant concern for her well-being and concerns about her feelings about herself. Understanding the impact of Clare's past experiences, particularly her developmental experiences, on her current view of herself is essential in making an assessment of her current behaviour and needs and supporting her foster carers in caring for her. You need to listen to Clare and gain an understanding of her perception, wishes and feelings. You will also need to gain an understanding of other people's perception of her, for example her teachers, and how they might support both her and you. She will need considerable support in building her self-esteem and self-worth and in identifying alternative opportunities to develop other choices to that of her current lifestyle.

Two important parts of identity development are 'ethnic identity development' (Paludi, 2002) and 'gender role identity'. Between the ages of three and six years children generally think about ethnic difference in physical terms and they do not necessarily see race as a fixed or stable attribute. Between the ages of 6 and 10 children generally think that race is a matter of ancestry that affects not only one's appearance but also one's diet, language and leisure activities. Between 10 and 14, they make the link to social class and are aware of connections, for example between race and income, race and neighbourhood (Rathus, 2008).

Research summary

Phinney (1993) describes three stages in the development of ethnicity:

1   Unexamined ethic identity – Lack of exploration of ethnic identity. Existing models suggest that minority subjects initially accept the values and attitudes of the majority culture. These include the internalised negative views of their own group held by the majority.
2   Ethnic identity search/moratorium – The initial stage of ethnic identity is conceptualised as continuing until adolescents encounter a situation that initiates an ethnic identity search.
3   Ethnic identity achievement – The ideal outcome of the identity process, characterised by a clear, confident sense of one's own ethnicity. Identity achievement corresponds to the acceptance and internalisation of one's ethnicity.

You may like to consider the potential impact of these issues for your practice using the case study in Activity 5.5.

Activity 5.5

Think about the following and consider how you would respond.

Chris, aged 14, has been in a children's home for a year. Chris's mother is white and his father is African-Caribbean. Another child at the home has been making racist comments and bullying him. Chris expresses confusion and anxiety about feeling that he does not belong anywhere.

Chris will need support and guidance in acknowledging and coming to terms with his emerging sense of self as a person and the impact of his cultural and racial identity. The significance of ethnicity and culture on adolescents' self-esteem, self-concept and emotional development is highlighted by Paludi (2002). As a social worker you should be aware of any low expectations that you may have, for example about children in the looked after system and children from different cultures, and of ways in which you may, even inadvertently, communicate these. You need to ensure that Chris has positive images of his racial origin conveyed to him, not just by you but also by the others around him (for example the staff at the children's home). Racial comments and attitudes need to be firmly challenged. You may have to consider the environment in which Chris lives (for example the relationships and friendships he has that promote his positive well-being and image of himself). You could enlist the support of his school in supporting Chris in his interaction with others, and in learning about promoting positive images of people from different cultures and ethnic backgrounds. Above all you need to listen to his experience. Using the narrative approach (namely listening to Chris's 'story') will enable you to make links for him between his history and his personal understanding.

Gender, and the development of sexual identity, is a critical part of one's identity. As Cobb (1995) suggests, an individual cannot simply see themself as a child to which they add sexual feelings and identity but must revise their concept of self. Originally, experts such as Erikson and Freud believed that although sexual identity may be confused during puberty, gender identity meant identifying oneself as a heterosexual male or female by adulthood. However, later research has suggested that sexual orientation and gender identity are much more varied than a simple male–female division.

Additionally, in contemporary society the individual has more choices to make as the 'rules' that govern this behaviour are increasingly challenged. Gender is a critical component of one's identity. From birth children are socialised and stereotyped into their gender roles. Boys tend to be encouraged to be strong, brave, logical and independent, and girls are expected to be gentle, sociable and co-operative. Many of the sexual differences identified in adolescence may in part be due to biological reasons; however, they are also due to acceleration in adolescents' socialisation into their gender roles. It has been suggested that the issue is not one of achieving a mix between female and male qualities and roles, rather of achieving 'sex-role transcendence'. This refers to the capacity to look beyond sex-roles and to make use of strengths and talents, regardless of one's biological sex (Katz, 1979).

Research summary

Figures from the Office for National Statistics (2014) demonstrate that the number of teenage girls getting pregnant in England and Wales is continuing to fall, with 23 conceptions per 1,000 15 to 17-year-old girls in 2014, compared to a high of 55 in 1976, and this is attributed to education programmes and easier access to contraceptives.

- However England continues to lag behind comparable western European countries, and teenagers continue to be at greatest risk of unplanned pregnancy and outcomes for some young parents and their children remain disproportionately poor.
- There are differences between regions, with girls in the north east of England more likely to get pregnant than those living in the south east and south west.
- The estimated number of conceptions to girls under 18 fell to 22,653 in 2014 compared with 24,306 in 2013, a decrease of 6.8 per cent.
- An estimated 4,160 girls under 16 became pregnant in 2014, compared with 4,648 in 2013, a fall of 10 per cent.

- There were some 871,038 conceptions to women of all ages in 2014, compared with 872,849 in 2013, a slight decrease of 0.2 per cent.
- Conception rates in 2014 increased for women aged 25 and over, and decreased for women under 25.

The focus on teenage pregnancy seen in England during the last fifteen years has been a considerable success as demonstrated by the decline. However, it still remains higher than a number of other western Europen countries and progress has been uneven across England. There is a 63 per cent higher risk of living in poverty for children born to mothers aged below 20. Mothers under 20 experience higher rates of poor mental health for up to three years after the birth. By age 30, women who were teenage mothers are 22 per cent more likely to be living in poverty than mothers giving birth aged 24 or over. Compared with older fathers, young fathers are twice as likely to be unemployed, even after taking account of deprivation (Local Government Association and Public Health England, 2016). Growing up in disadvantaged circumstances (for example living in social housing and in low-income households) was a predictor of young parenthood. In addition, individual childhood attributes such as poor reading ability, having a conduct disorder and having a mother with low educational aspirations for her child were also predictive factors. These five factors combined to increase the probability of having a teen birth from 1 per cent when none of these risk factors was present, to 31 per cent when all five were present. In males they increased the probability of being a father at age 22 or under from 2 per cent to 23 per cent (Berrington *et al.*, 2005).

In a study by Wiggins *et al.* (2005), many teenage parents report positive experiences. For some, the pregnancy was either planned or wanted. For others, this was not overtly the case at the time, but in retrospect their teenage pregnancy came to be viewed as a positive occurrence. Much that was negative about the experience of teenage parenthood for the mothers, the fathers and the children resulted from factors related to their socially excluded lives rather than the teenage pregnancy per se.

- Disliking school is linked to greater risk of teenage pregnancy.
- Violence in school and the home is an important risk factor for teenage pregnancy.
- Most teenage mothers felt that any sex education they had received at school and at home had been inadequate.
- The key factors that characterised the lives of those mothers who had done well were: support from family; having a positive partner relationship; developing a career or having employment they liked; and the passage of time since the birth.

(Wiggins *et al.*, 2005)

Psychological approaches to development in adolescence

In this section we are going to explore the concept of autonomy. We will look at different explanations for how and why adolescents respond to situations through their behaviour, particularly through an exploration of the concept of autonomy.

The development of autonomy in adolescence is gradual and progressive. Steinberg (1993) identifies three types of autonomy:

1. Emotional autonomy – aspects of interdependence in relation to changes in the individual's close relationships, for example, changes in expression of affection, interactions and patterns of power.

2. Value autonomy – changes in the adolescent's concept of moral, political, ideological and religious issues.

3. Behavioural autonomy – changes in decision-making abilities and changes in conformity and susceptibility to influence, for example from parents and peers.

Thom *et al.* (2007) discuss the concepts of 'dependence–autonomy' within their chapters which develop a critical analysis of children's and young people's development and the impact of risk.

The establishment and maintenance of a healthy sense of autonomy is a lifelong concern from early childhood; for example, you may recall that Erikson (1995) identified the development of autonomy as a stage that happens in the second and third year of life, into adult life. Developing autonomy during adolescence is more acute as it involves a range of interdependent processes placing adolescence in new roles and responsibilities which then require choices and decisions. Physical changes associated with puberty require choices about such things as sexuality and the development of sexual relationships. Cognitive changes (e.g. the concept of 'formal operation' defined by Piaget, 1936) provide the foundation for changes in the adolescent thinking systematically and in abstract terms about social, moral and ethical issues. Critical to this are the friendships and relationships that are formed with others.

Activity 5.6

Think about the friendships you had during your adolescence. How were these different from the friendships you had as a child? What kind of relationships did you have as an adolescent with members of the opposite sex? What kind of relationship did you have with your parents/carers?

Comment

Your experience will probably reflect changes in your relationships with friends – closer, more personal, and more emotionally expressive. A critical feature will be the development of more intimate relationships. Whilst this is an important concern throughout our lives, during adolescence they became more 'real' as the individual develops greater autonomy outside the family context. You may have been able to identify changes in your relationship with your family, especially as they and you 'adapted' to the different relationships that supported your growing autonomy.

Research summary

Robert L. Selman (Selman and Schultz, 1990) proposed five stages of children's friendship development, with his theoretical approach based on the model of Jean Piaget and the constructivist view (Rubin, 1980).

Stage One (3 to 7 years) Momentary Physical playmate – A close friend is one who may live nearby and who the child is playing with at that moment. There is no clear conception of an enduring relationship, other than specific encounters.

Stage Two (4 to 9 years) One way assistance – A friend is someone who does something that pleases you. A close friend is someone who you know better than other people.

Stage Three (6 to 12 years) Fair weather cooperation – There is a new awareness of interpersonal relationships. Friendship becomes reciprocal, but is still focusing on specific incidents rather than an enduring relationship (Rubin,1980).

Stage Four (11 to 15 years) Transitioning stage – In the transformation from stage 2/3 to this stage, children reflect on intimacy and mutuality within a continuing relationship.

Stage Five (12 to adulthood) Advancement – Perspectives can be shared between two people on common interests and deeper feelings. Perspectives among people form a network, which in turn becomes generalised.

It should be noted, however, that these stages are not concrete: chronological age is not reliable; a child does not have to go through every stage; and when asked about friendships there are often inconsistencies.

(Continued)

(Continued)

A study by the University of Minnesota study tracked 78 people from infancy through to their mid-20s. Researchers found that individuals who had been securely attached at 12 months were rated by their elementary school teachers as more socially competent. These more socially competent young people were also more likely to have secure friendships by the time they were 16 (Simpson *et al.*, 2007).

The development of social behaviour

One of the misconceptions is that adolescents demonstrate their independence or 'autonomy' by rebelling against their parents. Autonomy is often confused with rebellion and breaking away from the values and 'norms' of their families. However, there is no doubt that changing relationships within a family can cause conflict and difficulties.

Activity 5.7

Think about the following and try to identify the reasons that may be contributing to the behaviours described;

Tony, aged 15, is a boisterous, outgoing adolescent. June, his mother, describes him as 'out of control' – he never does as he has been told. June says, 'He's going to turn out like his father.' Terry, his father, is currently serving a prison sentence for a violent assault.

Eleanor, aged 14, is a bright and studious child who enjoys reading. Her teacher describes her as an able child, whose intelligence is well above average. Her parents cannot understand Eleanor's ability. 'She certainly does not take after us or our families,' they tell you. She spends a lot of time in her room and appears to have few friends.

Shelly, aged 13, gets frustrated and upset when she does not get her own way. She screams, shouts and hits others. Shelly was adopted by the Browns last year.

Blake, aged 14, is quiet and compliant. He has few friends. His teacher has noticed that he is stealing objects from the other children. When confronted he denies everything.

Gill, aged 16, has a learning disability. At school she is described as presenting no behaviour problems. However, at home her parents find her behaviour increasingly difficult to manage. When Gill does not 'get her own way' she kicks, spits and throws things. Gill often pinches and punches her brother Shaun, aged 9.

Understanding the reasons that underlie these behaviours will depend on your perspective. You may have merely attributed them to being a 'normal' adolescent. You may have viewed them as a parent-based issue: lack of appropriate response, inconsistent responses or, alternatively, over-control. You may have a view that this is about the genetic make-up of the child, individual personalities, the previous experiences that the young person has had or the behaviour that the young person has seen and learned. You may even have viewed it as a combination of all of these factors. As a social worker your response to each of these cases will depend on your assessment of a range of factors. Planning a response and supporting children, young people, parents and others to understand and manage their behaviour is a key role for social workers.

Case study 5.1

Read the following case and identify the motivations expressed by Johnny for taking drugs.

> Johnny, 15, says, 'I just like smack, or 'e' when I can't get it, and the buzz it gives me. My mates and I just hang out; there's nothing to do. Drugs make you feel good. Everyone does it around here. No one cares what we do anyway. My Dad's off his head most of the time anyway.'

Comment

Clearly there are a number of motivations from Johnny's perception to take drugs, including: influence of peers; feeling of 'fitting it'; boredom; availability of drugs; his father's use of drugs. In the study undertaken by Dillon et al. (2007), they identify three theories that are concerned with the thoughts that influence young people's resilience to involvement in drug-using behaviour, and subsequently the factors that facilitate them in putting these decisions into practice.

The three theories identified by Dillon et al. (2007) concerning the thoughts that influence young people's resilience to drug use are as follows:

1. *Schema theory* (Piaget, 1970) – Schema theory suggests that all people have a set of categorical rules or a script that they use to organise their knowledge about a particular concept in order to interpret the world. There appears to be evidence of young people operating a 'drugs as harmful to self' schema in order to remain resilient.

2. *Self-regulation theory* (Cochran and Tessor, 1996) – This theory refers to the internal and external process that allows individuals to carry out goal-focused actions over time, and in different social contexts. There is evidence to suggest that the young people in the current study employed three forms of approach goals in order to justify and maintain their resilience.

i. Ways in which drug use was perceived as incompatible with their career aspirations. Young people suggested that if they were to use drugs this may prevent them from attending classes and, in turn, stop them achieving the qualifications necessary to follow their chosen career path.

ii. Some young people made extensive use of their spare time to play sports, pursue hobbies and work in part-time jobs. As a result, this left them little time to be involved in situations where drug use may take place.

iii. The young people who were parents suggested that their role was not compatible with using drugs.

3. *Self-efficacy theory* (Bandura, 1977, 1986) – Self-efficacy can be conceptualised as people's beliefs about their capabilities of putting their decisions about what they want to do into practice. It is proposed that strong self-efficacy enhances feelings of accomplishment and overall well-being in people (Bandura, 1977, 1986). Young people were successful on two levels:

i. They managed to refuse an offer of a drug.

ii. They did not compromise their position within a friendship or relationship, for example.

This provides support for the suggestion of strong self-efficacy resulting in feelings of well-being and mastery.

Dillon *et al.* (2007) summed up resilience and risk factors in a helpful table (see Table 5.1).

Table 5.1 Summary of factors young people identified as facilitating or impeding resilience to drug use

Other people's motivations to use	Contextual risk factors	Factors making it easier/more difficult to refuse offers	Motivations not to use
Following example of others	In trouble with the police/ school	Reputation as 'resilient' to drug use	Other people's disapproval
To fit in	Alcohol use	Type of drug offered	Fear of effect on health
Peer pressure	Boredom	Reputation as a smoker or drinker	Fear of addiction
Alleviate boredom	Familial substance use	Age	Alternative sources of support/coping mechanisms
The 'buzz'	Mental health issues	'Happy to be the odd one out'	Current health conditions
Curiosity about effects	Problematic family relationships	Being drunk	Fear of losing control
Ease physical pain		Offered by friends or strangers	Role as a parent
'To look hard'			Availability of time
To feel more confident			Financial cost
			Personal experiences with drugs

Understanding and making sense of behaviour must be seen in the context of their development. Theorists take different approaches to explaining why children think and behave as they do.

Temperament

Temperament refers to the individual difference in the basic psychological processes – the apparent in-built tendencies in relation to reactions and behaviours. Children and young people who develop aggressive tendencies are inclined to have a difficult temperament from an early age. Psychologists studying this area have described key dimensions of temperament. Buss and Plomin (1989) suggest that there are three differences:

1. Emotionality – variations in the tendency to become distressed or upset easily, with fear or anger.

2. Activity – variations in tempo, vigour and endurance.

3. Sociability – variations in the tendency to seek and be gratified by rewards; high level of responsibility towards others.

Thomas and Chess (1977) believe that individuality in temperament is established by the time the child is three months old. They describe nine dimensions, which they organise into three types:

 i. The easy child.

 ii. The difficult child (unhappy, hard to distract, difficult to settle).

 iii. The slow-to-warm-up child (unwilling to be approached or adapt to new experiences).

Theories of temperament argue that individual differences are biologically or genetically determined, with studies of twins providing the strongest evidence. They show that identical twins are more alike in their temperament than fraternal twins.

'The Big Five' are a central group of personality traits that seem to be evident in all humans, no matter what their group or culture. The five-factor model comprises five personality dimensions and is held to be a complete description of personality:

1. Openness – imaginative, curious and artistic attitude; welcoming new experiences.

2. Conscientiousness – organised, deliberate and conforming impulses.

3. Extroversion – outgoing, assertive and active behaviour.

4. Agreeableness – kind, helpful and easy-going feelings.

5. Neuroticism – anxious, moody and self-punishing thoughts.

This is often referred to by the mnemonic OCEAN (Berger, 2014, p. 634).

These studies are not conclusive: individual differences in temperament should be seen as tendencies and may influence experiences. Temperament could be weakened or strengthened by a child's experience, for example the reactions of their caregiver. Some traits may be regarded as appropriate and encouraged in children (for example physically active boys and quiet, sedate girls). Children who are described by adults as having a difficult temperament, such as displaying irritability and being hard to comfort, could be affected by a more punitive reaction to their behaviour. However, temperament does not inevitably determine personality; rather it may suggest a bias towards certain patterns. A difficult temperament can be modified over time with appropriate caregiving. Thomas and Chess (1986) describe the concept of 'goodness to fit' to explain how temperament can change. 'Goodness to fit' refers to the fit between a child's behaviour and caregivers' expectations and behaviour towards that child (for example, if a parent has an expectation of a sociable happy child, they may have difficulties adapting to a difficult child). Additionally, they may not have the resources to draw on to support them (for example, coping skills and social support). Consequently, parents' behaviour may reinforce a child's undesirable behaviour. Where parents are able to respond patiently, caringly and positively to this behaviour, the child is able to progress well with their development.

Socialisation within the family

Children and young people learn from the modelling and communication of values within their family. Children need opportunities to participate in helping activities in which they learn how to co-operate, share and receive positive encouragement and praise for their actions. They imitate the behaviour of adults, particularly of those with whom they have a positive relationship. This includes values such as fairness and caring (Oliner and Oliner, 1988). Consequently, if parents are punitive, the expectation is that young people are more likely to model this. Additionally, parents who are inconsistent in administrating and following through on discipline are more likely to have aggressive and difficult children.

Activity 5.8

Do you have a view on smacking? Do you believe that children should never be smacked? Or do you think that a smack is an appropriate measure of discipline? What is your view on the following article?

Leader, Sunday 4 May 2003, *Observer*

> *As we report today, the Government wants to make it illegal throughout the United Kingdom for childminders to smack children in their care. The antiquated defence of 'reasonable chastisement' will no longer be admissible – except for parents.*

> *We welcome the belated recognition that this 140-year-old justification for hitting young children has left Britain with one of the worst child-cruelty records in Europe and has offered carte blanche to sadists and abusers. But it is feeble of the Government not to take the argument to its logical conclusion and outlaw the hitting of children by anyone.*
>
> *Social workers and police have long complained that the 'reasonable chastisement' defence prevents them from intervening in cases of parental abuse, from which, shockingly, one child a week still dies in the UK. In Sweden, in the ten years following a ban on smacking, not a single child died as a result of parental physical abuse.*
>
> *Striking other adults (whether 'reasonable chastisement' or not) is unlawful. Why then do we persist in finding it acceptable to visit violence on children? It is time for an outright ban. Hitting children is never right.*

The impact of parental discord, for example being exposed to verbal and physical violence, will have an impact on children's behaviour. Research demonstrates the impact of domestic violence on children (Hester and Pearson, 1998; Humphreys and Mullender, 2000; Hester *et al.*, 2007). These reports show that children are aware of and responsive to domestic violence to a greater degree than had previously been thought. Although many develop coping strategies, their social, emotional and educational development may be hindered where processing of their destructive experience is not facilitated.

A number of studies have identified the overlap of domestic violence and child abuse:

- The domestic violence perpetrator may also be directly abusive to the child.
- Witnessing violence to their mothers may have an abusive and detrimental impact on the children concerned.
- The perpetrators may abuse the child as a part of their violence against women.

Children (even within the same family) may be affected in quite different ways due to age, gender, temperament and so on which may also act as mediating factors. Factors which could eliminate any harm to children and young people include:

- ensuring the safety of the mother;
- focusing on safety and quality in deciding on and arranging child contact;
- listening to children and counselling support;
- primary prevention – in schools.

(Holt *et al.*, 2008)

Research summary

- Professional understanding of, and responses to, domestic violence should be informed by the perspectives of children and young people.
- Practitioners need to recognise that domestic violence may be a cause of a range of physical, emotional and behavioural difficulties for children and young people.
- The complex relationship between domestic violence and safeguarding children requires respectful and sensitive handling.
- Children and young people aware of domestic violence have the right to be listened to and need help to understand what is happening.
- Some children and young people cope well despite their experiences of domestic violence.
- Work with perpetrators, though controversial, is an important aspect of reducing domestic violence and its impact on children and young people.

(SCIE, 2008)

As a social worker you will need to take into account the impact of all of these factors, especially the role and attitudes of the carers, in your assessments of children who are at risk of abuse and/or may be in trouble, for example with the law.

The impact of socio-economic status, for example poverty, adds to the stressors for families and may mean that there are limited resources, both physically and emotionally, to support and engage children in their development.

Increasing research is being undertaken into the impact of television and video games on the levels of violence demonstrated by children and young people. Some research suggests that this has an impact on children's behaviour; other research contradicts this view.

Research summary

Research carried out by Dawson *et al*. (2007) into why people play video games and what impact they think playing games has on them has been published by the British Board of Film Classification (BBFC). This qualitative research project consisted of interviews and discussions with people who play games and involved video games players ranging from children as young as 7 through to players in their early 40s, parents of young games players, games industry representatives, and games reviewers. The interviews were carried out in Edinburgh, Birmingham, Leeds, Newcastle upon Tyne, Radlett in Hertfordshire, Croydon and Greater London.

The following is an extract taken from parts of the report, where the findings have been analysed in respect of the impact of violence in games on the players' behaviours:

> *A few gamers fear that the violence in games may have regrettable effects on some people's behaviour, principally people who become obsessed with games and spend too much time playing them.*

> *'If someone's got that violent side in them they'll sit and play computer games with violence in them for hours and hours and it's not going to do them any favours.'*

It is sometimes argued that playing violent games can make a player aggressive in the short term, again particularly if he plays 'too much'.

> *'I would say that your emotional mood definitely changes when you play a violent game. If you're not winning you can get quite aggressive.'*

> *'I don't like (violent) games because my brother plays them and it makes him really aggressive. There's this boy who lives near us... and he plays like 18 games, for 18s and over. Before he played them he was all right but since he's been playing them he's become a bit aggressive. It's really changed him quite a bit.'*

HOW WAS HE BEFORE?

> *'He was normal. He would get angry if someone made him angry but he wouldn't try to punch them... He used to be quite good at work and he used to really like maths and now he doesn't.'*

It is generally only boys and men who are regarded as being at any sort of risk in this way, but one young girl in this sample seemed to say that playing games made her feel aggressive.

> *'When you're playing one of those {violent} games you're so controlled that you think it's like real... I've played it before, not like a really old one, just like a 12 one, and you do switch off the rest of the world and just focus on the telly. When I stop playing it it's all weird and you feel like punching someone.'*

It sometimes seems to be suspected that playing too much, becoming obsessed with video games, might tip someone over the edge into violence.

> *'You get some people that get too into it. You get problems and they go out and do something stupid in real life... You hear about it on the news. They go out on a killing spree... It frustrates me because it's not the computer game's fault.'*

(Continued)

> *(Continued)*
>
> *A few gamers put the counter argument – that games can provide a safe outlet for aggression that might otherwise find unfortunate expression in real life.*
>
> > *'If you're in a mood and want to hit someone, then you can play the game and it releases you.'*
>
> *Most gamers have a robust conviction that only people with some exceptional propensity to be violent are susceptible to influence by the violence in video games. People who commit violent acts are not ordinary gamers but 'idiots' and 'nutters'.*
>
> (Dawson *et al.*, 2007, pp. 78–79)

The whole of the research report from which the extract is taken can be downloaded at www.bbfc.co.uk. You may be interested to read the entire report or other parts of it, but for the purposes of this chapter it is sufficient to develop your understanding and ability to critique the different influences on the development of young people in contemporary society.

Activity 5.9

Having read the research summary above, reflect upon your views of this issue.

Consider not only video games, but also the greater role of the media and internet communication; how significant do you believe the impact of these issues is on the social and behavioural development of young people?

It can be seen that there is little doubt that the various new technologies have some form of influence on young people's lives and their experiences. However, to what extent and to what effect can be debated. In the research extract, you can read different views from people who are themselves gamers, so there is a range of perspectives. With respect to developing as a social being, one of the most influential developments in recent years is arguably the widespread, extensive use of mobile telephones, text and internet communication facilities. Young people have new, different and innovative ways to communicate with each other, to source information and to be listened to (for example, the internet provides a wide range of ways in which young people can voice their views, source information and express their ideas).

Behaviourism and social learning theory

We have introduced the basic concept of behaviourism and social learning theory in Chapter 2. The focus in this section is to apply some of these principles to an understanding of children's behaviour. The focus of the approaches to a young person's behaviour is to study what is actually going on in the situation. The basic principles are that children learn new behaviour through modelling – copying the actions of others. This behaviour is strengthened by reinforcement, which increases the likelihood that the behaviour will be repeated. 'Positive reinforcement' refers to a positive addition to the situation, such as praise, a hug or a reward. 'Negative reinforcement' refers to the removal of something unpleasant or unwanted from the situation.

In behaviourist terms, this is not the same as punishment; punishment is the removal or denial of something pleasant from the situation. For example, Karl's mother may have said that he could not have any sweets that day if he does not clean his room. This may have prompted Karl to clean his room and may work in the short term. However, behaviourists would argue that this might have unintentional emotional effects such as frustration and anger (for example an outburst of temper). Consequently, it may increase rather than reduce the unwanted behaviour.

Case study 5.2

Sophie, aged 13, has been fostered by the Green family for the last six weeks. She has been subject to emotional and physical neglect by her parents. Sophie finds it difficult to sit at the dinner table. She eats her food as fast as she can and constantly gets up from her chair. Recognising that Sophie has not had any pattern at mealtimes, Jonathan and Pauline, the foster parents, talk to her about her experience of mealtimes and the importance of them as an opportunity to be together, within their family. Sophie admits that her experience of mealtimes in her family has been non-existent – there was no pattern to mealtimes and you had to 'grab' food when it was available. They agree that they will support Sophie in building up a pattern of sitting at the table. The first week she must sit on her chair for five minutes, building up to staying at the table for the whole meal. Each day that she achieves her goal the Greens say she can have a small treat, with a week's achievement resulting in a bigger reward. Additionally, they ensure that she is encouraged and praised privately for sitting at the table.

Cognitive-developmental approach

The cognitive explanation of children's and young people's behaviour is concerned not only with what is actually happening, but also with their understanding and mental representations of what is going on. They are also concerned within everyday interactions in their social environment – with other children and with key adults in their lives.

Case study 5.3

Karl, aged 14, is told to go and clean his room. He whines and moans as he does it, deliberately creating more mess. His mum persists in telling him to clean his room. She eventually gives in, lets him go and cleans the room herself. Karl has learned that whining works in avoiding unpleasant tasks.

Case study 5.4

Susan, aged 13, comes in late. Her parents talk to her about the importance of time-keeping and how concerned they were about her. Peter, aged 15, remarks, 'That is different from what you would say to me! I would get shouted at and grounded for a week!' 'Well, that is because you are just trouble and always doing things to annoy us,' replies Dad.

Children and young people are treated differently for a whole range of reasons. In this case it may be because of Susan's age and the parents' expectations and response to her gender. However, Peter is aware that the quality of interaction between himself and his parents is different. He recognises that he is treated differently from his sibling. Differences in treatment are an important ingredient in the child's developing internal model of self and contribute towards differences in behaviour between children in the same family.

Moral development

Moral development is concerned with the development of values relevant to how we treat other people and how we get treated. Children's and young people's behaviour needs to be grounded in an expectation that they are able to grasp and manage moral issues in their social world. In the first eight years of their life children develop a network of social relationships with people – their family, other adults and children. They develop different relationships based on their expectations and the constraints of different settings and different people.

Babies are born morally neutral. As they begin to be more mobile they also begin to discover the rights and wrongs of situations. This is based on adult approval or disapproval as they do not understand the adults' moral judgement. For example, when a toddler is urged 'not to touch' an ornament they do not grasp the adult's moral judgement, rather that the adult will disapprove. Initially children will learn through direct observation about 'rules' and move on to understand general principles about tasks and situations. As their experience develops, their judgements move from being definite and fixed to being more qualified – 'ifs', 'buts' and 'what ifs'. They move from seeing everything from their own viewpoint to taking a broader perspective. By five and six years children have a clear understanding and working assumption about how the social world works.

Piaget (Birch, 1997) emphasises the cognitive aspect of moral development, believing that a child's moral development is linked to their stage of cognitive development. He concludes that there are two broad stages of moral development:

- Stage 1: heteronomous morality or moral realism – Rules are seen as strictly to be complied with. An act is judged on the consequence rather than intention. It is 'naughtier' to break several cups rather than just one.

- Stage 2: autonomous morality or moral relativism – This occurs around the age of 7 or 8. Rules are established and maintained through negotiation within the social group. Intention and consequence are linked.

Subsequent researchers have used different methodologies in testing children's and young people's moral thinking, which have confirmed Kohlberg's three levels. However, they have also identified the potential impact of two other features: the impact of culture as it affects moral judgement, and differences in morality relating to gender. Some critics believe that Level 3 thinking in particular reflects liberal western intellectual values. Some cultures, for example the Turkish culture, place great emphasis on the community and community values. Consequently, this could be considered a higher form of moral thinking than the individualism emphasised by Kohlberg (Walker *et al.*, 1995).

Carol Gilligan (1982) believed that Kohlberg overlooked significant differences in approach attributed to gender as his very research was based on male values; for example, he only used boys in his original research. Gilligan argued that there were two distinct orientations towards morality: a morality of care, which females are more likely to orientate towards, and a morality of justice, which males are more likely to orientate towards.

- Morality of care – the tendency for females to be reluctant to judge rights and wrongs in absolute terms because they are socialised to be nurturing.

- Morality of justice – the tendency of males to emphasise justice over compassion, judging right and wrong in absolute terms.

Research summary

Lawrence Kohlberg (1976) studied the moral reasoning of children and young people building to develop a stage model of moral development. He proposed three levels of moral development, with two stages in each:

(Continued)

(Continued)

Level 1: Pre-conventional morality (middle childhood)

Stage 1: Punishment and obedience orientation – children keep rules in order that punishment may be avoided.

Stage 2: Instrumental morality – children follow rules when it is in their immediate interest to do so. Although they are able to consider others, it is only when the results are favourable to themselves.

Level 2: Conventional morality (approximately 13–16)

Stage 3: Mutual expectations within relationships – being good is worthwhile for its own sake.

Stage 4: Social systems and conscience – the source of morality is placed in a wider social, 'societal' context.

Level 3: Principled or post-conventional morality (approximately 16–20)

Stage 5: The social contract – rules may not be absolute but take into account the good of the many rather than individual wants. Moral and legal viewpoints may conflict with each other.

Stage 6: Universal ethical principles – individuals have developed a personal system of moral principles, which guide personal beliefs and actions.

Gilligan raises an important debate about the 'voices' of men and women. Why should the experience of the definition and routes to morality be different for men and women? How do we ensure that both of these 'voices' are placed alongside each other in order to develop an integrated approach to justice and care?

Individual difference in adolescence

You will be aware that as a social worker you need to have an understanding of 'normal' child growth and development. This will allow you to compare, contrast and assess the development of a child with whom you will be working with that of the average child. Additionally, it will help you to judge the role of others, especially parents, in their development (for example their ability to meet the demands of the different stages of development, their ability to respond to the competing demands of parenting, their values and attitudes and the impact that these have on the child and so on).

Throughout this and previous chapters we have attempted to identify issues that may specifically impact on the individual's experience of adolescence – issues of gender, issues of race and culture and disability. Drug and alcohol use is increasing among young people.

For the majority of young people this may be experimentation associated with peer culture and peer pressure. For others it may be a more serious issue. Young people who use substances may demonstrate low self-esteem and self-worth, rebelliousness and a lack of aspiration in relation to academic achievement. You will also need to consider and work with children who present with more challenging behaviour, and you will need to work with children who present with emotional issues. A distinction needs to be made.

There are those young people who present with a range of anti-social behaviour, such as criminal activity, aggression, defiance and a refusal to comply (for example with authority). These behaviours may be labelled 'conduct issues'. Other young people may present with emotional issues, such as depression and anxiety. A distinction needs to be made between those that might be associated with developmental issues and those that may be more serious. For example, a small proportion of young people will present with psychiatric disorders such as suicide attempts associated with depression, schizophrenia, anorexia or bulimia nervosa.

Research summary

Beinart *et al.* (2002) undertook a survey of 14,000 students in English, Scottish and Welsh secondary schools in order to assess their involvement in crime, drugs and alcohol misuse and other anti-social activities. The survey described 17 major risk factors and six protective factors, summarised in Table 5.2.

Table 5.2 Youth crime and anti-social behaviour: risk and protective factors (Beinart *et al.*, 2002)

Risk factors	Protective factors
Poor parental supervision and discipline	Strong bonds with family, friends and teachers
Family conflict	Healthy standards set by parents, teachers and community leaders
Family history of problem behaviour	Opportunities for involvement in families, schools and the community
Parental involvement/attitudes condoning problem behaviour	Social and learning skills to participation
Low income and poor housing	Recognition and praise for positive behaviour
Low achievement beginning in primary school	
Aggressive behaviour including bullying	
Lack of commitment including truancy	
School disorganisation	

(Continued)

(Continued)

Risk factors	Protective factors
Community disorganisation and neglect	
Availability of drugs	
Disadvantaged neighbourhood	
High turnover and lack of neighbourhood attachment	
Alienation and lack of social commitment	
Attitudes that condone problem behaviour	
Early involvement in problem behaviour	
Friends involved in problem behaviour	

Chapter summary

In this chapter you have explored human life course development in respect of adolescence, focusing on the use in practice of human growth and development theories and knowledge. The chapter started by putting adolescence into the context of the society in which we live and considering the way the term is socially constructed in our society.

The chapter then worked through a range of theories that explain human development during adolescence. Exploration of social development in adolescence included consideration of the transition into adulthood, changing roles and the growth of independence and maturity. Biological development focused on physical, bodily changes such as puberty, sexuality and growth. You also looked at learning theories that explain development in adolescence as shaped by predictable processes of learning.

Whilst considering your own thoughts about being a teenager, you looked at examples of individual difference, such as gender, race, culture, disability and difficult behaviours and how these issues can impact on an individual's experience of adolescence. Throughout the chapter, you developed your understanding of the range of influences that impact on a person's experience of adolescence. However, you also saw the importance of recognising that whilst there are certain expected changes within this period of life, there are no pre-determined pathways that lay out predictable ways in which people will experience or behave in their adolescent years. This then reinforces the importance of developing an understanding of the individual's perspective, the meanings they attach to their life events and the impact this has had for them. The significance of personal biographical accounts cannot be underestimated.

Further reading

Coleman, JC (2011) *The Nature of Adolescence* (4th edn). Hove: Routledge.

This successful textbook provides an introduction to all of the key features of adolescent development.

Daiute, C, Beyont, Z, Higson-Smith, C and Nucci, L (2006) *International Perspectives on Youth Conflict and Development.* New York: Oxford University Press.

This text may be of interest as it will widen your studies to take account of difference in an international context. This edited volume of essays considers the social, political and economic contexts of youth conflict across 14 countries on seven (sic) continents. The range of international authors introduce case studies and use research to examine social practice embedded in local, national and international processes, through analysis of young people's participation in armed conflict, fighting and social exclusion in the context of their local environments. Whilst this text will expand your reflections on youth development, it is simply a very interesting and informative read.

Daniel, B and Wassell, S (2002) *Adolescence: Assessing and Promoting Resilience in Vulnerable Children.* London: Jessica Kingsley.

This practical resource for work with vulnerable adolescents shows ways of promoting resilience and encouraging pro-social behaviour.

Kroger, J (2007) *Identity Development: Adolescence Through Adulthood* (2nd edn). London: Sage.

Kroger presents an overview and analysis of general theoretical orientations to the question of what constitutes identity, including narrative, psychological, and sociocultural approaches. The book also describes the key biological, psychological and contextual issues due in each phase of adolescence and adulthood.

Websites

The National Youth Agency: www.nya.org.uk

According to the information provided on their website, the National Youth Agency (NYA) was founded in 1991 and is funded primarily by the Local Government Association and relevant government departments. Their aim is to support those involved in young people's personal and social development, and to promote young people's voice, influence and place in society, thus enabling all young people to fulfil their potential within a just society. The website provides a range of resources including publications and information about policy development.

6: Using life course development knowledge in social work practice with adults

Achieving a social work degree

This chapter will help you begin to meet the following capabilities, to the appropriate level, from the Professional Capabilities Framework:

- **Knowledge**
  - Apply knowledge of social sciences, law and social work practice theory.
- **Critical reflection and analysis**
  - Apply critical reflection and analysis to inform and provide a rationale for professional decision making.
- **Contexts and organisation**
  - Engage with, inform, and adapt to changing contexts that shape practice. Operate effectively within own organisational frameworks and contribute to the development of services and organisations. Operate effectively within multi-agency and interprofessional settings.

It will also introduce you to the following academic standards as set out in the social work subject benchmark statement:

3.1.1 Social work services and service users.
3.1.4 Social work theory.

Introduction

In this chapter, and the next, you will consider human life course development in respect of adults. The material has been separated into two chapters, the first being dedicated to considering adults in their early and middle years, and the second develops those ideas to consider life course knowledge as it relates to older adults. This chapter will begin by exploring what we mean by 'adulthood'. It will then develop your knowledge and understanding of the significance of life course development and life transitions in adult life and the implications for social work practice. Drawing on theories, illuminated by case examples including situations where adults experience a range of disabilities, the chapter will discuss how adult life course development can be explained. The value of a person's first-hand account of their life, their own explanations and meanings will also be considered. Following the life course perspective described in Chapter 1, you will consider how life transitions present opportunities for growth and development or, conversely, potential crisis points in people's lives.

Social work is seen as having a clear role in working with people to empower, protect and promote their well-being and inclusion and in its contribution to supporting people across the wider health and care system (DH, 2016). As *The Strategic Statement on Social Work With Adults in England 2016-2020* (DH, 2016) states, social workers deal with complex and challenging situations, requiring a distinct set of knowledge, skills and values, requiring compassion, empathy and analytical thinking, and an understanding of the positive impact they can have on people's lives. Social workers have a vital role in integrated health and social care systems and in working in multi-disciplinary teams, seeing the whole person and using a strengths and outcome-focused approach to support people's independence and well-being.

The Care Act 2014 is the most significant piece of legislation for social care since the establishment of the welfare state. Local authorities have a primary responsibility to promote individual well-being, with a shift of duty to provide services to meeting needs. A key part of the act is focusing on preventative services or delaying the need for support. Local authorities must facilitate a diverse, vibrant and sustainable market for care and support services to benefit the whole population. Carers (people who provide unpaid care and support, often a family member or friend) should be supported to maintain their caring role for longer. Needs or carer assessments must be carried out where it appears to an authority that these are relevant; they should be appropriate, proportionate, person-centred, and ensure a focus on the duty to promote well-being. Once an assessment has been carried out, there is a duty on the local authorities to provide care and support plans and offer a personal budget. Adult safeguarding is highlighted in the Care Act 2014, setting out a legal framework for how local authorities and other parts of the system should protect adults at risk of abuse or neglect. This includes setting up an Adults Safeguarding Board, to include key stakeholders. The act also requires local authorities to promote integration with the NHS and other key partners.

These documents, and others we will refer to, are hugely influential in our understanding of adulthood, and in influencing the language, assumptions and principles that are articulated via these documents.

What do we understand by the term 'adult'?

Before we can study the life course development of adults in detail, we need to consider what we mean by the word 'adult'. In the previous chapter you considered 'adolescence' as the transitional stage before adulthood; you will now think about how we define the point at which a person is deemed to have reached adulthood.

Activity 6.1

Let us presume that you consider yourself to be an adult. Write down the point in your life when you feel you made this transition. Now list the factors you believe made you an 'adult' as opposed to being a child or an adolescent.

Comment

You may have considered a number of factors as being important. Perhaps you have listed a certain birthday or a particular life event such as leaving home or something more difficult to define, like a feeling of having developed your own sense of individuality, however that may be defined.

It is likely that you thought that age was a factor. For example, in Britain the law permits various activities once an individual reaches certain ages. At the age of 16 a person can legally consent to sex, get married with parental consent and also leave full-time education. However, the right to vote or purchase alcohol is not legally granted until the age of 18. In our society people often celebrate their 21st birthday with the notion of getting the 'key to the door' as a particular transition point into independence. In other countries these events may be permissible at different ages (for example, in Spain you can legally purchase alcohol on reaching your 16th birthday, yet in Canada that right is not legally permissible until the age of 19).

Adulthood can also be linked to physical and biological changes. From this perspective we could define adulthood as the time when physical growth is complete and the individual has moved through puberty and is able to reproduce. However, the rate and point at which individuals reach physical maturity will vary greatly and may be difficult to determine.

Another aspect of being an adult could be defined in terms of psychological development. Yet recognising and measuring emotional, personality and identity development, in order to decide upon whether a person has reached adulthood, is also fraught with difficulties.

Whether you choose one or more of these areas to help define adulthood will depend upon your own perspective. What is clear is that the point at which we become an adult is contested. In social work practice, we need to be mindful of the ways in which individuals construct their own sense of self and the points along the life course at which they would locate themselves. We also need to be mindful of the ways in which laws, policies and agency remits affect how people are responded to, and indeed whether or not they will receive a social work service. However, for this chapter we shall consider early and middle adulthood within an age-frame of approximately between 18 and 65 years.

Stages of development through adult life

Separating the life course into easily definable segments is not straightforward. However, there are theories and models that explain adult life in terms of stages of development or tasks through which individuals progress. In Chapter 2 of this book we introduced you to Erik Erikson's (1997) model of life stages. We are going to explore this further, alongside other models that consider adult life in stages, namely those developed by Havighurst (1972) and Levinson (1978).

Activity 6.2

Think about adult life in our society, in particular your life and those of other adults known to you. Write down the answers to the following questions:

- Do you think of adult life as divided up into segments or stages of some kind?
- If so, what are these stages?
- How would you identify and define the stages of adult life? For example, when does one part of adulthood start and another end?

Comment

We cannot guess how many stages you have identified, but it is likely that you have used some age-related divisions, perhaps considering young adulthood, middle age and older age adulthood as main categories, with possibly more stages in between.

Erik Erikson's 'eight stages of man'

Erikson's theory arose from a psychosocial perspective on human life course development. He described 'eight stages of man' that represent a process of personality and identity development. His theory was developed from the concepts first described by Sigmund Freud (1949). Freud put forward a psychoanalytic theory to explain the development of personality through childhood stages of psychosexual development. Erikson took this a stage further, in that his theory covers the whole of life and incorporates the influence of the social context of people's lives, thus taking a psychosocial perspective.

Erikson's model explains human development as the process of forming our identity, our thoughts, emotions and personality, through the interaction between the individual, the society and situations in which they live. He suggests that people confront a series of developmental challenges or conflicts, each occurring at particular and predictable times or stages in their lives.

Research summary

Eric Erikson's (1902–1994) eight stages of development:

1 First year.
2 Second and third years.
3 Fourth and fifth years.
4 Six to 11.
5 Adolescence.
6 Young adulthood (20s and 30s).
7 Middle adulthood (40s to 60s).
8 Late adulthood.

Eric Erikson's stages of psychosocial development in adulthood

Young adulthood: intimacy versus isolation

(Age 20–30 years)

Erikson describes this life stage challenge as forming intimate relationships with other adults. The struggle in this stage is to experience intimacy, yet retain a sense of one's own identity. Successfully negotiating this challenge enables an individual to experience love and commitment to others, whilst unsuccessful movement through this stage may lead to isolation and the forming of superficial relationships with others.

Middle adulthood: Generativity versus stagnation

(Age 40–60 years)

This stage of life presents the challenge of contributing to society, being productive and creative. Thus it is linked with parenting, employment and occupation. Erikson stresses the importance of progression and the need for individuals to have contributed to the progression and future of society. The favourable outcome is stated as having the ability to be concerned and caring about others in the wider sense; however, the unfavourable outcome is that the individual may not grow or develop themself, becoming bored and over-concerned with themselves.

Case study 6.1

Jeanette is a single parent with two children, both under five years of age. She is 21 years old and lives with her children in a flat within a multi-storey complex. Largely due to lack of money, but also difficulties in securing childcare, Jeanette seldom goes out or socialises without her children. She has a number of friends, many of whom she has met through the local nursery; they are also single parents. Jeanette has very little contact with her mother, although she lives close by, as they fell out when Jeanette first became pregnant. Jeanette has never known her father, who left the family home when she was a baby. Things have become increasingly difficult for her; she is gradually getting into worsening debt to a local money lender and feels that she has no one she can discuss her problems with. She is considering turning to prostitution.

In negotiating each stage or life crisis, the challenges could be successfully or unsuccessfully met, leading to favourable or unfavourable outcomes. Erikson refers to this balance as a *favourable ratio* (1987). Where the outcome of moving through a life stage is unfavourable, the individual will find it more challenging to meet the trials of the next stage. Erikson states that at each of the developmental stages, it may be necessary for individuals to return to unsettled earlier points in their lives. This is similar to crisis theory as discussed in Parker and Bradley (2014).

Unlike many other theories, Erikson's model covers life from infancy to old age, although the crises associated with these ages may be experienced repeatedly at different chronological periods in an individual's life. For the purposes of this chapter though, we will explore the two of Erikson's stages that relate to early and middle adulthood. We shall look at the last of Erikson's stages in the next chapter.

Jeanette is in Erikson's 'young adulthood' life stage, within which he describes the challenge of 'intimacy versus isolation'. As we have discussed above, he stresses the significance of each life stage in preparing the person for the next stage and that where the person has experienced difficulties in negotiating one stage, they may revisit that point later in their lives. In Jeanette's situation, some of her difficulties may have arisen from her adolescence or even childhood experiences, for example where issues of attachment to her father may have been unresolved. Furthermore, her pregnancies during adolescence could be interpreted, using Erikson's model, as her way of attempting to meet the challenge of adolescence by developing her own identity and role in society. It could be argued, therefore, that Jeanette is now seeking to reduce the isolation she feels by considering forms of relationships that may also provide financial reward. Additional aspects of this case study that you should consider are the needs of her children and whether she is able to meet those needs, not only in terms of basic, practical resources such as food and warmth, but also in respect of their emotional and support needs. In other words, is Jeanette, in her current situation, able to adequately parent her children? This is not a straightforward issue and would require a detailed assessment of Jeanette's and her family's situation.

Case study 6.2

Ivy is a 44-year-old single woman who lives alone. Her parents died ten years ago. She has a younger brother who lives some distance away and has a young family and busy career. Ivy has a progressive physical illness and experiences episodes of severe pain and difficulties using her limbs. She finds that some days are worse than others, but on bad days her mobility and ability to take care of herself are substantially impaired. Through an individual budget (DH, 2006), Ivy employs a team of care staff to meet her needs in her own home. Throughout her adult life, she has successfully controlled and managed all of her own affairs. For a number of years she has been very active within a national voluntary organisation, campaigning for the rights of disabled people. Lately she has stopped attending the meetings and has not been responding to telephone calls. She does not readily engage in conversation with her care staff and appears low-spirited. When one member of the care team insisted on questioning Ivy about what was the matter, she angrily responded 'I think I'll give up and go into residential care!'.

Activity 6.3

Consider Ivy's current life situation. Explain the significance of events in Ivy's life using Erikson's model of life stages. You could do this by answering the following questions:

- Which of Erikson's stages is Ivy likely to be in?
- What might be the conflicts and challenges facing her at this time?
- What might be causing the difficulties that she faces?
- In what ways is Erikson's model helpful in explaining her situation?
- How would your understanding of her situation, using Erikson's approach, help you to think about social work practice with her?

We would suggest that Ivy is in the 'middle adulthood' stage. Erikson describes meeting the challenge of the conflict between 'generativity versus stagnation' as crucial to success at this stage of life. You may have thought that Ivy is facing a number of challenges at this point in her life. Her physical health may be declining as the progressive nature of her illness, alongside age-related changes, exacerbate her impairments. Ivy is also reaching other physical changes of middle adulthood, such as the menopause. The impending reduction of reproductive ability will lead to role and identity dilemmas, as Ivy will need to consider that she may never have children. Furthermore, Erikson's definition of 'generativity' extends beyond parenthood, to include productivity and developments for future generations. Ivy may feel disheartened that after many years of work and campaigning her efforts have effected little change. Thus her self-identity, role in society and the meanings she attaches to them are being challenged and redefined.

Erikson's theory leads us to think about whether or not Ivy has moved successfully through previous life stages: in other words, to look at whether there are outstanding or unresolved issues from an earlier point in her life. So, for example, during her young adulthood, how did Ivy meet the challenges of 'intimacy versus isolation'? It appears from the information that we have that she is isolated and self-absorbed within her experiences. She does not appear to have any intimate relationships or attachments. Therefore, according to this model, it could be seen that Ivy had not been able to successfully meet the challenges of young adulthood.

You may have felt that this model was helpful in suggesting explanations for the difficulties she faces. You may have thought that the model was less helpful as it restricted your ability to consider specific issues that may have been relevant, in that she may have a very close relationship and be in regular contact with her brother.

Your thoughts on this activity so far would all impact upon your assessment of Ivy's situation. Having applied Erikson's model to help you understand the issues for her, you were asked to think about the implications for social work practice. One of the areas of work would be to help Ivy identify, clarify and express her strengths, expectations and limitations. The basic principle of 'personalisation', central to the Care Act 2014, is that care and support should be individualised and tailored to fit around a person's specific needs, giving greater independence, choice and control over their life. This has led to greater choice in how care and support

> ## Case study 6.3
>
> Marcus is 43 years old; he is married and has two children. His son is 17 years old and has just left school and joined the armed forces. His daughter is 19 years old and is in her first year at university. Marcus was born and spent his childhood in Jamaica, moving to England to study when he was in his early 20s. Marcus's father was taken ill and died in Jamaica four months ago. Shortly afterwards his mother had a stroke, resulting in some long-term impairments. As Marcus is her only family, she has moved to England to live with Marcus and his wife.

Using Levinson's model, Marcus could be seen to be in the stage of entering middle adulthood, which Levinson describes as a transitional phase, characterised by change. Levinson used the popular term 'mid-life crisis'; this term is often linked to some of the challenges and responses apparent in the middle years of adulthood. Marcus is experiencing a number of changes and new challenges in his life, through which he will need to reconsider his own identity and role. On the one hand his children are becoming independent and his role as 'father' may need to take a different approach. On the other hand his identity and role as 'son' has also changed. He may previously have visited his mother for holidays, but will not have lived with her for many years. His relationship with his mother will change due to her level of dependency and their new living arrangements. Additionally, Marcus may have to renegotiate roles with his wife in order to encompass the evolving changes in their family situation. For Marcus, successfully having moved through previous stages in life will also be significant, for example, how his relationship with his mother and later his children developed through other stages in his life.

Therefore, Levinson's model could be seen to be helpful in explaining the situation that Marcus is experiencing. However, given that Levinson based his theory on original research that was undertaken with only male participants, you should consider whether the model would be as useful if Marcus were female, for example. Levinson's work has been criticised for only being relevant to white, middle-class males (Bee, 1994), with the later studies that included women being considered as only providing weak support for the model. In Case Study 6.3, however, the transitional issues of change, challenge and role adjustment facing Marcus could be described and explained using Levinson's model if this case study were based upon a female.

Robert Havighurst's developmental tasks

We shall now look at a third staged model of life development, as proposed by Robert Havighurst (1972). Like Erikson, Havighurst divided the whole life course into stages, with the additional concept of 'developmental tasks'. He defined these as tasks that occur during life and need to be successfully achieved if the person is to move on to succeed in completing later tasks. Failure in the tasks will lead to unhappiness, disapproval by society and problems with later tasks. You will note some similarities with Erikson's approach to life stages and 'crises' in this respect.

Research summary

Havighurst's developmental tasks

Robert Havighurst describes six life stages and related 'developmental tasks'. Two of these are stages of adult life, and each has a number of 'developmental tasks' associated with that phase:

1. Infancy and early childhood.
2. Middle childhood.
3. Adolescence.
4. Early adulthood.

Development tasks are:

- selecting a mate;
- learning to live with a marriage partner;
- starting a family;
- rearing children;
- managing a home;
- getting started in an occupation;
- taking on civic responsibility;
- finding a congenial social group.

5. Middle age.

Development tasks are:

- achieving adult social and civic responsibility;
- assisting teenage children to become responsible and happy adults;
- reaching and maintaining a satisfactory performance in one's occupational career;
- developing adult leisure time activities;
- relating to one's spouse as a person;
- accepting and adjusting to the physiological changes of middle age;
- adjusting to ageing parents.

6. Later maturity.

Case study 6.4

Marcia is a single, 50-year-old woman who has a learning difficulty. She has lived in a small residential care unit for many years. Her behaviour can be challenging as she gets frustrated and angry when she cannot meet her own needs; this can result in aggressive, sometimes violent, outbursts. With regular support, encouragement and guidance, Marcia can meet her own daily self-care needs. However, she cannot read or write, she is unable to appreciate danger, and needs a great deal of support with practical tasks such as money management. Marcia attends a local day centre, where she participates in adult education classes. She has a number of good friends at the centre, as she has been attending for a long time.

According to Havighurst's model, Marcia has not been able to achieve the developmental tasks in early adulthood, such as managing a home or starting a family. Additionally, she is now not able to engage in many of the tasks of middle age, such as achieving adult social and civic responsibility. Havighurst would therefore suggest that her failure to complete these tasks would result in unhappiness and disapproval by society. Marcia, though, has many friends and lives a settled and seemingly contented lifestyle.

Therefore, it could be argued that Havighurst's model cannot adequately help us to understand Marcia's life course. This may be because it lays out expectations that apply to all people, assuming a particular path of fixed events and tasks along the life course. These assumptions of what might be considered 'a normal life course' can result in the devaluing and oppression of individuals who deviate from that course and are therefore seen as different. Marcia's voice, her views on her life so far, and her personal hopes and goals, are paramount when looking at her situation and life course development. There is a recognition that children, young people and adults with learning disability and/or autism have the right to the same opportunities as everyone else to be treated with dignity and respect and to have a home within their community in order to be able to develop and maintain relationships and have the support needed to live healthy, safe and rewarding lives (LGA, ADASS and NHS England, 2015b). It can be seen, therefore, that Marcia's voice, her views on her life so far, and her personal hopes and goals, are paramount when looking at her situation and life course development.

The impact on life course development of having a disability

In this section you will explore how the experience of having an impairment or disability in adulthood can change your life course and affect how you move through transitions.

Cree and Davis state that, for individuals who experience a physical or learning disability:

identity differs markedly from those around the individual and is characterised by difference, stigma, exclusion, loss of power and the denial of citizenship. It is then sustained through diagnosis and the social welfare and economic arrangements that are made for disabled people by the society in which they live.

(2007, p.108)

Research summary

The BBC Panorama programme *Undercover Care: The Abuse Exposed* (May 2011) showed mismanaged Winterbourne View Hospital staff mistreating and assaulting adults with a learning disability and autism. A serious case review (Flynn, 2012), commissioned by South Gloucestershire Safeguarding Board, highlighted significant issues about the abuse and care of vulnerable adults. Under the Care Programme Approach (CPA) in the role of care co-ordinators, social workers have to monitor the care and progress of people placed at Winterbourne. Further, as safeguarding staff they responded to 40 concerns from October 2007–2011. The safeguarding review highlighted that people at Winterbourne View should have benefited from the involvement of social workers, rather than professional input confined to medical staff. As the review highlights, social workers and social services have a key role to play in supporting, commissioning and reviewing support for vulnerable people:

Providing timely expertise and reliable social care support to people whose behaviour may challenge their relatives, colleagues and services in their homes and/or localities of origin has to become the default commissioning stance. The long-stay hospitals demonstrate that medicalising people's lives under the supervision of nurses and psychiatrists produces poor physical and mental health outcomes. These are far removed from the known aspirations of people with learning disability and autism.

(Flynn, 2012, p. 145)

The Winterbourne Review highlights the importance of the role and responsibility of social workers in working with adults, particularly those who are vulnerable. This further reflects the importance of taking account of whole life course planning. The *Winterbourne View Review: Good Practice Examples* (DH, 2013a) illustrates examples of good work.

We have already found that staged models of life development can be seen to be problematic, in that they do not incorporate issues of difference. So, as an example, we shall look in more depth at the period of becoming an adult. Each of the models explored earlier in the chapter includes a stage of becoming an adult and gaining some independence, as part of identity and personal development. For Erikson, the period of 'young adulthood' was characterised by the conflict between intimacy versus isolation; for Levinson, 'entering the adult world' required the development of life goals; and for Havighurst, 'early adulthood' required the completion of development tasks such as getting an occupation and selecting a mate.

These notions of independence, leaving the family of origin and setting out in occupational pathways, are potentially in conflict with the possible need for ongoing care and support that may characterise physical, learning or mental health difficulties. The expected transition of 'leaving parents' may be delayed or perhaps not happen at all. The challenge of developing meaningful, intimate and physical relationships might also be hampered or not 'allowed', particularly where individuals with learning difficulties or several physical and sensory impairments have difficulties expressing their own wishes and feelings and may be deemed vulnerable or at risk.

In addition there are separate but related issues in respect of the development of individuality, self-image and sense of personal identity. Young adults with learning difficulties and physical disabilities in particular can have problems being accepted with the status of adult; this can be compounded by the use of language which denies an adult status – 'a mental age of three'. All of these issues can potentially be more apparent where the person lives in supported care environments, such as residential care, as issues of safety, segregation and stereotyping may be more evident.

So, having a disability could significantly alter a person's opportunities for growth and development throughout their lives, further supporting the argument that prescriptive, staged models of development are not able to explain life development for all adults. Added to this, as you have seen, the presence of a disability can impact upon a person's ability to cope with transitions. Of course, the onset of a disabling condition would, in itself, be a life event or transition.

The value of taking the narrative approach when working with adults who experience disabilities is again evident. The individual is the only person who can truly know and explain what having those impairments means to them and their life. The person's own account of their life history will be unique and, as such, will facilitate the valuing of difference and diversity.

Research summary

The National Service Model (LGA, ADASS and NHS England, 2015a) was developed with people with learning disabilities, families and carers. It sets out how services should support people with a learning disability and/or autism who display behaviours that challenge.

1   People should be supported to have a good and meaningful everyday life – through access to activities and services such as early years services, education, employment, social and sports/leisure; and support to develop and maintain good relationships.
2   Care and support should be person-centred, planned, proactive and coordinated – with early intervention and preventative support based on

sophisticated risk stratification of the local population; person-centred care and support plans; and local care and support navigators/keyworkers to coordinate services set out in the care and support plan.

3   People should have choice and control over how their health and care needs are met – with information about care and support in formats people can understand; the expansion of personal budgets; personal health budgets and integrated personal budgets; and strong independent advocacy.

4   People with a learning disability and/or autism should be supported to live in the community with support from and for their families/carers as well as paid support and care staff – with training made available for families/carers; support and respite for families/carers; alternative short term accommodation for people to use briefly in a time of crisis; and paid care and support staff trained and experienced in supporting people who display behaviour that challenges.

5   People should have a choice about where and with whom they live – with a choice of housing, including small-scale supported living, and the offer of settled accommodation.

6   People should get good care and support from mainstream NHS services, using NICE guidelines and quality standards – with Annual Health Checks for all those over the age of 14; Health Action Plans; Hospital Passports where appropriate; liaison workers in universal services to help them meet the needs of patients with a learning disability and/or autism; and schemes to ensure universal services are meeting the needs of people with a learning disability and/or autism (such as quality checker schemes and use of the Green Light Toolkit).

7   People with a learning disability and/or autism should be able to access specialist health and social care support in the community – via integrated specialist multi-disciplinary health and social care teams, with that support available on an intensive 24/7 basis when necessary.

8   When necessary, people should be able to get support to stay out of trouble – with reasonable adjustments made to universal services aimed at reducing or preventing anti-social or 'offending' behaviour; liaison and diversion schemes in the criminal justice system; and a community forensic health and care function to support people who may pose a risk to others in the community.

9   When necessary, when their health needs cannot be met in the community, they should be able to access high-quality assessment and treatment in a hospital setting, staying no longer than they need to, with pre-admission checks to ensure hospital care is the right solution and discharge planning starting from the point of admission or before (LGA, ADASS and NHS England 2015a, p. 25).

A service model to support the commissioning of relevant support and services has been developed to support this (see Figure 6.2).

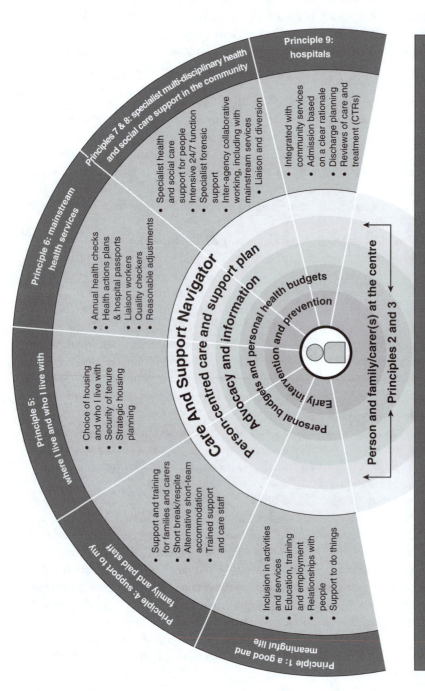

Figure 6.2 Service model

Critique of staged theories of adult development

The strengths of these psychosocial-staged approaches to explaining human development are that they can help to provide reference points for the descriptions people give of their life experiences and to our understanding of their life course. However, they have been criticised for the following reasons:

- Not incorporating difference and diversity – These theories are culturally specific, in other words, it does not always make much sense if you attempt to apply these models to adults who are not from western cultures. Furthermore, other areas of difference, such as sexuality and gender, are not easily explained; these models were developed mostly from a male perspective. So, for example, in Erikson's stage of young adulthood (intimacy versus isolation), theories of homosexuality and the social significance of stigma and oppression are not integrated.

- Being too fixed and deterministic – Life stage models are seen as being fixed, simplistic and determined, whereas in reality it is not possible to divide real life neatly into stages. Erikson's model was popular and influential in the mid-twentieth century. However, it has been criticised for being set in a particular period in history with no acknowledgement that things will change over time, in different societies and across different cultures. In other words, life stages or transitions are socially constructed and value-laden. The models suggest that there are universal experiences which all people encounter. However, in reality, whilst human biological and physical changes are relevant, the meaning and significance of these transitions will vary considerably. Anthony Giddens (1991), a sociologist, lays out a compelling argument that modern society is continually changing and that people pursue many different paths through their lives. According to Giddens, it is no longer possible to draw on traditional ideas of previous generations and we have to work out our identities for ourselves as we go through life.

- Reinforcing socially constructed expectations – These models thus reflect many of the expectations and values of our society and culture. In this way, by reinforcing these expectations people who move through their lives in different ways can be left to feel as if they have failed (for example, if they continue to live with their family of origin beyond their mid-20s, or if they are not in a mature sexual relationship in adulthood).

It is important to remember, therefore, that whilst theories of human development can be particularly useful from a social work perspective, when considering an individual's life experiences and the meaning they put on their life and own development, the stages outlined in the models are socially, culturally and historically defined. In other words, life stages are not fixed and accepted universally.

Life events as transitions

One of the common themes across these models is that they consider life in stages, often with an age-related dimension. The theorists then explain how each stage or period of transition is moved through and the impact this may have on a person's life development.

In Chapter 1 of this book the concept of transitions was introduced as phases or stages within a person's life course when people move through life events. We also explored how different people may experience the same life event, yet their response and subsequent development through the transition will be different. Therefore, it is important for social workers to understand the potential impact of transitions within a person's life course in order to help us work with people at different times in their lives.

The theoretical models we have explored so far in this chapter have provided a framework for describing and predicting certain transitions that might be expected as part of the life course. However, as we have seen, these theories suggest fixed life course stages that form a common experience for all adults. They do not, then, easily account for unexpected life events that may have social or personal significance, nor do they consider the impact and challenges of multiple life events.

Challenges and opportunities

Transitions are processes of change within the life course; they demand personal change and often result in role readjustment. In this way, transitions present considerable challenges and opportunities for growth and development. In order to inform social work practice, it is necessary to understand the influences and factors that enable individuals to adapt and cope with changes in their lives to positive effect.

All transitions or life events have the potential to be stressful and challenging, even those that we might plan for and welcome. In order to determine some indication of the potential challenges and stresses in your life at the time, using the Holmes and Rahe (1967) social readjustment rating scale (see Table 6.1), you should add together the total of all the units related to the life events you have experienced in the past 12 months. Where this figure is over 300, it is said to imply that you have a significantly increased chance of major health breakdown in the following two years.

This model, as with the other theories explored in this chapter, presents an explanation of people's reactions to transition as being predictable and universal. It also suggests only the negative perspective of stress and challenge, without the potential for growth and development being reflected. Furthermore, whilst the social readjustment rating scale considers the cumulative effect that major life events may have, it does not account for the fact that the influence upon our development depends not only on the life event but also on social, physical and psychological factors.

Research summary

The Holmes and Rahe social readjustment rating scale

In the mid-1960s, researchers Holmes and Rahe concluded that an accumulation in a 12-month period of life-changing events scoring 200 or more on a scale (see below) could increase the risk of stress and ill health. Holmes and Rahe developed a tool to identify, rank and score the accumulative potential stressors in a person's life. The social readjustment rating scale lists 43 life events; the top 12 are presented in Table 6.1.

Table 6.1 Top 12 potential stressors in the social readjustment rating scale (adapted from Holmes and Rahe, 1967)

Rank	Life event	Life change units
1	Death of spouse	100
2	Divorce	73
3	Marital separation	65
4	Jail term	63
5	Death of a close family member	63
6	Personal injury or illness	52
7	Marriage	50
8	Fired from job	47
9	Marital reconciliation	45
10	Retirement	45
11	Change in health of family member	44
12	Pregnancy	40

Activity 6.4

Consider the Holmes and Rahe social readjustment rating scale for yourself. Have you experienced any of the life events listed in Table 6.1 over the past 12 months? Do you feel that this grading of stressful events reflects your own experiences or the experiences of adults known to you?

The staged models of life course development introduced earlier in this chapter suggest that each period of transition has to be, in some way, successfully negotiated or undertaken in order to develop and move on through further life stages. In this section of the chapter we are going to consider other factors that may affect the outcome of a person's move through a period of transition, in particular the importance of individual and personal resources and the influence of societal factors.

Personal resources

Personal resources can take many different forms. They may be characteristics within the individual or more tangible resources that are available, from outside of the individual. Individual characteristics would be a personal, psychological or inner strength, resilience and confidence that may enable that person to cope with and adapt to changes in their life. As we have discussed in previous chapters, the development of this strength of personality may have arisen through the individual's life course and the experiences of previous life events. This would support Erikson's approach to life stages in that, according to his approach, the successful completion of each stage prepares the person for subsequent challenges. Another factor to consider is the extent to which an individual has control over their own life and the decisions they make. Léonie Sugarman describes research into personal resources and their effect on effective coping mechanisms. She states that:

> A *cluster of personality characteristics has been identified as being associated with more effective coping, including self esteem, self efficacy, mastery, internal locus of control {i.e. the extent to which an individual believes she can influence events}, self confidence and flexibility.*

> (1986, p. 156)

Another factor to consider at this individual level is the person's access to physical, external resources. These may be financial resources, material assets or social support networks. Sugarman describes the latter as '*interpersonal networks in which the individual is embedded*' (1986, p. 148).

These support networks may include close family, friends, people in the community, mutual or peer support systems or professional and voluntary support. The extent of the person's access to internal, emotional and psychological resources and external, material resources can shape how they move through life transitions. Further potential influences are factors in society, which may make transition and life development more challenging for certain individuals. We have considered how a person's own interpretation of what is going on in their life is an important factor in shaping their response to change. Their interpretation, however, and the perspectives of those around them, will have been formed in the context of the society in which they live and their previous life experiences. In other words, the meaning they put on their own life will be influenced not only by their own values and experiences but also by the values, views and expectations of society at that time. This is particularly significant for individuals who experience care needs, impairments or oppression and discrimination in our society. In summary, therefore, the way in which a transition is experienced and the extent to which it is successfully negotiated will depend upon an individual's access to resources, their interpretation of what is going on, their previous experiences of transitions in life, and the social construction of a transition.

Activity 6.5

Think about a life transition that you have experienced; it may be moving your family home, changing a job or school, for example.

- Do you feel that you moved through this transition successfully? If so what were the resources you used to enable you to negotiate this life event?

Whatever life transition you chose to consider, you will have had access to resources of some kind. This is likely to have been a mixture of personal resources (e.g. inner strength, self-esteem, confidence) and external resources (e.g. social networks, friends, family, financial resources and mutual help). The significance of specific resources and their influence on your passage through the transition will be very personal and dependent upon the many factors discussed above.

Activity 6.6

Reflect upon your learning about the concept of transitions and their impact on the life experiences and development of adults. As just one example, consider how significant transitions (for example moving house or starting a new job) might impact upon an adult who is physically disabled.

As you have seen, the impact of transitions will be different for all individuals and that impact will be influenced by a range of issues. However, there may be some additional potential complexities for people who experience particular needs within our society. So, for example, a person who is physically disabled and moves house may need to rearrange different support services or adaptations in the home. Taking up a new job may mean specific assessments and arrangements for equipment or specific support services. All of these things often take time and can be complex to set up, adding to the potential for stress and anxiety.

In this section you have explored life events and transitions. This is particularly relevant to social work practice, in that social work service users are very likely to experience a number of such challenges. Sometimes people will access social work services as the result of complex transitions in their lives, or it may be that as service users they will experience transitions as a result of the service they receive. For many people, both of these situations will apply.

As has been highlighted earlier the Care Act 2014 requires local authorities to promote integration with the NHS and other key partners.

Activity 6.7

How would you 'define' integration? Why is it important? What contribution can an understanding of life course development make?

Integration can be described as '*the processes, methods and tools of integration that facilitate integrated care. Integration involves connecting the health care systems (acute, community and primary medical) with other service systems (such as long term care, education and housing)* (Leutz, 1999, pp. 77–78). Integrated care requires '*[imposing] the patient perspective as the organising principle of service delivery*' (Lloyd and Wait, 2006, p. 7). What is critical is that the focus of integration should be on the patient's/service user's perspective, that they received the care services they were in need of when and where they needed them (Van Raak *et al.*, 2003). The National Collaboration for Integrated Care and Support (DH, 2013b) outlined a narrative of integrated care and support developed by national voices, with an emphasis on service user leadership and service user outcomes:

> *My care is planned with people who work together to understand me and my carer(s), put me in control, co-ordinate and deliver services to achieve my best outcomes.* (p. 15)

Integration across health and social care has long been sought as a solution to delivering coordinated and comprehensive care to people, particularly those with complex needs:

> *Person-centred coordinated care and support is key to improving outcomes for individuals who use health and social care services. Too often, we don't communicate properly with each other, don't work together as a team or don't treat people as whole individuals. As a result, care and support is often fragmented, delayed or duplicated, which can result in missed opportunities to prevent needs from escalating and intervening early... People deserve better than this and we all need to play our part in delivering services that are better coordinated around preventing and meeting their needs.* (DH, 2013b, p. 6)

This includes the need for:

- better planning to ensure services are seamless – in that there is no obvious divide between health and social care support;

- holistic care – in that support plans will cover all key areas of a person's day-to-day life;

- greater personal involvement and empowerment of people using the services – in that users will have control of their support plan and be able to choose and direct the various elements of that support plan.

This is also reflected in other policies. For example, the NHS's five year *Delivering the Forward View: NHS Planning Guidance 2016/17–2020/21* (NHS England *et al.*, 2015) requires new partnerships with local communities, local authorities and employers, with service integrated around the patient/service user. All local authorities are required to have Health and Well-Being Boards (established under the Health and Social Care Act 2012) which are the only forum where clinical, political, professional and community leaders come together to plan how best to meet health and care needs, and commission appropriately. Health and Well-Being Board members are expected to collaborate to understand their local community's needs, agree priorities, and encourage commissioners to work in a more joined-up way to produce a Health and Well-Being Strategy unique to each local area. The Strategy details what priorities have been set based on a Joint Strategic Based Assessment (JSNA) – a shared evidence-based consensus on key local priorities. The Better Care Fund was established to incentivise the NHS and local government to work more closely together around people, placing their well-being as the focus of health and care services, and shifting resources into social care and community services for the benefit of people, communities and health and care systems (Local Government Association and NHS England, 2013).

A life course approach emphasises a chronological and social perspective, looking across a person's life experiences or across generations for evidence for current behaviours, whilst also recognising that both past and present experiences are shaped by the wider social, economic and cultural context.

Chapter summary

In this chapter you have explored human life course development in respect of adults in the early and middle years of adulthood, focusing on the use in practice of human growth and development theories and knowledge. We examined the problematic nature of the term 'adult' before looking at three examples of theories that take a staged developmental approach to explaining human life course and identity development.

(Continued)

(Continued)

Using case examples, we considered the significance of transitions in adult life and evaluated the models in this context. Taking a life course perspective, we looked at how life transitions present opportunities for growth and development or, conversely, potential crisis points in people's lives. The significance of the resources available to the individual in determining their passage through the transition was discussed before looking at the potential impact of disability on an adult's life development.

The following chapter develops these themes further, as it sets out knowledge in respect of older adults. It will consider older age in terms of opportunities for growth and development and address issues related to ageing, older age and how it is constructed in our society. By exploring the themes introduced in this chapter, particularly the significance of transitions in later life, you will develop an understanding of effective ageing and end-of-life issues.

Further reading

Chisnell, C and Kelly, C (2016) *Safeguarding in Social Work Practice*. London: Sage.

This book examines safeguarding and what it means across the life course, bringing together common themes and knowledge in safeguarding across children, young people and adult social work. Its approach is intended for students to view the subject from a holistic perspective, helping them develop their understanding of core themes and transferable skills for practice.

Davies, M (ed.) (2012) *Social Work with Adults*. Basingstoke: Palgrave Macmillan.

This book examines policy, law, research and theory in relation to social work with adults. Exercises and case studies are provided to help you make connections and examine the challenges that social workers face.

Gardner, A (2014) *Personalisation in Social Work* (2nd edn). London: Sage/Learning Matters.

This text provides an overview of the personalisation agenda and reflects on the legislation, history, theories, values and collective voices that have influenced that agenda.

Grant, G, Ramacharan, P, Flynn, M and Richardson, **M** (eds) (2010) *Learning Disability: A Life Cycle Approach* (3rd edn). Maidenhead: Open University Press.

Recognising learning disability as a lifelong disability, this book is structured around the life course.

Katz, J, Pearce, S and Spurr, S (2011) *Adult Lives: A Life Course Perspective*. Bristol: Policy Press.

This book examines the past, present and future of adults' lives.

Rogers, J, Bright, L and Davies, H (2015) *Social Work With Adults.* London: Sage.

Social work with vulnerable adults is becoming increasingly centred on a key piece of legislation: the Mental Capacity Act. This provides a framework for protecting the vulnerable while allowing those who may lack capacity to have certain safeguards enshrined in law. It will help support students to learn two things: first, how the Mental Capacity Act operates and what its key principles are when applied to safeguarding adults; and second, which compassionate skills and values need to be interwoven with legislative knowledge.

Sugarman, L (2001) *Life Span Development: Concepts, Theories and Interventions* (2nd edn). London: Methuen.

Léonie Sugarman's book remains a relevant and important text for students of human life course development. It is particularly useful for further reading related to this chapter, as it has a chapter on life events, transitions and coping.

Websites

Association of Directors of Adult Social Services (ADASS): www.adass.org.uk

This website has been established by the Association of Directors of Adult Social Services. It contains the whole range of policy initiatives, press releases and consultation responses for the Association's members, and is regularly updated.

Department of Health: www.dh.gov.uk/government/policies

The policy and guidance section of the Department of Health website is a useful starting point for looking at the policy context of adulthood, with particular relevance to social and health care, in our society today. The site offers a range of downloadable reports and bulletins, all of which will have further references that might direct your additional reading.

7: Using life course development knowledge in social work practice with older adults

---

Achieving a social work degree

This chapter will help you begin to meet the following capabilities, to the appropriate level, from the Professional Capabilities Framework:

- **Knowledge**
  - Apply knowledge of social sciences, law and social work practice theory.
- **Critical reflection and analysis**
  - Apply critical reflection and analysis to inform and provide a rationale for professional decision making.
- **Values and ethics**
  - Apply social work ethical principles and values to guide professional practice.
- **Diversity**
  - Recognise diversity and apply anti-discriminatory and anti-oppressive principles in practice.

It will also introduce you to the following academic standards as set out in the social work subject benchmark statement:

3.1.1 **Social work services and service users.**
3.1.4 **Social work theory.**

Introduction

In this chapter you will consider human life course development in respect of older adults. Globally, with widespread falls in fertility rates, and significant rises in life expectancy, the proportion of those aged 60+ has risen from only 8 per cent of the world population (200 million people) in 1950 to around 11 per cent (760 million) in 2011, with a dramatic increase still ahead as those aged 60+ are expected to reach 22 per cent (2 billion) by 2050 (United Nations, 2015). Population ageing is set to be one of the most significant social transformations of the twenty-first century, with far reaching economic, political and social implications and for all sectors of society, including social protection, family structures and intergenerational attachments. There is concern worldwide about how we respond positively to ageing, actively promoting the value of older people to their communities and wider society.

The Office for National Statistics states that the population of the UK is ageing. The population aged 65 and over has grown by 47 per cent since mid-1974 to make up nearly 18 per cent of the total population in mid-2014, while the number of people aged 75 and over has increased by 89 per cent over the period and makes up 8 per cent of the population. The Office for National Statistics census data for England in 2011 tell us that:

- in 2011, 9.2 million (16 per cent) of usual residents of England and Wales were aged 65 and over, an increase of almost one million from 2001;

- 57 per cent (5.3 million) of those aged 65 and over in 2011 were married or in a civil partnership, but the proportion of those aged 65 and over who were divorced almost doubled from 5.2 per cent in 2001 to 8.7 per cent in 2011;

- just under one-third (31 per cent) of those aged 65 and over were living alone in 2011 – this was a decrease from 34 per cent in 2001;

- 10 per cent of people aged 65 and over were economically active, 90 per cent were economically inactive, including 86 per cent retired, but the proportion of the population aged 65–74 who were economically active in 2011 (16 per cent) was almost double the proportion in 2001;

- half (50 per cent) of all usual residents in England and Wales aged 65 and over living in households reported very good or good health in 2011 compared with 88 per cent for those aged under 65;

- 14 per cent of older people living in households in England and Wales provided unpaid care in 2011, compared to 12 per cent in 2001. The largest increase in proportion was for those aged 65 and over providing 50 hours or more unpaid care a week: up from 4.3 per cent (341,000) in 2001 to 5.6 per cent (497,000) in 2011. (Office for National Statistics, 2013)

The ageing population of the UK mirrors those in many other European countries. It is partly a consequence of the age structure of the population alive today, in particular the ageing of the large number of people born during the 1960s baby boom. It also stems from increased longevity – a man born in the UK in 1981 had a cohort life expectancy at birth of 84 years. For a boy born today, the figure is 89 years, and by 2030 it is projected to be 91. The trend for women is similar. A girl born in 1981 was expected to live for 89 years and one born today might expect to live to 92. Cohort projections suggest a girl born in 2030 might live to 95. Healthy life expectancy has not, however, increased as fast, resulting in proportionally greater demands on public services such as social care and the NHS.

This chapter will start by exploring what we mean by the terms 'older adults' and 'old age' and consider where these meanings originated. It will then develop your knowledge and understanding of the significance of life course development in later adulthood. You will explore theories and explanations of development in later adulthood that examine social, biological and cognitive processes. Some of the theories introduced in Chapter 6 will be revisited and their relevance to life course development in later life will be considered. Using a range of case studies you will examine the concept of successful ageing and what this means for professional social work practice. As shown in earlier chapters, practice is embedded within a social, cultural, policy-driven context. In particular, as with the previous chapter, social work practice with older people is informed by key policy and strategic developments. Policy is increasingly directed at examining the future impact of an ageing population and ensuring that services can respond. In particular, there has been an increasing focus on ensuring appropriate responses to the care and treatment of older people.

The House of Lords Select Committee's *Ready for Ageing?* (2013) highlighted the fact that that the UK population is ageing rapidly. While the fact that we are all living longer represents progress and the contribution of older people to society can be even greater, '*in order to make a success of these democratic shifts, major changes are needed in our attitude to ageing*' (2013, p. 8), with challenges for individuals, employers, social and health services and for the government and political parties.

The Government Office for Science's *Future of an Ageing Population* (2016) report highlights that the UK population is ageing rapidly, with nearly one in seven people projected to be over 75 years old by 2040. This will require a co-ordinated response to ensure the interconnectedness of policies and practice affected by ageing. This includes:

- a need for significant improvements in health, as chronic condition, multi-morbidities and cognitive impairments become more common;
- support for unpaid carers as families face increasing pressures to balance care with other responsibilities, particularly work;

- enabling people to work longer to support the growing numbers of dependents, while providing individuals with the financial and mental resources needed for increasingly long retirements;

- opportunities for life-long learning and training helping us to participate for longer in the labour market;

- appropriately designed housing that can adapt to people's changing needs as they age;

- physical, social and technological connectivity, allowing people to care for others, interact socially, participate in society and access services.

A number of reports have expressed concern about the ability of services, particularly with regard to adult social care systems, to meet rising demands. The King's Fund and Nuffield Trust's *Social Care For Older People: Home Truths* (Humphries *et al.*, 2016) states that social care for older people is under massive pressure, with an increasing number of people not receiving the help they need. The Ready for Ageing Alliance's *Still Not Ready for Ageing* (2016) also states that there is an urgent need for government action on tackling the challenges and maximising the opportunities of ageing.

The Care Act 2014 and other important documents, which are having a significant impact on the way that services are being planned, commissioned and delivered for adults, have been outlined in the previous chapter. It could be argued that our understanding of later adulthood is, in some ways, influenced by the terminology chosen, assumptions made and principles espoused in the policy agenda.

Throughout the chapter you will have opportunities to consider your own thoughts about growing older and the importance of each individual's life story within a life course perspective. Again, building on your reading in earlier chapters, you will look at the impact of life transitions in later adulthood, considering how such events may present challenges and opportunities for older people. This part of the chapter will incorporate a discussion about end-of-life issues.

Defining 'later adulthood'

In order to explore life course development in the later stages of life, we need to have a clear understanding of the different terms that are used to describe people who may be considered to have reached this stage of life. You considered the term 'adulthood' in Chapter 6 and reflected on how difficult it can be to agree on a firm definition of this notion. The concept of 'later adulthood' is no different. As stated in Chapter 6, as social workers we need to appreciate how individuals understand themselves, their identity, their own lives and place in society. We need to consider whether or not they would see themselves as older adults and what meaning this has for them. We also need to consider how our society, its laws, policies, expectations and agency requirements, can affect how older people are responded to.

Activity 7.1

Write down your first thoughts in response to the following:

- So far, we have used the terms 'later adulthood' and 'older people' to describe people who are considered to be in the later stages of adulthood. Write down any more words or phrases you have heard being used.
- Name some people that you know and would consider to be at this stage in their lives. Think about these people and write down what it is about them that makes you consider them to be defined in this way.

You may have thought of many different words or phrases that are used to describe older adults, for example 'people who are ageing', 'old aged', 'senior citizens', 'old age pensioners', 'elders' or 'elderly people'. As you will see from the title of this chapter, the term 'older adults' has been chosen. You may also have identified a number of different features that would lead you to think of a person as an older adult. As with other stages of life, a common starting point is to think of chronological age (for example, you may have thought that anyone over the age of 65 years could be described as an older adult). Linked to this, you may have listed some social aspects of ageing, such as being a person who has retired from employment, or can receive certain entitlements such as a pension or travel pass, due to their age. You may also have listed some biological changes, perhaps some of the more visible changes such as hair or skin changes, or aspects of ability. Finally, you may have included changes in people's ways of thinking or understanding as they grow older, with issues about the life they have lived and their life coming to an end being prevalent. These ideas would reflect aspects of cognitive changes associated with ageing. Through this chapter you will explore each of these perspectives in more detail as you consider some theoretical perspectives on development in older adulthood.

Regardless of the range of responses you may have made to Activity 7.1, it could be suggested that most people have a common understanding of what is meant by 'older adults' and who might be included in that group. In other words, the meanings of these terms are taken for granted in our society. In earlier chapters of this book you were introduced to the concept of 'social construction'. The 'social construction of old age' refers to the way in which meanings, interpretations and images that emerge from our society affect our understanding of older age.

These meanings and images that are entrenched in the structures of society, our history, culture and language, become so powerful that people see them as 'fact'.

In this chapter we will challenge the assumptions that arise from the way in which society gives meaning to ageing. We shall do this by demonstrating that older adults are not a single homogeneous group, but instead are diverse individuals, who have made many life choices, having moved through distinct and very different life courses, therefore reinforcing the importance for social work practice to take account of how individuals think of themselves and the meanings they attach to their own lives.

Case study 7.1

Margaret lives with her husband Charles in the south of England. Margaret is 76 years old and Charles is nearing his 78th birthday. They have two children, a son who lives with his wife and three children in Australia and a daughter who lives near them. Their daughter is a single parent of two children aged 10 and 12. Margaret retired from a career as a part-time administrator in the public sector ten years ago. Charles retired shortly before his wife, having worked in engineering for most of his working life. As their daughter works full-time, Margaret and Charles enjoy spending a lot of time taking care of their grandchildren. They take them to and from school and care for them during school holidays. They talk to their son and his family regularly via Skype, and have planned a two-month holiday to visit them this year. Margaret likes the children to call her 'Peggy' rather than Grandma, whilst Charles is happy for his grandchildren to call him 'Gramps'. When the children are at school, Margaret and Charles take pleasure in participating in a variety of voluntary activities and hobbies. Charles enjoys swimming at the local sports centre and is a governor at the school his younger grandchild attends. Margaret works in a voluntary capacity at the Citizens Advice Bureau and also delivers meals-on-wheels twice weekly. She also likes going to yoga classes one evening a week.

Margaret and Charles are both within the chronological age group that could be defined using the words you have explored. In terms of the social aspects of ageing, they have both experienced the transition of retirement and would be entitled to any benefits linked to their age. It is also likely that they are aware of some of the physical changes of ageing. However, it is apparent that this couple have a positive outlook on their lives. It is possible that they would not describe themselves as 'older people' or in any way dependent or vulnerable.

Therefore, the danger of constructing one definition of older adulthood is that it does not allow for individuality. Margaret and Charles do not neatly fit the stereotypical meanings attributed to being an older person in our society. Such definitions imply beliefs about later life and how an individual older person should look, behave and live in our society.

Activity 7.2

We all expect to grow into older adults. Think about the following questions and write down short answers to each one:

- When you think about your own life and the prospect of growing older, what is your attitude towards this time of life? In other words, do you think your life as an older adult will be enjoyable? Is it something that you look forward to or are fearful of?
- How do you think your attitude and thoughts have been developed?
- Complete the following sentence, with at least six different endings: 'Getting older means …'

Comment

It is probable that your responses to the first part of this activity have been developed by thinking about the lives of older adults you know, perhaps your grandparents, neighbours or friends, or you may have thought of older adults in the media, politicians and soap-opera actors. It would be useful to ask the older adults in your family what growing older means to them. You will have completed the sentence in a range of ways, some of which may be similar to the examples below, but the ways in which older adults themselves would complete the sentence are the most meaningful.

- 'Growing older means freedom from work and more opportunities.'
- 'Growing older means being able to take time to do things and enjoy companionship.'
- 'Growing older means having less hair and more wrinkles.'
- 'Growing older means having accumulated a wealth of life experiences and knowledge.'

Thus some people will think about later life with some excitement, as an opportunity to have time for themselves, time to travel or relax. Others may have expressed some concerns about growing older, as the experience is something of an unknown and it may appear to be a long way off.

Your responses to this activity will have been shaped not only by your experiences, but also by the expectations and meanings that society has given to later life. In other words, as stated earlier, the experience of being an older adult is socially constructed and through this older adults become stereotyped. Furthermore, the generalisations about older adults may lead to negative assumptions about development in older age and consequently older adults being devalued in our society. Such negative generalisations often include concepts of physical weakness, loneliness, vulnerability, depression, a lack of cognitive ability and overall dependency on other people and society. Through the discussion, activities, case studies and examples as you progress through this chapter, we will challenge these notions and demonstrate that later life is a time of opportunity for growth and development. It can be argued that:

> *chronological age has a powerful effect on how we are perceived, the expectations of others and the opportunities that may be available to us.*

> (Crawford and Walker, 2004, p. 10)

Negative generalisations like those mentioned above can result in discrimination against individuals on the grounds of their age. This is called 'ageism' and can refer to discrimination at any age, but the social construction of old age and the negative connotations mean that ageism in respect of older age is particularly prevalent in our society. Prejudice and inequality related to older adulthood can be seen at a number of different levels, from the attitudes and behaviours of individuals through to the structural policies and cultural beliefs in our society:

> *Ageism ... in our bloodstream — and the most commonly experienced form of discrimination.*

> (Ray *et al.*, 2006)

Activity 7.3

> *Ageism is a set of beliefs ... relating to the ageing process. Ageism generates and reinforces a fear and denigration of the ageing process, and stereotyping presumptions regarding competence and the need for protection. In particular, ageism legitimates the use of chronological age to mark out classes of people who are systematically denied resources and opportunities that others enjoy, and who suffer the consequences of such denigration, ranging from well-meaning patronage to unambiguous vilification.*

> (Bytheway, 1995, p. 26)

> *Ageism is used to describe stereotypes and prejudices held about older people on the grounds of their age. Age discrimination is used to describe behaviour where older people are treated unequally (directly or indirectly) on grounds of their age.*

> (Ray *et al.*, 2006, p. 8)

> *Ageism is broader than age discrimination. It refers to deeply rooted negative beliefs about older people and the ageing process, which may then give rise to age*

> *(Continued)*

(Continued)

> discrimination. Such beliefs are socially created and reinforced, embedded as they are in functions, institutions, rules and everyday social life.
>
> (Hewstone 1989 in McGlone and Fitzgerald, 2005, p. 8)

- What are the common themes within these definitions?
- Do you agree or disagree?
- Why?

Our lives are defined by age; ageism is powerful and largely unchallenged. More people (29 per cent) reported suffering age discrimination than any other form (AgeUK, 2005). Ageism is the most widely experienced form of discrimination across Europe (AgeUK, 2011).

At a structural level, chronological age is the determining factor for a number of socially and legislatively determined transitions (for example the age of retirement or holding a driving licence). Therefore, an age limit is being used to justify individuals' access to or exclusion from a service, facility or entitlement. This is discriminatory and is an example of ageism. The Human Rights Act places all public authorities in the UK under a duty to respect the rights it contains in everything that they do. Public authorities must:

- not deprive anyone of their liberty except in certain, predefined circumstances, such as following a conviction by a criminal court or if someone lacks the mental capacity to consent to care or treatment and it is in their best interests to deprive them of their liberty;

- have an appropriate, legally-based procedure in place to protect an individual's rights.

Any deprivation of liberty must be lawful, proportionate, and continue for no longer than is necessary. For a person to be classed as being deprived of their liberty, they must be subject both to continuous supervision and control and not be free to leave. Under the Mental Capacity Act 2005, there are procedures in place to make sure that people's rights to liberty are protected if a public authority decides that someone does not have the capacity to consent to necessary care or treatment. These safeguards, which have been developed by the courts, are called Deprivation of Liberty Safeguards (DOLS).

Research summary

The Mental Capacity Act 2005, including DOLS, promotes a person-centred approach which highlights autonomy and, for those who lack mental capacity, ensures that decisions made on their behalf are made in their best interests and with the least possible restriction of freedoms. Practitioners are expected to promote the least restrictive course of action possible to support liberty and autonomy.

Baroness Hale, in the Supreme Court judgement relating to deprivation of liberty P v Cheshire West and P & Q v Surrey County Council, said *'It is axiomatic that people with disabilities, both mental and physical, have the same human rights as the rest of the human race … This flows inexorably from the universal character of human rights, founded on the inherent dignity of human beings'*. This means that physical liberty is the same for everyone and is disability neutral.

The Equality Act 2010 makes discrimination on the basis of age, sometimes called ageism, unlawful. The act also protects a person from discrimination on the basis of race, sex, gender reassignment, disability, religion or belief, sexual orientation, marriage or civil partnership, pregnancy and maternity.

Activity 7.4

How would you challenge some of these myths about older people?

Older people do not have the same social needs as 'us'.

Older people just want to be left alone.

Older people do not remember what it is like to be young.

Older people are not interested in sex.

Comment

These kinds of statements are often repeated, but not backed up by evidence. Rather they reflect the social influences which support the belief that old age is a 'miserable decline'. These stereotype older people as a specific group with the same attributes. They provide a 'blanket analysis', as if older people were a single entity – which they certainly are not. Often language is used as a form of benign prejudice (for example that older people should 'take it easy, now you are old' and that they are 'doddery but dear'). Whilst there may be respect for older people, this can too easily shift to neglect. Older age is often seen as concerning other people rather than us; however, we too will one day become older people.

Research summary

The age span for older people is potentially considerable (from 60 years to potentially beyond 100 years). Some authors have identified age-related 'phases' within this age span: the young old (60 to 69), the middle old (70 to 79), and the very old (80+) (Forman *et al.*, 1992). Gilleard and Higgs (2015a) identify a

(Continued)

(Continued)

fourth age which can be understood as a feared imagery of old age, which has been likened to a metaphorical 'black hole' where human agency is no longer visible. The concept of social death has been observed by researchers, in which the person is no longer an active agent in other people's lives, a loss of social identity, a loss of social connectedness, and losses associated with disintegration of the body. Sweeting and Gilhooly (1997) drew links with, while making distinctions between, the loss of self or personhood ascribed to dementia and the idea of social death. The implication is that 'social death' does not so much describe as ascribe a negative status to the person with dementia, contributing in effect to the exclusionary othering of people with dementia (Kitwood, 1993b, 1997; Kitwood and Bredin, 1992). It is suggested that *'giving space to persons with dementia, respecting their wishes, supporting their identity and recognising their individuality seem crucial in preventing such individuals' de-personalisation and their social dying'* (Gilleard and Higgs, 2015b, p. 269).

A report from the Commission on Improving Dignity in Care for Older People (from the LGA, NHS Confederation and AgeUK) highlighted the importance of ensuring that services are focused on the individual needs of people:

> *Delivering dignity will mean changing the way we design, pay for, deliver and monitor care services as the numbers of older people in care continues to grow. Alongside the consistent application of good practice and the rooting out of poor care, we need a major cultural shift in the way the system thinks about dignity, to ensure care is person-centred and not task-focused.*
>
> (Commission on Improving Dignity in Care for Older People, 2012, p. 3)

Whilst the Francis Report (2013) was primarily concerned with failures in an acute hospital setting, it was a timely reminder of the importance of working together to develop a culture of care, support, dignity and respect, with a clear focus on people.

The Francis Report

The Francis Report followed an earlier independent inquiry on the failings in the Mid Staffordshire NHS Foundation Trust between 2005–2009, and revealed a catalogue of failures in the care of older people:

> *There was a lack of care, compassion, humanity and leadership. The most basic standards of care were not observed, and fundamental rights to dignity were not respected. Elderly and vulnerable patients were left unwashed, unfed and without fluids. They were deprived of dignity and respect. Some patients had to relieve themselves in their beds when they*

were offered no help to get to the bathroom. Some were left in excrement-stained sheets and beds. They had to endure filthy conditions in their wards. There were incidents of callous treatment by ward staff. Patients who could not eat or drink without help did not receive it. Medicines were prescribed but not given. The accident and emergency department, as well as some wards, had insufficient staff to deliver safe and effective care. Patients were discharged without proper regard for their welfare.

(Statement by Robert Francis, QC, 06.02.2013)

Another aspect of life in which older adults may be considered to be disadvantaged due to the policies and structure of society relates to financial security. Later adulthood is often characterised by stereotypical images of poverty and social exclusion. However, within our society there is substantial variation in the amount and sources of income and also living standards. Patterns of income distribution in later adulthood most usually continue to reflect the distribution of income throughout the life course, although inequalities can be seen to become greater with increasing age. So, for example, income differences that have been identified in relation to gender, disability and ethnicity continue to be evident in later adulthood, but the disparities become greater.

So far in this chapter we have stressed the uniqueness of each older person and their situation. We have also highlighted the ways in which attitudes, ideas, concepts and beliefs about later life might be developed. Added to this, the whole of this book has been underpinned by social work values, the importance of listening to the perspectives of individuals and the narrative tradition. For social work practice with older people and for developing an understanding of their life course, the narrative, biographical approach is particularly valuable and enables us to gather some appreciation of their 'chronosystem', in other words, the influence of their life course and the history of their growth and development (see Chapter 2). As stated by Cree and Davis (2007, p. 8), *'the narrative turn builds on the oral history and life history tradition'*. So, consider this poem written by Roy Barker, aged 80, which is about his life growing up in Doncaster.

Where we live

Doncaster town or Donny to proper folk
Been a good place to grow up in
From the time of gaslights flicker to neon brightness
Milk in jugs home made bread
To sliced loaf tightly packed
Pantomime at Christmas black and white pictures that moved
To television in living colour

Seeing a man taking a step on the moon

Whilst eating crisps – sat on the sofa in the room

Going to work on yu bike – Now busy roads full of cars

Remember club trips tu Cleethorpes on train

Now it's planes that land and take yu tu Spain

Oh! and wine that makes yu dizzy

Who now – gets their beer in a jug carried home – from the landlord's pub

Have yu noticed now that coal's not burned

The sky is clearer up above

Doncaster built mainly on level ground

Better than Sheffield – wi all its ups and downs

Sunny Donny is the place of memories sweet

Parkinsons – Nuttalls – Do you still recall the taste?

Mmm!!!

(Roy Barker, aged 80, as cited on the Age Concern
website at www.ageconcern.co.uk)

Activity 7.5

Roy's poem is, at the same time, amusing, poignant and informative. What were
your initial thoughts, given the little bit of information you have here, about Roy's
story? Does this tell you very much about Roy and his life course so far?

Comment

Of course, this is a very short poem, but it does tell you some things about
Roy's background, his thoughts and his experiences. It certainly highlights the
range of changes and developments that he has experienced and been part of
through his lifetime so far. It is also useful to consider that 'stories', narratives
or biographies do not always have to be in oral form – they do not always have
to be heard through interviews or discussions; there are other very effective ways
of 'listening' to people and enabling them to express themselves. As the chapter
moves on to consider different ways in which later adulthood is theorised or
explained, you may find it useful to remember Roy, or perhaps return to his
poem, as a real example.

Theories and explanations of development in (later) adulthood

In the first activity of this chapter, you thought about how you might define later adulthood in terms of the main characteristics or features that it encompasses. We commented that your responses might have come from a range of different perspectives that focused on social, biological or cognitive aspects of growing older. We shall now explore each of these approaches to ageing in more depth, using models from key theorists and case examples. You should note, however, that whilst you will look at each approach separately here, it is important for social workers to take a holistic approach to understanding life course development for older adults: '*The life course is central to any understanding of ageing*' (Ray and Philips, 2012, p. 32). Therefore, in developing your understanding of later life, you should be mindful that an individual's life course development and life experiences are affected by a range of factors; these include social and economic aspects, cultural, historical, psychological, cognitive and physiological influences.

Social development in later adulthood

In Chapter 6 you examined Erik Erikson's (1982) theory of the 'eight stages of man', the eighth and final stage being 'late adulthood'. As with the earlier life stages, Erikson theorises that late adulthood is a developmental challenge or conflict, which can be successfully or unsuccessfully met, resulting in favourable or unfavourable outcomes (see Figure 7.1).

Erikson describes the demands of later life as requiring the individual to look back over their life experiences and draw them together into a form of self-acceptance that he calls 'ego integration'. Where the individual feels that they have not had a successful life, they may sense some regret about not being able to 'turn the clock back' and do things again. Such regrets, according to Erikson, lead to 'despair' and ultimately a fear of the end of life.

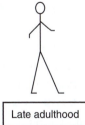

Late adulthood

Late adulthood (aged 70+ years): integrity versus despair

Erikson describes this last life stage crisis as one of integrity versus despair, the struggle in this phase being to experience a sense of wholeness and acceptance of one's own life and the choices that were made, without harbouring regrets or feelings of having inadequately fulfilled life's expectations. Successfully negotiating this challenge by reaching a stage of self-acceptance and comfort with one's life enables the individual to come to terms with death.

Figure 7.1   Erikson's stages of psychosocial development in late adulthood

Case study 7.2

Henry Jones (aged 85) was widowed ten years ago and shortly afterwards moved into a bungalow, in a supported housing complex, where he now lives. Henry has two children, both of whom have families and careers; they live about 60 miles away from him. Henry is finding it increasingly difficult to care for himself. He needs regular assistance with practical tasks and is starting to have problems attending to his personal needs. Since the death of his wife, Henry appears to have gradually alienated all of their friends and family. He is considered by many to be difficult, demanding, often angry and sometimes extremely rude to people who have offered support and friendship.

Following many minor disputes and difficulties, his family no longer visit him. Henry has also rejected support services from a range of carers as, for one reason and another, he has disapproved of or disliked each service. Now the only support that he will accept is from the housing support warden. The warden visits regularly and, due to his increasing level of need, Henry finds that he is becoming gradually more dependent upon her, to the extent that her support role is far beyond that which a warden would usually undertake. An example of this is that Henry will telephone the warden frequently at her home, when she is off-duty, or has left his home only minutes before. These calls are not usually urgent matters and could have waited until the next planned call.

Activity 7.6

Think about the challenges that face Henry. Write down a few sentences that answer the questions below:

- Using Erikson's model, how would you briefly explain Henry's situation?
- Having formed an understanding of Henry's situation using Erikson's approach, what are the implications for the way in which you as a social worker would work with him?

From the information you have on Henry's life, it is not possible to know about his whole life course and whether he has moved successfully through the previous life stages described by Erikson, or whether there are outstanding issues for him. Henry's behaviours could be seen as the result of feeling angry and discontent with his life. Perhaps the loss of his wife, the subsequent change of role and feelings of having no purpose or worth in life could result in the bitterness and contempt that are exhibited. The move to sheltered accommodation may also have been a difficult transition for Henry, as this happened shortly after his wife's death. He also has to adjust to his changing physical capabilities, which potentially threaten his independence and the self-identity that he has known. The apparent dependency on one individual, and the unreasonable behaviours described, may be explained through difficulties at earlier life stages, which may be exacerbated now. For example, having no contact with his family means that he is not aware of their development and contribution to society, this being a key element of 'generativity' at the middle adulthood stage.

The implications of this knowledge for social work practice are immense. The most significant concept though, would be for social workers to work to encourage and enable the development of 'ego integrity'. This can be achieved by valuing the individual, their experiences and their own interpretation of their life events through active listening. Therapeutic work through reminiscence and biographical approaches to life reviews can help a person to integrate past life experiences and enable them to form a realistic acceptance of their life course. We have also noted that Henry may have low self-esteem and feel that he has no purpose in life. Therefore, enabling him to seek a purpose or role in life could be beneficial. At the same time, considering ways to increase and maintain his independence would be valuable in restoring his feelings of self-worth.

There is some disagreement amongst theorists, however, as to the value of maintaining activity, or conversely reducing activity, in later adulthood. In this context, the term 'activity' is taken to have a wide meaning, encompassing not only physical activity but also mental activity, involvement, engagement and interactions within society. The two approaches to the debate on the value of activity in later adulthood are 'disengagement theory' and 'activity theory'.

Henry's life situation could be seen to demonstrate some elements of disengagement theory (Cumming and Henry, 1961). Henry has distanced himself from previous friends and family and appears to reject most opportunities to interact with people. He appears to be isolated and to have chosen to withdraw from active involvement in earlier social roles and networks. From the perspective of disengagement theorists, these behaviours are not indicative of physical change or impairment, but demonstrate a change of emphasis to focus on other tasks that are prioritised. This corresponds with Erikson's later adulthood challenge, where the importance of focusing on reviewing one's life and reaching a point of acceptance and 'ego integration' is seen as paramount at this stage of life.

Disengagement theory attempts to dispel the negative myths of ageing as a period of loneliness and reducing ability, by reframing these notions as natural, appropriate and purposeful processes that enable the individual to move through later adulthood successfully. Thus, according to this approach, by reducing social and emotional interactions and becoming increasingly preoccupied with themself, an older adult is thought to be able to increase their satisfaction with life.

Disengagement theory, however, is directly opposed by activity theory. According to the views of activity theorists, the more active, occupied and involved the older adult is, the more likely they are to be satisfied with their life. Activity theory proposes that older adults should maintain either the same or substitute activity patterns that they established in middle adulthood.

The case example of Margaret and Charles from earlier in this chapter provides a useful example of how older adults might continue to be active in a broad sense as they develop in later life. So Margaret and Charles have substituted the activities, commitment and involvement in their careers with their roles and activities as grandparents and volunteers and their participation in leisure pursuits.

Critics of disengagement and activity theories would highlight the constraints posed by the structural expectations of society. For example, retirement and institutional care could be seen as mechanisms that enforce disengagement and do not enable continued activity. Disengagement theory is then accused of providing a political tool in that it legitimises such policies. However, activity theory could also be seen to promote the involvement of older adults in voluntary activities, which again can be argued to be a useful political mechanism for maintaining the high number of unpaid, yet productive citizens in the economy.

Biological development in later adulthood

Throughout the life course, increasing age is associated with certain physical bodily changes. Such biological developments are associated with normal expectations of the ageing process.

Activity 7.7

Think about people you know who are becoming older adults, perhaps your parents or grandparents. List the physical or biological changes they may be experiencing.

Comment

You may have associated a whole range of physical changes with increasing age. Perhaps you noted some of the more familiar age-related physical changes such as sensory changes. So you may have noted that as people grow older, they may need to have their sight corrected with spectacles, despite not having needed spectacles earlier in their lives, or have a more complex prescription than previously required. You may also have included a possible reduction in hearing ability. Changes related to the person's joints or bones, such as osteoporosis or arthritis, that gradually impact upon their ability to do certain physical tasks, are another area you may have covered.

There may be a number of other physical changes that you have thought of. However, it is important that you appreciate that whilst many of these biological changes appear to be commonplace this does not mean that as we age these changes can be predicted or considered inevitable.

The common aspect in any of the physical changes that can be linked to later adulthood is that they are related to changes taking place within the cells of the body, most usually degenerative changes.

Research summary

The Hayflick limit

Dr Leonard Hayflick, a biologist, researched the biology of ageing. He suggested, following laboratory tests, that human cells can divide or repair up to a maximum of 50 times before they degenerate and die. This led to the concept of there being a maximum capacity for cell regeneration, known as 'the Hayflick limit'. This biological approach presents a form of cellular clock, ticking away, that has been individually programmed into the person's physical make-up. The Hayflick limit puts human lifespan at a maximum of 120 years (Hayflick, 1977).

These notions of a cellular clock, physical degeneration and progressive age-related changes can be used to support ideas of increased frailty and dependency in older age, with no possibility for growth and development. It is for this reason that biological perspectives should not be taken in isolation. Such changes are not universal, in that they do not affect all individuals in the same way through a predictable pathway. Other aspects of people's lives also impact upon and interact with their individual development, for example, social, environmental and psychological factors.

Case study 7.3

At 80 years of age, Michael Aimable ran and completed the London Marathon in 2007. He is a dedicated runner and through his running supports the Muscular Dystrophy Campaign. He is a regular London Marathon runner, having taken part in events since the 1980s. Michael

→

did not take up running until 1980, when he was 54 years old. Since then he has notched up an incredible 90 marathons and 132 half-marathons. That's well over 4,000 miles in the last twenty-six years, and not counting all the other races, plus an average of 40 miles a week of training. A former cipher operator in the army for twenty-two years, he caught the running bug after he decided on an urgent need to lose weight:

> I was 15 stone and overweight. I was getting violent pains down my left arm and heart and I knew I had to do something. It took me a month to be able to run a mile, and then one day a friend said they would give me five pounds if I did a half marathon for charity. It was a blessing in disguise.

(www.muscular-dystrophy.org/index.html)

This example of the marathon runner is a powerful illustration of the potential for physical development and renewal in later life. However, whilst only a small minority of people, at any age, are physically active to this degree, the majority of people in later life do lead active lives.

So far, in this section of the chapter you have mostly considered visible biological changes in later adulthood. However, another change that faces some older adults is deteriorating intellectual ability.

Severe loss of memory associated with other changes, such as personality change, and problems related to overall functioning, is termed 'dementia' and is given a biological or medical interpretation. Dementia is then described as a symptom of a disease, such as Alzheimer's disease or Parkinson's disease. There is considerable debate, though, as to how dementia can be explained. On the one hand it is seen as a clinical disease, linked to the biological ageing process, which comes about due to changes in the cells in the brain, and is therefore a diagnosable and treatable pathological condition. The contrasting view suggests that a biological interpretation alone is not comprehensive and that social, environmental and individual or personal factors can be significant.

Research summary

Dementia is not a single disease. Dementia is a syndrome and refers to the impairment of cognitive brain functions of memory, language, perception and thought. There are many diseases that cause dementia, such as Alzheimer's disease, dementia with Lewy bodies and Parkinson's disease-associated dementia. The majority are degenerative but not all, for example, vascular dementia.

The *World Alzheimer's Report 2013* (Prince *et al.*, 2013) states that systems should be in place to monitor the quality of dementia care in all settings – whether in care homes or in the community. Autonomy and choice should be promoted at all stages of the dementia journey, prioritising the voices of people with dementia and their caregivers, and further that health and social care systems should be better integrated and co-ordinated to meet people's needs.

The Alzheimer's Society's (2013) report suggests that 80 per cent or more of residents in care homes have dementia or significant memory problems and also indicates that expectations for dementia care are low. While 68 per cent of respondents feel that the quality of care is good, only 41 per cent feel the quality of life for the residents is good. The report reinforces other research findings that the level of activity for residents with dementia in care homes leaves room for improvement, with only 41 per cent saying the opportunities for activity are good.

Tom Kitwood (1993a, p. 102) has written about and researched dementia; he states that *it is being realised that a purely technical frame has had its day*. Kitwood develops the notions of *malignant social psychology* and *personhood* as he argues that dementia results from the interplay between cell deterioration in the brain and the interpersonal, psychological and social environment. His work provides a strong incentive for social work practice that offers a person-centred approach that actively acknowledges an individual's perception of their life and their situation.

Marshall and Tibbs add to this by developing a 'citizenship approach' to dementia, which understands that people with dementia are fellow citizens who make a contribution to society as well as receive services. It is the detailed and practical everyday issues, addressed with care and attention, which contribute to genuine person-centred care for people with dementia (2006, p. 16).

Research summary

A joint publication by the National Institute for Health and Clinical Excellence (NICE) and the Social Care Institute for Excellence (SCIE), *Dementia – Supporting People with Dementia and their Carers in Health and Social Care* (2006/ updated 2016), states that dementia is a progressive and largely irreversible syndrome that is characterised by a widespread impairment of mental function. It can be viewed as one of the ways in which an individual's personal and social capacities change with age. Changes in such capacities are only experienced as disabilities when environmental supports are not adaptable to suit changing needs and capacities.

(Continued)

(Continued)

As the condition progresses, people with dementia can present carers and social care staff with complex problems including: aggressive behaviour; restlessness and wandering; eating problems; incontinence; delusions and hallucinations; and mobility difficulties.

It is estimated that there are 700,000 cases of dementia in the UK and approximately one million people caring for people with dementia. Demographic changes in the next thirty years, with a substantial increase in the proportion of people in the 'old old' age groups, mean that the prevalence of dementia is set to more than double in the next thirty to fifty years. The report made the following recommendations:

- People with dementia should not be excluded from any services because of their diagnosis, age or coexisting learning disabilities.
- Health and social care professionals should always seek valid consent from people with dementia. This should entail informing the person of options, and checking that they understand there is no coercion and they can continue to consent over time. If a person lacks the capacity to make a decision, the provisions of the Mental Capacity Act 2005 must be followed.
- Health and social care practitioners should discuss with the person with dementia, while they still have capacity, the use of advance decisions to refuse treatment and lasting powers of attorney, which are made under the provisions of the Mental Capacity Act 2005. People with dementia and their carers should be informed about the availability and role of local and national advocacy services.
- Health and social care managers should ensure that the rights of carers to receive an assessment of needs as set out in the Carers and Disabled Children Act 2000 and the Carers (Equal Opportunities) Act 2004 are upheld.
- Health and social care managers should co-ordinate and integrate working across all agencies involved in the treatment and care of people with dementia and their carers.
- Care managers and care co-ordinators should ensure the co-ordinated delivery of health and social care services for people with dementia.
- Memory assessment services should be the single point of referral for all people with a possible diagnosis of dementia.
- People with dementia who develop non-cognitive symptoms that cause them significant distress or who develop challenging behaviour should be offered an assessment at an early opportunity.

- Health and social care managers should ensure that all staff working with older people in the health, social care and voluntary sectors have access to dementia-care training that is consistent with their roles and responsibilities.
- Acute and general hospital trusts should plan and provide services that address the specific personal and social care needs and the mental and physical health of people with dementia who use acute hospital facilities for any reason.

If you wish to develop your understanding of issues in relation to dementia, SCIE have developed an excellent web learning resource available at www.scie.org.uk/publications/misc/dementia/.

Research summary

The Prime Minister's Challenge on Dementia 2020 (established under David Cameron) is to make England the best country in the world for dementia care and support and for people with dementia to live, as well as to conduct dementia research (DH, 2016b, p. 8). There are more than 50 specific commitments across four core themes:

1   Risk reduction – to educate more people earlier about the risks of developing dementia and the steps to reduce those risks.
2   Health and care – joined-up plans for health and care support in every area and personalised care plans for every person with dementia; dementia-friendly health and care settings.
3   Awareness and social action – increasing the total number of Dementia Friends and establishing more Dementia Friendly Communities.
4   Research – establishing a Dementia Research Institute.

There is also the intention to establish a Dementia 2020 Citizens Panel – putting the views and lived experiences of people with dementia and carers at the forefront of planning and practice.

The Alzheimer's Society's Dementia Friends programme is the biggest ever initiative to change people's perceptions of dementia. It aims to transform the way the nation thinks, acts and talks about the condition. If you are interested in learning more about dementia and becoming a Dementia Friend (learning a little bit more about what it's like to live with dementia and to then turn that understanding into action) or Dementia Champion (a volunteer who encourages others to make a positive difference to people living with dementia in their community), here is the link: https://www.dementiafriends.org.uk/

Cognitive development in later adulthood

In this section you will look at age-related intellectual and cognitive changes in later adulthood. As with the biological changes discussed earlier, it is important that you appreciate that ageing does not automatically correspond with a significant decrease in cognitive functioning or intelligence.

Intelligence can be described as encompassing a range of cognitive abilities or thought processes. These are sometimes known as 'crystallised' and 'fluid' abilities. Crystallised intellectual abilities refer to the individual's knowledge that has been acquired over the life course, usually familiar material and general knowledge. Fluid intellectual abilities relate to the ability to reason, analyse, evaluate and process complex information. Older adults are thought to be less proficient with tasks that require fluid intellectual abilities, whilst retaining the crystallised abilities (see Figure 7.2). However, these are generalisations and there are differences in intelligence across individuals that may demonstrate age-related effects, life course events, social or cultural differences.

Cognitive abilities can also be described as the result of the interaction between information from the senses: concentration, short-term memory, long-term memory, learning and recall.

Thus, whilst certain cognitive processes may decline with age, ageing, by itself, does not result in significant decreases in intelligence. It is a myth that older adults become less intelligent with age. The possible changes to cognitive processing described above are not universal characteristics, and many older adults can develop ways to compensate for any difficulties that they do experience (for example writing things down in order to remember them). Furthermore, individual difference in cognitive ability at any age is enormous. As with the other areas you have looked at in this chapter, cognitive development in later life is interrelated to many other aspects of life, including general physical health, social and environmental factors. As a social worker, therefore, it is important to consider the most effective ways in which to enable the older adult to maximise their cognitive abilities by attending to all of these interrelating factors.

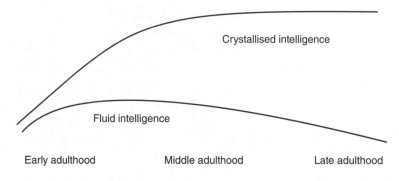

Figure 7.2 Crystallised and fluid intellectual abilities as they develop in the adult life course

Research summary

Baltes' life course model

Professor Paul Baltes (1987), a German researcher, proposed that intelligence develops in relation to biological, social and cultural forces. Biological influences on intelligence include the brain cell development that occurs throughout the life course.

> *As an individual ages, the capacity to read, execute calculations, draw abstractions, and make judgements develops in relation to biological and social experiences. Baltes' life course model also suggests that intelligence becomes increasingly diverse over time. The majority of older adults can read, perform calculations, draw abstract inferences and exercise independent judgement. However, the performance of these intellectual abilities is much more varied than it would be within a group of children.*

(Baltes, 1987).

Case study 7.4

In 1938, after studying mechanical sciences at university, Colonel Michael Cobb joined the army and saw action at Dunkirk, in North Africa and in the Far East during the Second World War. In 2008, at the age of 91, Colonel Cobb graduated from Magdalene College, Cambridge, with a PhD. He had earned his PhD by creating an atlas which recorded and mapped the railway stations built in Britain between 1807 and 1994 (*Daily Mail*, 19.7.2008).

Joe Bartley, from Paignton, South Devon, is due to start work at a cafe in the town after placing an advert in a local paper asking for part-time work to stop him 'dying from boredom'. It read, 'Senior citizen, 89, seeks employment in Paignton area. 20hrs+ per week. Still able to clean, light gardening, DIY and anything. I have references. Old soldier, airborne forces. Save me from dying of boredom!' He said he had been overwhelmed by the response to the advert, which he described as 'not unusual, just an old guy looking for work'. He also said he had lived alone since his wife, Cassandra, had died two years previously, and had been lonely: 'When you live on your own there is no one to speak to. Since she died I've moved into a flat and it's a big block. Once you walk into that flat it's like solitary confinement' (*Guardian*, 29 November 2016).

The University of the Third Age (U3A) is a learning co-operative of older people, which enables members to share many educational, creative and leisure activities. Activities are organised mainly in small groups that meet regularly, often in each other's homes. Members, through sharing their knowledge, skills and experience, learn from each other. Its vision is to make lifelong learning, through the experience of U3A, a reality for all third agers. (See the website at http://u3a.org.uk/)

Significance of transitions in later life

Throughout this chapter you have looked at some of the ways in which development and change in later adulthood can be explained and understood. In previous chapters you have also considered changes in terms of transitions or phases within a person's life course development. You will now look at how transitions and life events impact on a person's development in later adulthood.

As social workers it is important to appreciate that each individual will experience transitions in a different way. Even where the life event or transition is something that is common to many people in our society (for example retirement), each person will respond and adjust to that change in a unique way. Furthermore, all transitions – whether predictable and expected or sudden and unplanned – present considerable challenges and opportunities for the individual, their growth and development. Therefore, social workers who work with older adults need to understand not only the changes that may occur in later adulthood, but also the variety of factors that influence how people adapt to such changes in their lives.

In earlier parts of the chapter you will have seen how older adults may experience a range of changes in their lives; some of these are physical and psychological changes, others are related to the expectations and rules of society, and some changes are transitions or personal events that impact on a person's life. In this section, you will look at different ways of explaining how people adjust to these changes in later adulthood.

As you have seen, the model of life development proposed by Erik Erikson (1997) suggests that later adulthood presents a challenge between integrity and despair. Erikson's approach is to argue that individuals can move successfully through transition at this stage in their lives if they develop a measure of self-acceptance and feel fulfilled with the life they have lived. So, by presenting life stages as challenges to be negotiated and met successfully or unsuccessfully, Erikson's approach provides a way of explaining how individuals might grow older 'successfully'.

Activity 7.8

Think about the phrase 'successful ageing':

- What does 'successful ageing' mean to you?
- Write down your own definition of 'successful ageing'.

Comment

The term 'successful' is a subjective one, in that your interpretation of success will be different from another person's perspective. However, you may have felt that there are many potential areas of life that can impact on whether you feel that you are ageing 'successfully'. Aspects such as having good physical and mental health, being independent, feeling content and happy, having enough money, suitable accommodation, having friends, family and social outlets may all have featured in your thoughts. The term 'successful ageing', as used in the literature and research related to later adulthood, originally arose from the work of Rowe and Kahn (1987).

Research summary

Successful ageing

Doctors John Rowe and Robert Kahn (1987) based their ideas on studies of groups of people as they moved through middle adulthood into later adulthood. They proposed that there is great variation in how people experience ageing and that an understanding of 'usual' or 'pathological' ageing will help us to develop preventative strategies with older adults so that they are more likely to achieve 'successful ageing'. Rowe and Kahn suggest three measures that will enhance the quality of life in later adulthood:

1   Avoid disability and disease.
2   Maintain high cognitive and physical functioning.
3   Stay actively involved with life and living.

It can be seen that Rowe and Kahn connected the concept of 'successful ageing' to being free of disease or ill health. This is a biological approach, as described earlier in the chapter. From this perspective, health promotion strategies, good diet and exercise would be seen as important ways in which to enable the body to successfully adapt to the changes of later adulthood. However, this viewpoint can be seen as very restrictive, in that it does not take account of the many other aspects of an individual's development that impact on how they experience transitions, as we have seen from Activity 7.8. It could also be argued that this biological perspective would disadvantage individuals who experience impairment or disease.

Bowling and Dieppe (2005) undertook a systematic literature review of 'successful ageing'. They acknowledgd Rowe and Kahn's model as the most widely used approach, but highlighted that it fails to address the implications of the fact that a disease-free older age is unrealistic for most people. While the biomedical model emphasises the absence of disease and the maintenance of physical and mental functioning as the keys to ageing successfully, socio-psychological models emphasise life satisfaction, social participation and functioning, and psychological resources, including personal growth. Satisfaction with one's past and present life has been the most commonly proposed definition of successful ageing, and is also the most commonly investigated. Older people's views of successful ageing include a number of different criteria. They summarise the main constituents of successful ageing as follows.

Theoretical definitions

- Life expectancy.
- Life satisfaction and well-being (includes happiness and contentment).
- Mental and psychological health, cognitive function.
- Personal growth, learning new things.
- Physical health and functioning, independent functioning.
- Psychological characteristics and resources, including perceived autonomy, control, independence, adaptability, coping, self-esteem, a positive outlook, goals, sense of self.
- Social, community, leisure activities, integration and participation.
- Social networks, support, participation, activity.

Additional lay definitions

- Accomplishments.
- Enjoyment of diet.
- Financial security.
- Neighbourhood.
- Physical appearance.
- Productivity and contribution to life.
- Sense of humour.
- Sense of purpose.
- Spirituality.

> *...successful ageing needs to be viewed, not only multidimensionally, but as an ideal state to be aimed for, and the concept itself should be placed on a continuum of achievement rather than subject to simplistic normative assessments of success or failure.*

> (Bowling and Dieppe, 2005, p. 1550)

Case study 7.5

Doreen Shepherd, 68, moved into Reeve Court Retirement Village in Rainhill, St Helens, Merseyside, 18 months ago, and takes a keen part in the activities on offer:

I'm very happy that I moved to the village, *says Doreen.*

There's lots to do. I belong to the choir, the knitting group and the discussion group. I've made lots of friends here and feel very secure.

→

While Reeve Court was being built, the managing company, Extra Care Charity Trust, worked in partnership with the local authority to find older people who would benefit from this active, independent environment.

There are lots of people in residential and nursing care homes because there's nowhere else for them to go, explains manager Lesley Blowers, when, with the right support, they could live independently. While we were building the village, we gave people information about it because, together with the local authority, we wanted to give older people a choice. Social services identified people in residential care who they thought would benefit from the environment we offer.

(DH, 2006, p. 17)

It is clear that issues of choice, control, quality of life and access to resources have been significant in Doreen's situation. We do not know any more about the types of resources that may have been available to her in making the decision to move to Reeve Court, but in Chapter 6 you read about the different types of resources that individuals may be able to draw upon to support and assist them as they move through life transitions. The availability of internal, emotional, psychological resources and external, material resources remains significant in determining how individuals will experience transitions in later adulthood. Also in Chapter 6 you read about how the experience of having an impairment or disability in adulthood can change your life course and affect how you move through transitions. Again, the issues remain relevant in later adulthood. It may be helpful for you to re-read pages 162–5 of Chapter 6 at this point.

End-of-life issues

One area of life course development that is most often associated only with later adulthood relates to end-of-life issues. That is not to discount that people may die at any age from a range of causes, but that in the later stages of adulthood the end of life becomes expected. You have already seen how Erikson's model considers that individuals who move successfully through the later stage of adulthood will be prepared for the end of life and will face their death without fear. You have also explored how biological approaches to human development, such as the Hayflick limit, describe a 'cellular clock' putting a time limit on human life (Hayflick, 1977).

A discussion about end-of-life issues in respect of human life course development provides the opportunity to draw together many of the themes that have been raised throughout this chapter. Death is, in pure terms, the end of the body's biological and physical functioning. However, end-of-life issues raise a complex, interacting range of emotions, meanings, interpretations and beliefs both at a personal level and in a wider societal context. Therefore, for social work practice the individual's perspective on nearing the end of their life, their response to the issues that this raises for them and the effect on their life are the paramount concerns. The way in which each individual perceives the prospect of the end of their life will depend upon a range of influences in their life. A person's values, outlook and beliefs are constructed through their life experiences and through cultural and societal expectations.

The attitudes, values and beliefs of the society and culture in which people's lives develop, and in which they are currently living, will strongly influence their thoughts about what the end of their life means to them. In our society, death in later adulthood is likely to take place in an institutional setting, either in hospital, residential or nursing care or in a hospice.

Thus dying and death could be seen to be part of a professionalised process, which is managed and controlled by the professionals, their theories, perspectives and interests. The logical conclusion of this view is that the individual older adult has, in these circumstances, little control over the process of their own death. This is, however, not necessarily the case as – particularly with the growth of the hospice movement philosophy – practitioners work towards user empowerment, enabling choice and control in all aspects of one's death.

Research summary

Around 470,000 people die each year in England and this is projected to rise by 20 per cent over the next twenty years. More people are expected to die at an older age and have more complex needs (ONS, 2016a). At the same time, 40,000 children and young people in England now live with a life-shortening or life-threatening health condition (Fraser *et al.*, 2011).

The main places of death for older people in England and Wales are, in descending order of prevalence, hospitals, care homes, own home and hospices. However, while some people experience excellent end-of-life care in hospitals, hospices, care homes and in their own homes, many others do not. Research shows that many people experience unnecessary pain and other symptoms, being treated with a lack of dignity and respect, and many do not die where they would choose to (AgeUK, *End of Life Evidence Review*, 2013).

As the *Ambitions for Palliative and End of Life Care: A National Framework for Local Action 2015– 2020* (National Palliative and End of Life Care Partnership, 2015) highlight, how we care for the dying is an indicator of how we care for all sick and vulnerable people. It is a measure of society as a whole and it is a litmus test for health and social care services (DH, 2008b, p. 2). They set out six ambitions for palliative and end of life care:

1   *Each person is seen as an individual: I, and the people important to me, have opportunities to have honest, informed and timely conversations and to know that I might die soon. I am asked what matters most to me. Those who care for me know that and work with me to do what's possible.*

2   *Each person gets fair access to care: I live in a society where I get good end of life care regardless of who I am, where I live or the circumstances of my life.*

3   *Maximising comfort and wellbeing: being in familiar surroundings: My care is regularly reviewed and every effort is made for me to have the support, care and treatment that might be needed to help me to be as comfortable and as free from distress as possible.*

4   *Care is coordinated: I get the right help at the right time from the right people. I have a team around me who know my needs and my plans and work together to help me achieve them. I can always reach someone who will listen and respond at any time of the day or night.*

5   *All staff are prepared to care: Wherever I am, health and care staff bring empathy, skills and expertise and give me competent, confident and compassionate care.*

6   *Each community is prepared to help: I live in a community where everybody recognises that we all have a role to play in supporting each other in times of crisis and loss. People are ready, willing and confident to have conversations about living and dying well and to support each other in emotional and practical ways.* (DH, 2008, p. 11)

The government's response, *Our Commitment To You for End of Life Care: The Government Response to the Review of Choice in End of Life Care* (DH, 2016c), commits to care for everyone approaching the end of life, to receiving care that is personalised and focused on individual need and preferences. In summary this requires: honest discussions about needs and preferences; being able to make informed choices about a person's care; a personalised care plan; sharing the personalised care plan with relevant professionals; involving, to the extent the individual wants, family, carers and other important people to the person in decisions about care; and knowing who to contact for help and advice.

It can be argued that death is an unmentionable subject in our society; it is both denied and stigmatised. Within the medical doctrines, for example, methods for prolonging human life and curing disease are dominant, although, as stated above, with the growth of the hospice movement, goals of pain control and dignity in death have become recognised and valued. In our language too, we could be accused of avoiding or denying death. We allude to death, but choose euphemisms such as 'passing on' and 'passing away', rather than being open, acknowledging and discussing death as an inevitable element of life itself.

Death is construed in some parts of society as a punishment. This is reinforced through some religious writings that connect death and dying with sin and retribution. However, many religious teachings also suggest that death is another significant transition, a transition from physical life to another form of life, where one's spirit lives on: 'life after death'. Religion and culture also provide structure and meanings to the way in which death is ritualised. Thus funerals, burials and the grieving process take place within a social and often religious context that gives meaning and importance to death as a life event.

So, social, cultural and religious beliefs and expectations impact on the community, family and social networks of the individual, as much as they do on the individual themselves. The death of any one person usually results in the roles and identities of those around them having to be renegotiated and changed. In other words, the death of one individual can be a major life event or transition for the friends and relatives they leave behind. In this way, the older adult's perspective on death will be influenced by the behaviours and attitudes of those for whom they care. At a personal level, death is frequently related to loss, not only the loss of bodily functions but also the loss of an opportunity to achieve certain things.

All of this means that for social care practice it is vital that an individual's perspective, wishes and feelings are fully understood and acted upon. An advance care plan (ACP) is a process of discussion between an individual and their care providers irrespective of discipline. If the individual wishes, their family and friends may be included. With the individual's agreement, this discussion should be documented, regularly reviewed and communicated to key persons involved in their care. The notion of ACP is the focus of the NHS publication *Advance Care Planning: A Guide for Health and Social Care Staff* (NHS, 2008). A specific subset of the ACP is in regard to medical treatments: Advance Directives (Advance Decisions, Living Wills). This is a statement explaining what medical treatment the individual would not want in the future, should that individual 'lack capacity' as defined by the Mental Capacity Act 2005. An advance decision or living will is legally binding:

> *Ensuring that everyone has a good life until they die and a good death and that those close to them receive the support they need must be everybody's business. Social Workers have an important contribution to make to this.*

> (Association of Palliative Care Social Workers *et al.*, 2016. p. 33)

Watts (2013) identifies the social work role as integral to the professional practice of the multi-disciplinary palliative care team. Research by Beresford *et al.* (2008) found that service users overwhelmingly valued their experience of specialist palliative care social workers, highlighting the quality of the relationship between service user and social worker, the personal qualities of the social worker and the nature and process of the work with them. Brown and Walter (2014) challenge the social work profession to help develop a more adequate model of end-of-life care, as a profession that is well placed to draw upon its values, culture and experiences, recommending a social model that builds on the resources and networks already surrounding individuals.

Case study 7.6

Eleanor Jacobs is 79 years old; she was widowed some thirty-five years ago, when her husband died after a long and painful progressive illness. Eleanor has four children but she has lived alone for many years. Her eldest daughter, Maria, married an Australian man and settled in Auckland over fifteen years ago. It is ten years since Eleanor saw her daughter, although they speak on the telephone and Maria writes long letters regularly.

$\longrightarrow$

Maria has two children that Eleanor has never seen. Eleanor's other children live within easy trav-
elling distance from their mother and visit occasionally. However, Thomas and Benjamin, her sons,
have never had a good relationship with each other, and more latterly Eleanor has become aware
that they argue about their responsibility to her and her care needs. She also believes it is very
likely that they have argued about their possible shares of an inheritance after her death. Ann is
the youngest child and Eleanor has always felt close to her. Eleanor has tried on several occasions
to talk, with Ann, about planning her funeral and what will happen after her death. Ann finds this
distressing and very difficult, and always closes down the discussion by smiling jokily and saying 'Don't be silly Mum, you're not going to die, you'll live on forever!' However, in the past year
Eleanor's health has deteriorated rapidly and she has become more acutely aware that the end of
her life may not be far away. Being alone for long periods has given her plenty of opportunity to
think about her death. The thoughts are gradually filling her with dread, anxiety and distress as
she finds she is unable to discuss or plan for the end of her life with those close to her.

It can be seen, therefore, that each person's perspective on the end of their life is influenced by
a complex interaction between the social and cultural images and ideologies through which
they have lived their lives. The images may depict a process within which the individual has
little control; added to this there may be connotations of punishment, denial and stigma. It
would, then, seem reasonable for individuals to develop a fear of death. However, older adults
do not often express a fear of death, although some describe a concern about the manner in
which they might die. Citing evidence from a range of writers and research, Moyra Sidell
explains that most older people have reached *some stage of acceptance*, which reminds us of
Erikson's notion of ego-integrity (Sidell, 1993). Perhaps this relates to death being inevitable
and expected in later adulthood and thus people are prepared for the end of their life.

Research summary

The Role of Social Workers in Palliative, End of Life and Bereavement Care (Association of
Palliative Care Social Workers *et al.*, 2016) provides an overview of the context and
explanation of what palliative social work is, and sets out the particular capabilities
(knowledge, skills and values) that palliative social workers have and the general
capabilities that all social workers have in relation to end of life and bereavement.

The capabilities for all social workers are:

- *Professionalism*: Social workers are ready to apply their knowledge, skills and
  values to recognise and support people who are dying, facing loss or bereaved.
- *Values and Ethics*: Social workers recognise the impact of people's values and
  beliefs, including their own, on death, dying and loss; and are committed to the
  principle of living well until the end of life, whatever that means for someone.

(Continued)

(Continued)

- *Diversity*: Social workers value people as individuals, and ensure their wishes and needs are respected at the end of life and when bereaved.
- *Rights and Justice*: Social workers ensure that people who are dying or bereaved, especially from marginalised or disadvantaged groups, can empower themselves and be enabled to get the support they need.
- *Knowledge*: Social workers are aware of the impact of loss from a person knowing that they or someone close is dying, from physical and other changes, from grief and from bereavement. They know how to use the law, evidence and systems to support and protect dying people and those close to them.
- *Critical Reflection*: Social workers are able to judge when specialist support is needed for people they work with who are dying or bereaved, and when they themselves need additional support.
- *Intervention and Skills*: Social workers are able to engage with people who are dying or bereaved and those close to them to ensure they have the practical, emotional, psychological and spiritual support they need. This includes working with individuals, groups and communities.
- *Contexts and Organisations*: Social workers are able to access advice, information and input from palliative care social workers when these are needed in their organisation.
- *Professional Leadership*: Social workers remind others of the need to recognise and respond effectively to people who are dying and bereaved, act as mentors, and share learning about how to do this well. This includes advocating for people's rights and supporting them to access the information and help they need.

Diversity in later adulthood

Throughout this chapter you have considered life course development in later adulthood from a range of perspectives, yet the overriding theme has been that whilst there may be trends and patterns to growing older, there are no predetermined pathways that lay out predictable ways in which increasing age will affect people. The only way of understanding an individual's development and the issues that later adulthood may hold for them is to listen to their life story, as they tell it and perceive it. In other words, to value the individual's own narrative and biographical account.

In this way, you will be able to appreciate the impact of life transitions for the individual and take account of differences between older adults. Life course development happens across the whole of life, being a gradual and progressive accumulation of influences, crises, transitions and growth, each of which can in turn be seen as a process of social, biological and cognitive development. Each older adult's experience of late adulthood, therefore, is not only moulded by the complex interactions of their current life, it is also influenced by their own life history and their subjective interpretation of it. For example, the experience of being an older black woman in contemporary British society may hold many challenges, but each older black woman will deal with those challenges differently, dependent to some extent upon how she has experienced and thinks about her life as a black woman.

Reflection point

- What do I know, or can I do now, that I did not know or could not do before I did this section of studying?
- Is there anything I do not understand or want to explore further?
- What else do I need to know to extend my professional development and learning in this area?

Chapter summary

In this chapter you have explored human life course development in respect of older adults, focusing on the use in practice of human growth and development theories and knowledge. We examined the problematic nature of some of the words used to describe this stage of human development and considered how late adulthood is constructed in our society, before looking at some approaches that explain human life course development in late adulthood. You have looked at the significance of transitions for older adults and considered how access to resources may influence their experience of life changes. This incorporated studying the concept of successful ageing and end-of-life issues. Throughout the chapter we have presented older adulthood as an opportunity for growth and development.

Further reading

AgeUK (2013) *Agenda for Later Life: Improving Later Life in 2013*. London: AgeUK.

Each year, AgeUK stands back and takes an overview of how society is meeting the needs of people in later life and sets out the agenda for public policy in that year.

Bartlett, R and O'Connor, D (2010) *Broadening the Dementia Debate: Towards Social Citizenship*. Bristol: Policy Press.

Dementia has been widely debated from the perspectives of biomedicine and social psychology. This book broadens the debate to consider the experiences of men and women with dementia from a sociopolitical perspective. It brings to the fore the concept of social citizenship, exploring what it means within the context of dementia and using it to reexamine the issue of rights, status(es), and participation and how it can be applied in practice.

Cann, P and Dean, M (eds) (2009) *Unequal Ageing: The Untold Story of Exclusion in Old Age.* Bristol: Policy Press.

This book analyses the vital dimensions of money, health, place, quality of life and identity, and demonstrates the gaps of treatment and outcomes between older and younger people, and between different groups of older people.

Moore, D and Jones, K (2012) *Social Work and Dementia.* London: Sage/Learning Matters.

This book enables social work students to consider the various ways that people can be supported to live well with dementia.

Payne, M and Reith, M (2009) *Social Work and End-of-life and Palliative Care.* Bristol: Policy Press.

This book focuses on practice interventions, advocating open communication and skilled interpersonal practice to help dying and bereaved people, their families and carers. It reviews sociological and psychological ideas about dying and bereavement, incorporating spiritual care, multi-professional practice and ethical issues likely to face social workers in end-of-life and palliative care.

Ray, M, Bernard, M and Phillips, J (2009) *Critical Issues in Social Work with Older People.* Basingstoke: Palgrave Macmillan.

This text highlights the importance of informed and critical practice in social work with older people.

Websites

AgeUK: www.ageuk.org.uk

AgeUK is a federation of about 400 independent charities working together with and for older people, locally, regionally and nationally. On their website you will find a wealth of information and research for students and for older people themselves and their carers. You will find that the section headed 'Policy' is particularly helpful in providing statistical information and information on government policy.

AgeUK commissions research and has networks across a wide range of related research organisations.

Joseph Rowntree Foundation: https://www.jrf.org.uk/

This site has a number of critical resources. Specifically in relation to older people there is an examination of how poverty affects older people in our society.

The National Council for Palliative Care: www.ncpc.org

The National Council for Palliative Care (NCPC) is the umbrella charity for all those involved in palliative, end-of-life and hospice care in England, Wales and Northern Ireland. You can find a range of very useful documents at: www.ncpc.org.uk/freedownloads.

New Dynamics of Ageing: www.newdynamics.group.shef.ac.uk/

The New Dynamics of Ageing programme is an eight-year multi-disciplinary research initiative with the ultimate aim of improving quality of life of older people. The overall aim of this programme is to advance understanding of the dynamics of ageing from a multi-disciplinary perspective. There is a wealth of resources on the website.

The Social Care Institute for Excellence: www.scie.org.uk

SCIE have also commissioned practical guidance for best interest decision making and care planning at the end of life.

SCIE has a range of very helpful e-learning resources about older people, and other resources too. For example, in relation to older adults, the Open Dementia Programme is an in-depth programme examining issues in relation to people living with dementia. There is also a Dementia Gateway, with a wide range of resources. End of Life Care has resources to explore high quality care at the end of life.

8: Conclusion

The content of this fifth edition of *Social Work and Human Development* meets the core elements of the requirements for social work education. The book has been primarily written for student social workers who are beginning to develop their skills and understanding of the requirements for practice in their first year or level of study.

The book also set out to meet subject skills identified in the Quality Assurance Agency's academic benchmark criteria for social work (2016). These include understanding the nature of social work and developing knowledge and understanding under the following headings:

- Social work services and service users.
- Values and ethics.
- Social work theory.
- The nature of social work practice.

Furthermore, this book aimed to enable you to meet the requirements of the Professional Capabilities Framework (PCF) (TCSW, 2012a). As (former) The College of Social Work (TCSW) states, the PCF:

- sets out consistent expectations of social workers at every stage in their career;
- provides a backdrop to both initial social work education and continuing professional development after qualification;
- informs the design and implementation of the national career structure;
- gives social workers a framework around which to plan their careers and professional development.

This book will have given you a firm grounding in and understanding of theories and models related to social work and human life course development. In essence, it has developed your knowledge and understanding of human development throughout the life course and its importance to social work practice.

Book structure

This fifth edition preserves the same overall logical structure as the first edition. However, I have aimed to update each chapter with additional links to current policy agendas and developing legislative frameworks. Furthermore, there is additional and updated 'Further reading' at the end of each chapter to include annotated references to recent texts and internet resources.

Through an interactive approach with additional diagrams, activities, case studies and updated research information, this edition set out to help you reflect on, evaluate and progress your learning.

The chapters within this book will have developed your understanding of a range of explanations of human life course development and their impact upon social work practice. Additionally, research and theory summaries have been included to reinforce your developing knowledge and understanding.

Within the chapters of this book you have been encouraged to start by examining your own views and perspectives and to think about the origins of these. The book has taken a whole of life course approach, drawing out the concept of taking a biographical, sometimes called a 'narrative', approach. This is about listening to the first-hand interpretation of individuals and their constructions of their own life course. The *PCF Capability Knowledge – End of Last Placement* (former TCSW, 2012c) states that students must *demonstrate and apply to practice a working knowledge of human growth and development throughout the life course.*

Understanding and adopting the biographical approach to understanding an individual's life course development will enable you to meet the criteria for this standard. Additionally, you have learnt about other key elements of the prescribed curriculum, such as knowledge of child development and legal intervention to protect.

Each of the seven chapters of this book has concentrated on a different aspect of human development through the life course. In Chapter 1, you explored the reasons why knowledge and understanding of human development throughout the life course are important to social work practice. This included consideration of the importance of recognising the impact that your values and life events can have upon your practice. Within this chapter the concept of life events and transitions was introduced and the links between practice and public inquiries into social and health care were made. In this chapter you will have considered the role of social work practice in working with individuals through transition periods in their lives.

The broad overview of a range of theoretical approaches to human life course development and the significance of knowledge from other disciplines provided within this chapter created the links to the later practice-focused chapters.

Chapter 2 concentrated on an introduction to theoretical models for understanding development across the life course. This chapter, as required by the social work subject benchmarks, offered an outline of research-based concepts and critical explanations from the theoretical approaches commonly used by social workers and other professionals when working with people in a variety of settings, across the whole life course. The connections, similarities and differences between the theories were considered, using the case study approach to enable you to compare and contrast models and apply them to social work practice situations.

The chapter reinforced the importance of listening to an individual's perspective on their life course and understanding the range of theories that attempt to explain the complexities of human life course development. Having introduced a range of perspectives and developmental theories in this chapter, the remaining chapters of the book developed these ideas further as they focused on specific phases in the human life course.

Chapter 3 examined life course development knowledge in social work practice with infants, young children and their families, setting out knowledge in respect of early child development. Through an exploration of pre-natal, peri-natal and neo-natal periods of life development, you considered the relative importance of hereditary factors and environmental factors in determining an individual's development. Human life course development knowledge and its use in social work practice with children in need and children in need of protection were considered in this chapter.

Chapter 4 examined life course development knowledge in social work practice with older children and their families. The chapter assisted you to develop your understanding and ability to evaluate and analyse theories that explain human development taking a systemic approach. The chapter also discussed the role of the social worker in supporting children to express their views and feelings, and to develop a positive sense of self-identity and independence.

In Chapter 5 you looked at life course development knowledge in social work practice in respect of young people in their teenage or adolescent years. The chapter considered issues related to the transition to adulthood and the particular significance this may have for young people with disabilities. Social work practice in supporting young people and their families to understand and manage behaviours is considered within this chapter. Theories that explain human life course development, taking a behavioural and social learning approach, were explored and critiqued in this chapter.

In Chapter 6, life course development knowledge in social work practice with people in early and middle adulthood was examined. In particular, the significance of transitions in adult life was considered, drawing on situations related to adults experiencing physical disability, adults with learning difficulties and adults who have caring responsibilities. The chapter looked at how transitions present opportunities for growth and development or, conversely, potential crisis points. Within this chapter you considered factors that may affect the outcome of a person's move through a period of transition, in particular the importance of resources or support networks, and the influence of societal factors. Chapter 6 also developed your understanding and ability to critique theories that explain life course development in stages or phases.

The final chapter examined ways in which an understanding of the theories of human development is essential to effective social work practice with older people and their families. Late adulthood was considered as an opportunity for growth and development, with issues related to ageing and how this is constructed in our society being addressed. An exploration of the significance of transitions in later life enabled you to consider effective ageing and end-of-life issues. Social work practice in palliative care settings is considered within this chapter. The theoretical approaches in this chapter built upon the models examined in Chapter 6 and considered their application in explaining life course development in later adulthood. As with all chapters in this book, this final chapter will have helped you to meet a range of elements of the Professional Capabilities Framework (former TCSW, 2012a), as outlined at the beginning of the chapter.

Professional development and reflective practice

This book has provided an introduction to human life course development and social work practice. It set out to develop your knowledge and skills by assisting you to take a critical approach, to reflect on your work and participate in the development of your learning, through the interactive approach taken in the book. We would now encourage you to look back over the chapters, reflecting and reviewing your progress by charting and monitoring your learning. Reflecting about, in and on your practice and your learning is not only important during your social work education, it is also considered key to continued professional development (CPD). This continuation of your development and lifelong learning includes keeping up to date, ensuring that research informs your practice and that you continually improve your skills and values for practice. The importance of professional development is clearly demonstrated through the PCF and in the Health and Care Professions Council's *Standards of Proficiency: Social Workers in England* (HCPC, 2017).

By taking responsibility for your learning and reflecting on your progress, you will always be in a position to consider your further learning and developmental needs. At this stage in your learning, you will have developed an appreciation of the knowledge you have gained, your understanding and ability to apply this learning to practice, and hence your future learning needs. This appreciation of your own learning will prepare you for further development as you work through the other books within this *Transforming Social Work Practice* series.

Appendix

Professional capabilities framework

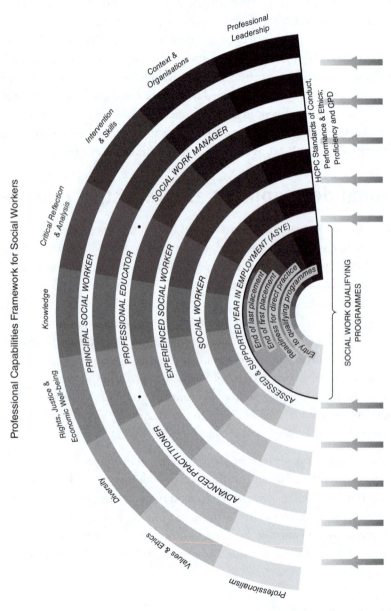

Professional Capabilities Framework diagram reproduced with permission of The College of Social Work.

Glossary

Accommodation   The process of modifying existing schema to fit new experiences or to create new schemas (Piaget).

Adolescent development   The physical changes associated with puberty; the process of development of 'self' and the changing nature of relationships with others.

Ageism   Where negative generalisations, assumptions or stereotypes result in people being treated unfairly, or discriminated against because of their age.

Assimilation   The process of taking in new elements of experiences and information in terms of the schemas that a child already possesses (Piaget).

Attachment   A positive emotional link of affection between two or more people.

Attachment theory   Theory that explains the significance of attachment and relationships, in particular the bonds between children and caregivers.

Behaviourism   Theories that focus on our behaviours and how these behaviours and the consequences of our actions influence our learning (e.g. Skinner, Bandura).

Bonding   The formation or strengthening of a bond between the mother and child (or child and significant other).

Cabinet Office: Social Exclusion Task Force   The role of the Task Force is to co-ordinate the government's drive against social exclusion, ensuring that the cross-departmental approach delivers for those most in need. Their stated aim is to ... *champion(s) the needs of the most disadvantaged members of society within Government, ensuring that as with the rest of the public service reform agenda, we put people first* (www.cabinetoffice.gov.uk/strategy.aspx).

Cabinet Office: Strategy Unit   The role of the Unit is to provide a cross-departmental perspective on the major challenges facing the UK, to work with departments in developing their key policies, and to provide strategic advice and support to the prime minister/No 10 (www.cabinetoffice.gov.uk/social_ exclusion_task_force.aspx).

Cognitive development   The mental processes by which we acquire and process knowledge (e.g. Piaget).

Department for Children, Schools and Families (DfCSF)   Government department whose stated purpose is to ... *make this the best place in the world for children and young people to grow up* (www.dcsf.gov.uk).

Department of Health (DH)   Government department that provides health and social care policy, guidance and publications, and whose defined purpose for social care is to ... *(work) to define policy and guidance for delivering a social care system that provides care equally for all, whilst enabling people to retain their independence, control and dignity* (www.dh.gov.uk).

Development   A complex, continuous, progressive series of changes that occur as a result of maturation and experience.

Developmental   Relating to growth, progression and advancement.

Developmental pathways/Developmental trajectories   Both of these terms relate to the different courses or routes, through a range of experiences and transitions that individuals may take as they grow and progress through the life course.

Developmental psychology   How people develop across the life course exploring their thoughts, ideas, feelings and behaviours.

Disengagement theory   A theory built on the premise that withdrawal from social participation and interaction is an expected and natural process in later adulthood. Disengagement and detachment are perceived as positive and normal for older people.

Ecological   Relating to the environment in which people live their lives.

General Social Care Council (GSCC)   The workforce regulator and guardian of standards for the social care workforce in England. They were established in October 2001 under the Care Standards Act 2000. They are responsible for the codes of practice, Social Care Register and social work education and training.

Generativity   A concept that relates to *generating* or being productive and contributing in some way to a future society. This is discussed in detail in Chapter 5 of this text.

Holistic   An approach that focuses on the whole of something; in the case of social work, this would usually be the whole of the person's life and current circumstances, and not just one element. Holistic approaches view the different aspects of a person as being closely interconnected and understandable only by making reference to the whole.

Identity development   A process of forming an awareness of 'who we are'. Understanding oneself as a person, developing our own personality and a concept of self in relation to others in the social world. Becoming conscious and confident about one's personal life history, sexuality, race, gender and ethnicity.

Life course   The progression and path an individual takes from conception to death.

Life course perspective   A viewpoint that considers the whole of a life (from conception to death) as offering opportunities for growth, development and change.

Life cycle   An alternative term used to describe the life course.

Life span   An alternative term used to describe the life course, often used in developmental psychology.

Life stage development   How people develop their identity as they move through stages or 'crisis' points in their lives (e.g. Erikson).

Milestones   Expected stages of sequential development of skills and abilities, usually in children and commonly related to age. These stages are based upon that which is deemed 'normal' and are used to gauge children's development and identify potential developmental problems.

Multi-dimensional (human development)   Human development across the life course that is recognised as complex and influenced by the interaction of biological, social, psychological and environmental factors.

National Service Framework (NSF)   The national service frameworks are national strategies which set out goals and programmes for change within specific areas of health and social care. The National Service Frameworks for Children (2004) and the one for Older People (2001) are particularly pertinent to this book.

Narrative or biographical approach   The narrative approach is a way of working with individuals that focuses on the importance of their own first-hand account of their life, their experiences and the meanings they attach to them.

Personalisation   This is intended to mean starting with the person as an individual with strengths, preferences and aspirations, and putting them at the centre of the process of identifying their needs and making choices about how and when they are supported to live their lives.

Post-registration training and learning (PRTL)   This is the term used by the GSCC and is taken here to mean the activities that individuals may undertake in order to achieve continuing professional development (CPD).

Psychosocial theories   Theories that arise from aspects of both sociological and psychological perspectives.

Puberty   A stage of human development which is defined by biological, physical change – the reproductive organs, in males and females, become functional.

Reflective practice   A form of mental processing – a form of thinking that we may use to fulfil a purpose or to achieve some anticipated outcome; or we may simply 'be reflective' and then an outcome may be unexpected (see Crawford, 2006).

Transition   Phases, stages or life events that people move through during their life course.

Social Care Institute for Excellence (SCIE)   The Institute's mission is to identify and spread knowledge about good practice to the large and diverse social care workforce and support the delivery of transformed, personalised social care services.

Schemas   The basic building blocks and the internal representation of a physical or mental action (Piaget).

Social construction   Where a common understanding or meaning of a concept is taken for granted, so that the notion appears to be obvious to those who accept it. However, the meaning actually emerges from ideologies, images, values and beliefs in a particular culture or society.

Systems perspective   A theoretical stance that views individuals as part of social systems that are dynamic and interconnected. This perspective focuses on the interaction and relationships between people and their environment.

Bibliography

Age Concern (2005) *Death and Dying. Policy Position Papers.* London: Age Concern England.

AgeUK (2005) *How Ageist is Britain?* London: AgeUK.

AgeUK (2011) *A Snapshot of Ageism in the UK and across Europe.* London: AgeUK.

AgeUK (2013a) *End of Life Evidence Review.* London: AgeUK.

AgeUK (2013b) *Agenda for Later Life: Improving Later Life in 2013.* London: AgeUK.

Ainsworth, MDS (1973) 'The Development of Infant–Mother Attachment', in Cardwell, B and Ricciuti, H (eds) *Review of Child Development Research*, 3, 1–94.

Ainsworth, MDS, Blehar, MC, Waters, E and Wall, S (1978) *Patterns of Attachment: A Psychological Study of The Strange Situation.* Hillsdale, NJ: Erlbaum.

Aldgate, J, Jones, D, Rose, W and Jeffry, C (2006) *The Developing World of the Child.* London: Jessica Kingsley.

Alzheimer's Society (2013) *Low Expectations: Attitudes on Choice, Care and Community for People with Dementia in Care Homes.* London: Alzheimer's Society.

Ariès, P (1962) *Centuries of Childhood.* New York, NY: Vintage.

Association for Young People's Health (AYPH) (2013) *Key Data on Adolescence 2013.* London: AYPH.

Association of Palliative Care Social Workers in collaboration with the former College of Social Work and Making Waves Lived Experiences Network/OPEN FUTURES Research, with support from the British Association of Social Workers and Hospice UK (2016) *The Role of Social Workers in Palliative, End of Life and Bereavement Care.* London: BASW.

Baltes, P (1987) Theoretical propositions of life-span developmental psychology: On the dynamics between growth and decline. *Developmental Psychology*, 23 (5), 611–626.

Bandura, A (1977) Self-efficacy: Toward a unifying theory of behavioural change. *Psychology Review*, 84 (2), 191–215.

Bandura, A (1986) *Social Foundations of Thought and Action.* Englewood Cliffs, NJ: Prentice Hall.

Banks, S (2004*) Ethics, Accountability and the Social Professions*. Basingstoke: Palgrave Macmillan.

Baumrind, D (1971) Current patterns of parental authority. *Developmental Psychology Monograph 4, 1,* part 2.

Beckett, C and Horner, N (2016) *Essential Theory for Social Work Practice* (2nd edn). London: Sage.

Bee, H (1994) *Lifespan Development*. New York: HarperCollins College.

Bee, H (1995) *The Growing Child*. New York: HarperCollins.

Beinart, S, Anderson, B, Lee, S and Utting, D (2002) *Youth at Risk? A National Survey of Risk Factors, Protective Factors and Problem Behaviours Among Young People in England, Scotland and Wales*. London: Communities That Care.

Bengston, VL, Elder, GH and Putney, NM (2012) 'The Life Course Perspective on Ageing: Linked Lives, Timing and History', in Katz, J, Pearce, S and Spurr, S (eds) *Adult Lives: A Life Course Perspective*. Bristol: Policy Press (pp. 9–17).

Beresford, P (2007) *The Changing Roles and Tasks of Social Work from Service Users' Perspectives: A Literature Informed Discussion Paper*. London: Shaping our Lives National User Network.

Beresford, P, Croft, S and Adshead, L. (2008) 'We don't see her as a social worker': a service user case study of the importance of the social work relationship and humanity. *British Journal of Social Work, 38 (7)*, 1388–1407.

Beresford, P, Fleming, J, Glynn, M, Bewley, C, Croft, S, Bransfield, F and Postle, K (2011) *Supporting People: Towards a Person-Centered Approach*. Bristol: Policy Press.

Berger, KS (2014) *The Developing Person* (9th edn). New York: Worth.

Berrington, A, Stevenson, J, Ingham, R, with Borgoni, R, Cobos Hernández, MI and Smith, PWF (2005) *Consequences of Teenage Parenthood: Pathways which Minimise the Long-term Negative Impacts of Teenage Childbearing*. Southampton: University of Southampton.

Berryman, J, Smyth, P, Taylor, A, Lamont, A and Joiner, R (2002) *Developmental Psychology and You*. Oxford: BPD Blackwell.

Birch, A (1997) *Developmental Psychology: From Infancy to Adulthood* (2nd edn). Basingstoke: Palgrave.

Birmingham Safeguarding Board (2010) *Serious Case Review in Relation to a Child. Case Number 14*. Birmingham: Birmingham Safeguarding Board.

Boud, D, Keogh, R and Walker, D (1994) *Reflection: Turning Experience into Learning*. London: Kogan Page.

Bowers, H, Lockwood, S, Eley, A, Catley, A, Runnicles, D, Mordey, M, Barker, S, Thomas, N, Jones, C and Dalziel, S (2013) *Widening Choices for Older People with High Support Needs*. York: Joseph Rowntree Foundation.

Bowes, A and Daniel, B (2010) Introduction: Interrogation harm and abuse: A life span approach. *Social Policy and Society, 9 (2)*, 221–229.

Bowlby, J (1953) *Child Care and the Growth of Love*. Harmondsworth: Penguin.

Bowlby, J (1969) *Attachment and Loss: Vol. 1 Attachment.* New York: Basic Books.

Bowlby, J (1973) *Attachment and Loss: Vol. 2 Separation Anxiety and Anger.* New York: Basic Books.

Bowlby, J (1988) *A Secure Base: Clinical Application of Attachment Theory.* London: Routledge.

Bowling, A. and Dieppe, P. (2005) What is successful ageing and who should define it? *British Medical Journal, 331*, 1548–1551.

Boyd, DG and Bee, HL (2010) *The Growing Child.* London: Pearson.

Boylan, J and Ray, M (2012) *Curriculum Guide – Human Growth and Development.* London: TCSW. Available from: www.tcsw.org.uk/uploadedFiles/TheCollege/Media_centre/ Curriculum%20guide_HGD_%2017July2012_proofed.pdf (accessed 2/2/17).

Brandon, M, Bailey, S, Belderson, P and Larsson, B (2013) *Neglect and Serious Case Reviews.* London: NSPCC. Available from: www.nspcc.org.uk (accessed 2/2/17).

British Association of Social Work (BASW) (2012) *The Code of Ethics for Social Work.* Birmingham: BASW.

Bronfenbrenner, U (1979a) *The Ecology of Human Development.* Cambridge, MA: Harvard University Press.

Bronfenbrenner, U (1979b) Contexts of child rearing: Problems and prospects. *American Psychologist, 34*, 844–850.

Brown, L and Walter, T (2014) Towards a social model of end-of-life care. *British Journal of Social Work, 44 (8)*, 2375–2390.

Bunn, A. (2013) *Signs of Safety® on England. An NSPCC commissioned report on the Sign of Safety model in child protection.* London: NSPCC.

Buss, AH and Plomin, R (1989) 'The EAS Approach to Temperament', in Plomin, R and Dunn, J (eds) *The Study of Temperament: Changes, Continuities and Challenges.* Hillsdale, NJ: Erlbaum (pp. 67–80).

Butrym, Z (1976) *The Nature of Social Work.* London: Macmillan.

Bytheway, B (1995) *Ageism.* Buckingham: Open University Press.

Cann, P and Dean, M (eds) (2009) *Unequal Ageing: The Untold Story of Exclusion in Old Age.* Bristol: Policy Press.

Chamberlayne, P, Bornat, J and Weingraf, T (eds) (2000) *The Turn to Biographical Methods in Social Science: Comparative Issues and Examples.* London: Routledge.

Cleaver, H, Nicholson, D, Tarr, S and Cleaver, D (2008) *Child Protection, Domestic Violence and Parental Substance Misuse.* London: Jessica Kingsley.

Cleaver, H, Unell, I and Aldgate, J (2011) *Children's Needs – Parenting Capacity: Child Abuse, Parental Mental Illness, Learning Disability, Substance Misuse, and Domestic Violence* (2nd edn). Norwich: The Stationery Office.

Cobb, N (1995) *Adolescence: Continuity, Change and Diversity* (2nd edn). Mountain View, CA: Mayfield.

Cochran, W and Tessor, A (1996) 'The "What the Hell" Effect: Some Effects of Goal Proximity and Goal Framing on Performance', in Martin, LL and Tessor, A (eds) *Striving and Feeling: Interactions Among Goals, Affect and Self Regulation.* New York: Lawrence Erlbaum.

Codd, J (1997) 'Knowledge, Qualifications and Higher Education: A Critical View', in Olssen, M and Morris Matthews, K (eds) *Education Policy in New Zealand: The 1990's and Beyond.* Palmerston North: Dunmore Press.

Cole, M and Cole, SR (2001) *The Development of Children.* New York: Worth.

Coleman, J (2011) *The Nature of Adolescence* (4th edn). Hove: Routledge.

Coleman, J and Hendry, L (1999) *The Nature of Adolescence* (3rd edn). London: Routledge.

Commission on Improving Dignity in Care for Older People (2013) *Delivering Dignity: Securing Dignity in Care for Older People in Hospitals and Care Homes.* London: AgeUK

Conley, C (2003) A review of parenting capacity assessment reports. *Ontario Association of Children's Aid Societies (OACAS) Journal, 47(3),* 16–22.

Coopersmith, S (1967) *The Antecedents of Self-Esteem.* New York: Freeman.

Coulshed, V and Orme, J (2006) *Social Work Practice: An Introduction* (4th edn). Basingstoke: Palgrave Macmillan.

Cousin, G (2006) An introduction to threshold concepts. *Planet, 17,* December.

Coventry Safeguarding Board (2013) *Serious Case Review re Daniel Pelka. Overview report.* Coventry: Coventry Safeguarding Board.

Crawford, K (2006) *Reflective Reader: Social Work and Human Development.* Exeter: Learning Matters.

Crawford, K and Walker, J (2004) *Social Work and Older People.* Exeter: Learning Matters.

Cree, V (ed.) (2013) *Becoming a Social Worker: Global Narratives.* London: Routledge.

Cree, V and Davis, A (2007) *Social Work: Voices from the Inside.* London: Routledge.

Crittenden, P (1996) 'Research on Maltreating Families: Implications for Intervention', in Briere, J, Berliner, J, Bulkley, JA, Jenny, C and Reid, T (eds) *The APSAC Handbook on Child Maltreatment.* Thousand Oaks, CA: Sage (pp. 158–174).

Crittenden, P (2008) *Raising Parents: Attachment: Parenting and Child Safety.* Cullompton: Willan Press.

Croisdale-Appleby, D. (2014) *Re-visioning Social Work Education: An Independent Review.* London: Department of Health.

Cumming, E and Henry, W (1961) *Growing Old: The Process of Disengagement.* New York, NY: Basic Books.

Daiute, C, Beyont, Z, Higson-Smith, C and Nucci, L (2006) *International Perspectives on Youth Conflict and Development*. New York: Oxford University Press.

Daniel, B and Bowes, A (2011) Re-thinking harm and abuse: Insights from a lifespan perspective. *British Journal of Social Work, 41 (5)*, 820–836.

Daniel, B and Wassell, S (2002) *Adolescence: Assessing and Promoting Resilience in Vulnerable Children*. London: Jessica Kingsley.

Daniel, B, Wassell, S and Gilligan, R (1999/2010) *Child Development for Child Care and Protection Workers*. London: Jessica Kingsley.

Davies, C and Ward, H (2011) *Safeguarding Children Across Services: Messages from Research on Identifying and Responding to Child Maltreatment*. London: Jessica Kingsley.

Davies, M (ed.) (2012) *Social Work with Adults*. Basingstoke: Palgrave Macmillan.

Dawson, CR, Cragg, A, Taylor, C and Toombs, C (2007) *Video Games*. London: British Board of Film Classification.

Deacon, L. and Macdonald, S. (2017) *Social Work Theory and Practice*. London: Sage.

Department for Education (DfE) (2010) *Review of the Office of the Children's Commissioner* (England). Norwich: The Stationery Office.

Department for Education (DfE) (2011a) *An Action Plan for Adoption: Tackling Delay*. London: Department for Education.

Department for Education (DfE) (2011b) *Support and Aspiration: A New Approach to Special Educational Needs and Disability. A Consultation*. London: Department for Education.

Department for Education (DfE) (2013) *Common Assessment Framework*. London: Department for Education.

Department for Education and Skills (DfES) (2002) *Birth to Three Matters: A Framework to Support Children in Their Earliest Years*. Nottingham: DfES Publications Centre.

Department for Education and Skills (DfES) (2003) *Every Child Matters*. Norwich: The Stationery Office.

Department for Education and Skills (DfES) (2004a) *Children Act 2004*. Norwich: The Stationery Office.

Department for Education and Skills (DfES) (2004b) *Every Child Matters: Change for Children*. Norwich: The Stationery Office.

Department for Education and Skills (DfES) (2005) *Every Child Matters Change for Children: Young People and Drugs*. Norwich: The Stationery Office.

Department for Education and Skills (DfES) (2006) *Common Assessment Framework for Children and Young People*. Norwich: The Stationery Office.

Department for Education and Skills (DfES) (2007a) *Practice Guidance for the Early Years Foundation Stage*.

Department for Education and Skills (DfES) (2007b)*The Early Years Foundation Stage (EYFS): Setting the Standards for Learning, Development and Care for Children from Birth to Five.* London: DfES.

Department of Education (DoE) (2014) *Rethinking Children's Services: Department of Education Children's Social Care Innovation Programme.* London: Department of Education.

Department of Education (DoE) (2015) *Working Together to Safeguard Children: A Guide to Inter-Agency Working to Safeguard and Promote the Welfare of Children.* London: Department of Education.

Department of Education (DoE) (2016a) *Children's Social Care Reform: A Vision for Change.* London: Department of Education.

Department of Education (DoE) (2016b) *Putting Children First: Delivering Our Vision for Excellent Children's Social Care.* London: Department of Education.

Department of Education (DoE) (2016c) *Adoption: A Vision for Change.* London: Department of Education.

Department of Health (DH) (2000) *Framework for the Assessment of Children in Need and Their Families.* Norwich: The Stationery Office.

Department of Health (DH) (2004) *National Service Framework: Children, Young People and Maternity Services.* Norwich: The Stationery Office.

Department of Health (DH) (2006) *Our Health, Our Care, Our Say: A New Direction for Community Services: A Brief Guide.* London: Department of Health Publications.

Department of Health (DH) (2008) *End of Life Care Strategy: Promoting High Quality Care for All Adults at the End of Life.* London: DH Publications.

Department of Health (DH) (2013a) *Winterbourne View Review: Good Practice Examples.* Norwich: The Stationery Office. Available from: www.gov.uk/government/publications/winterbourne-view-hospital-department-of-health-review-and-response (accessed 2/2/17).

Department of Health (DH) (2013b) *Integrated Care and Support: Our Shared Commitment.* Norwich: The Stationery Office.

Department of Health (DH) (2015) *Working Together to Safeguard Children.* London: HMSO.

Department of Health (DH) (2016a) *The Strategic Statement on Social Work with Adults in England 2016–2020.* London: Department of Health.

Department of Health (DH) (2016b) *The Prime Minister's Challenge on Dementia 2020.* London: HMSO.

Department of Health (DH) (2016c) *Our Commitment To You for End of Life Care: The Government Response to the Review of Choice in End of Life Care.* London: HMSO.

Department for Work and Pensions (DWP) (2016) *Household Below Average Income 1994–1995 to 2014–2015.* Available from: www.gov.uk (accessed 23/3/17).

Dillon, L, Chivite-Matthews, N, Grewal, I, Brown, R, Webster, S, Weddell, E, Brown, G and Smith, N (2007) *Risk, Protective Factors and Resilience to Drug Use: Identifying Resilient Young People and Learning from Their Experiences*. London: Home Office.

Dodge, R, Daly, AP, Huyton, J and Sanders, LD (2012) The challenge of defining wellbeing. *Journal of Wellbeing, 2 (3)*, 222–235.

Doel, M (2010) 'Service User Perspectives on Relationships', in Ruch, G, Turney, D and Ward, A (eds) *Relationship Based Social Work: Getting to the Heart of Practice*. London: Jessica Kingsley (pp. 199–213).

Erikson, E (1987) *A Way of Looking at Things: Selected Papers from 1930–1986*. London: Norton.

Erikson, E (1995) *Childhood and Society*. London: Vintage.

Erikson, E (1997) *The Life Cycle Completed. The Extended Version*. London: Norton.

Eyer, DE (1993) *Mother–Infant Bonding: A Scientific Fiction*. New Haven, CT: Yale University Press.

Fahlberg, V (1991) *A Child's Journey Through Placement*. London: BAAF.

Farington, D (1996) *Understanding and Preventing Youth Crime*. York: Joseph Rowntree Foundation.

Flynn, M (2007) *The Murder of Steven Hoskins: A Serious Case Review*. Cornwall: Cornwall Adult Protection Committee.

Flynn, M (2012) *Winterbourne View Hospital: A Serious Care Review*. Bristol: South Gloucestershire Safeguarding Adults Board.

Fook, J (1996) *The Reflective Researcher: Social Workers' Theories of Practice Research*. Sydney: Allen & Unwin.

Fook, J (2002) *Social Work: Critical Theory and Practice*. London: Sage.

Forman, D E, Berman, AD, McCabe, CH, Baim, DS and Wei, JY (1992) PTCA in the elderly: The 'young-old' versus the 'old-old'. *Journal of the American Geriatrics Society, 40 (1)*, 19–22.

Francis Report (2013) *Report of the Mid Staffordshire NHS Foundation Trust Public Inquiry Volumes 1, 2 and 3*. London: The Stationery Office.

Fraser, L K, Miller, M, Aldridge, J, McKinney, PA and Parslow, RC, with Hain, R (2011) *Life-limiting and Life-threatening Conditions in Children and Young People in the United Kingdom: National and Regional Prevalence in Relation to Socioeconomic Status and Ethnicity*. Leeds: University of Leeds.

Freud, S (1949) *An Outline of Psychoanalysis*. London: Norton.

Gaine, C (2010) *Equality and Diversity in Social Work Practice*. London: Sage/Learning Matters.

Gardner, A (2011) *Personalisation in Social Work*. London: Sage/Learning Matters.

General Social Care Council (GSCC) (2005) *Post Qualifying Framework for Social Work Education and Training*. London: GSCC.

General Social Care Council (GSCC) (2017) *Codes of Practice for Social Care Workers and Employers*. London: GSCC.

Gesell, AL (1928) *Infancy and Human Growth*. New York: Macmillan.

Giddens, A (1991) *Modernity and Self-identity*. Cambridge, MA: Polity Press.

Gilleard, C and Higgs, P (2015) Social death and the moral identity of the fourth age. *Contemporary Social Science*, *10(3)*, 262–271.

Gilligan, C (1982) *In a Different Voice: Psychological Theory and Women's Development*. Cambridge, MA: Harvard University Press.

Gilligan, P and Furness, S (2006) The role of religion and spirituality in social work practice: Views and experiences of social workers and students. *British Journal of Social Work*, 36, 617–637.

Glendinning, C, Challis, D, Fernandez, Jacobs, S, Jones, K, Knapps, M, Manthorpe, J, Moran, N, Netten, A, Stevens, M and Wilberforce, M (2008) *Evaluation of the Individual Budgets Pilot Programme: Final Report*. York: Social Policy Research Unit, University of York. Available at: www.york.ac.uk/inst/spru/pubs/pdf/IBSEN.pdf (accessed 23/3/17).

Gordon, D, Levitas, R and Pantazis, C (2000) *Poverty and Social Exclusion in Britain*. York: Joseph Rowntree Foundation.

Government Office for Science (2016) *Future of an Ageing Population*. London: Government Office for Science.

Grant, G (2012) 'Safeguarding Vulnerable Adults Over the Lifecourse', in Katz, J, Pearce, S and Spurr, S (eds) *Adult Lives: A Life Course Perspective*. Bristol: Policy Press.

Grant, G, Ramacharan, P, Flynn, M and Richardson, M (eds) (2010) *Learning Disability: A Life Cycle Approach* (3rd edn). Maidenhead: Open University Press.

Gubrium, J and Holstein, J (eds) (2003) *Ways of Aging*. Oxford: Blackwell.

Harter, S (1999) *The Construction of Self: A Developmental Perspective*. New York: Guilford Press.

Havighurst, R (1972) *Developmental Tasks and Education* (3rd edn). New York: David McKay.

Hayflick, L (1977) 'The Cellular Basis for Biological Ageing', in Finch, CE and Hayfick, L (eds) *Handbook of the Biology of Aging*. New York, NY: Van Nostrand Reinhold (pp. 159–186).

Health and Care Professions Council (HCPC) (2012a) *Your Guide to Our Standards for Continuing Professional Development*. London: Health & Care Professions Council. Available from: www.hpc-uk. org/assets/documents/10003B70Yourguidetoourstandardsofcontinuingprofessionaldevelopment. pdf (accessed 13/1/14).

Health and Care Professions Council (HCPC) (2012b) *Your Guide to Our Standards for Continuing Professional Development*. *London: Health & Care Professions Council*. Available from: www.hpc-uk. org/assets/documents/10003B70Yourguidetoourstandardsofcontinuingprofessionaldevelopment. pdf (accessed 20/02/17).

Health and Care Professions Council (HCPC) (2017) *Standards of Proficiency: Social Workers in England.* London: Health & Care Professions Council. Available from: www.hpc-uk.org/assets/documents/10003B08Standardsofproficiency-SocialworkersinEngland.pdf (accessed 13/1/14).

Hester, M and Pearson, C (1998) *Preventing Child Abuse: Monitoring Domestic Violence.* Bristol: Policy Press.

Hester, M, Pearson, C and Harwin, N, with Abrahams, H (2006) *Making an Impact – Children and Domestic Violence: A Reader.* London: Jessica Kingsley.

Higgs, P and Gilleard, C (2015a) *Rethinking Old Age: Theorizing the Fourth Age.* London: Palgrave Macmillan.

Hockey, J and James, A (2003) *Social Identities Across the Life Course.* Basingstoke: Macmillan.

Hollis, F (1970) 'The Psychosocial Approach to the Practice of Casework', in Roberts, RW and Nee, RH (eds) *Theories of Social Casework.* Chicago, IL: University of Chicago Press.

Holmes, TH and Rahe, RH (1967) The Social Readjustment Rating Scale. *Journal of Psychosomatic Research, 11 (2)*, 213–318.

Holt, S, Buckley, H and Whelan, S (2008) The impact of exposure to domestic violence on children and young people: A review of the literature. *Child Abuse and Neglect, 32 (8)*, 797–819.

Horner, N (2009) *What is Social Work?* (4th edn). London: Sage/Learning Matters.

House of Lords Select Committee on Public Service and Demographic Change (2013) *Ready For Ageing?* London: HMSO.

Howarth, J (ed.) (2009) *The Child's World: The Comprehensive Guide to Assessing Children in Need* (2nd edn). London: Jessica Kingsley.

Howe, D (1987) *An Introduction to Social Work Theory.* Aldershot: Arena.

Howe, D (1995) *Attachment Theory for Social Work Practice.* Basingstoke: Macmillan.

Howe, D (1998) 'Psychosocial Work', in Adams, R, Dominelli, L and Payne, M (eds) *Social Work: Themes, Issues and Critical Debates.* Basingstoke: Macmillan.

Howe, D (2008) *The Emotionally Intelligent Social Worker.* Basingstoke: Palgrave Macmillan.

Howe, D (2009) *A Brief Introduction to Social Work Theory.* Basingstoke: Palgrave Macmillan.

Hughes, B and Mtezuka, EM (1992) 'Social Work and Older Women', in Langan, M and Day, L (eds) *Women, Oppression and Social Work: Issues in Anti-discrimination Practice.* London: Routledge.

Humphreys, C and Mullender, A (2000) *Children and Domestic Violence: A Research Review on the Impact on Children.* Dartington: Research in Practice.

Hunt, S (2005) *The Life Course: A Sociological Introduction.* Basingstoke: Palgrave Macmillan.

Humphries, R, Thorlby, R, Holder, H, Hall, P and Charles, A (2016) *Social Care for Older People: Home Truths.* London: The King's Fund and Nuffield Trust.

Hutchinson, C and Foster, J (2008) *Best Interests at End of Life*. Lancashire: Central Lancashire PCT & East Lancashire PCT. Available from: www.scie.org.uk/publications/mca/files/lancspct.pdf (accessed 2/2/17).

Ingleby, E (2010) *Applied Psychology for Social Work* (2nd edn). Exeter: Learning Matters.

Institute for Health Research (2005) *The Impact of Person Centred Planning*. Lancaster: University of Lancaster. Available from: http://www.learningdisabilities.org.uk/content/assets/pdf/publications/impact-person-centred-planning (accessed 13/1/14).

International Federation of Social Workers (IFSW) and International Association of Schools of Social Work (IASSW) (2013) *Global Definition of Social Work*. Available from: http://ifsw.org/get-involved/global-definition-of-social-work/ (accessed 2/2/17).

Johnson, F, Hogg, J and Daniel, B (2010) Abuse and protection across the lifespan: Reviewing the literature. *Social Policy and Society*, 9 *(2)*, 291–304.

Jowitt, M and O'Laughlin, S (2005) *Social Work with Children and Families*. Exeter: Learning Matters.

Karmiloff, K and Karmiloff-Smith, A (2002) *Pathways to Language: From Fetus to Adolescent*. Cambridge, MA: Harvard University Press.

Katz, J, Pearce, S and Spurr, S (eds) (2012) *Adult Lives: A Life Course Perspective*. Bristol: Policy Press.

Katz, P (1979) The development of female identity. *Sex Roles*, 5, 155–178.

Kellett, J and Apps, J (2009) *Assessments of Parenting and Parenting Support Need: A Study of Four Professional Groups*. York: Joseph Rowntree Foundation.

Kitwood, T (1993a) 'Frames of Reference for an Understanding of Dementia', in Johnson, J and Slater, R (eds) *Ageing and Later Life*. London: Sage (pp. 100–106).

Kitwood, T (1993b) Towards a theory of dementia care: The interpersonal process. *Ageing and Society*, 13 *(1)*, 51–67.

Kitwood, T (1997) *Dementia Reconsidered: The Person Comes First*. Buckingham: Open University Press.

Kitwood, T and Bredin, K. (1992) Towards a theory of dementia care: Personhood and well-being. *Ageing and Society*, 12 *(3)*, 269–287.

Kloep, M, Hendry, L and Saunders, D (2009) A new perspective on human development. *Conference of the International Journal of Arts and Sciences, 1(6)*, 332–343.

Kohlberg, L (1976) 'Moral Stages and Moralisation', in Linkons, T (ed.) *Moral Development and Behaviour: Theory, Research and Social Issues*. New York, NY: Holt, Rinehart and Winston (pp. 31–53).

Korbin, JE (2007) 'Issues of Culture', in Wilson, K and James, A (eds) *The Child Protection Handbook* (3rd edn). London: Baillière Tindall (pp. 134–141).

Kroger, J (2007) *Identity Development: Adolescence Through Adulthood* (2nd edn). London: Sage.

Laming, H (2003) *The Victoria Climbié Inquiry Report*. Norwich: The Stationery Office. Available from www.publications.parliament.uk/pa/cm200203/cmselect/cmhealth/570/570. pdf (accessed 2/2/17).

Laming, The Lord (2009) *The Protection of Children in England: A Progress Report*. Norwich: The Stationery Office.

Leutz, WN (2005) Five laws for integrating medical and social services lessons from the United States and the United Kingdom. *Milbank Quarterly, 77(1), 77–110.*

Levinson, D (1978) *The Seasons of a Man's Life.* New York, NY: Knopf.

Lloyd, J and Wait, S (2006) *Integrated Care: A Guide for Policy Makers.* London: International Longevity Centre.

Local Government Association, Association of Directors of Social Services and NHS England (2015a) *Supporting People with a Learning Disability and/or Autism who Display Behaviours that Challenge, including Those with a Mental Health Condition: Service model for commissioners of health and social care services.* London: LGA, ADSS and NHS England.

Local Government Association, Association of Directors of Social Services and NHS England (2015b) *Building the Right Support: A national plan to develop community services and close inpatient facilities for people with a learning disability and/or autism who display behaviours that challenge, including those with a mental health condition.* London: LGA, ADASS and NHS England.

Local Government Association and Public Health England (2016) *Teenage Pregnancy and Young Parents.* London: Local Government Association.

Lorenz, K (1970) *Studies in Animal and Human Behaviour,* Vol 1 (trans. Robert Martin). London: Methuen.

Luthar, S (2015) 'Resilience in Development: A Synthesis of Research Across Five Decades', in Cicchetti, D and Cohen, DJ (eds) *Developmental Psychopathology: Risk, Disorder and Adaptation* (2nd edn). New York, NY: Wiley (pp. 739–795).

Maccoby, E (2012) 'Parenting Effects: Issues and Controversies', in Borkowski, J, Landesman Ramey, S and Bristol-Power, M (eds) *Parenting and The Child's World: Influences on Academic, Intellectual and Social-Emotional Development.* Hillsdale, NJ: Erlbaum (pp. 35–46).

Maccoby, E and Martin, J (1983) 'Socialization in the Context of the Family: Parent–Child Interaction', in Hetherington, E (ed.) *Handbook of Child Psychology: Socialization, Personality and Social Development (*Vol. 4). New York: Wiley.

Main, M and Hesse, E (1990) 'Parents' Unresolved Traumatic Experiences are Related To Infant Dis-organized Attachment Status: Is Frightened and/or Frightening Parental Behavior the Linking Mechanism?', in Greenberg, MT, Cicchetti, D and Cummings, EM (eds) *Attachment in the Preschool Years: Theory, Research and Intervention.* Chicago, IL: University of Chicago Press (pp. 161–182).

Manthorpe, J and Martineau, S (2008) *Support Workers: Their Role and Tasks. A Scoping Review.* London: Social Care Workforce Research Unit King's College.

Marshall, M and Tibbs, MA (2006) *Social Work and People with Dementia: Partnerships, Practice and Persistence* (2nd edn). Bristol: Policy Press.

McGlone, E and Fitzgerald, F. (2005) *Perceptions of Ageism in Health and Social Services in Ireland.* Dublin: National Council on Ageing and Older People.

Meggitt, C (2006) *Child Development: An Illustrated Guide* (2nd edn). Oxford: Heinemann Educational.

Mezirow, J (1991) *Transformation Dimensions of Adult Learning.* San Francisco, CA: Jossey-Bass.

Michaelson, J, Abdallah, S, Steuer, N, Thompson, S and Marks, N (2009) *National Accounts of Well-being: Bringing Real Wealth onto the Balance Sheet.* London: New Economics Foundation.

Ministry of Justice and Department for Education (2011) *Family Justice Review: Final Report.* Available from: www.gov.uk/government/uploads/system/uploads/attachment_data/file/217343/family-justice-review-final-report.pdf (accessed 2/2/17).

Moon, JA (2004) *A Handbook of Reflective and Experiential Learning: Theory and Practice.* London: RoutledgeFalmer.

Moore, D and Jones, K (2012) *Social Work and Dementia.* London: Sage/Learning Matters.

Mulder. C (2015) From the inside out: Social workers' expectations for integrating religion and spirituality in practice. *Journal of Religion and Spirituality in Social Work, 34 (2),* 177–204.

Mullender, A and Morley, R (eds) (1994) *Children Living with Domestic Violence: Putting Men's Abuse of Women on the Child Care Agenda.* London: Whiting and Birch.

Munro, E (2010) *The Munro Review of Child Protection. Part One: A Systems Analysis.* London: Department of Education.

Munro, E (2011) *The Munro Review of Child Protection Final Report: A Child-centred System.* London: Department for Education.

Narey, M (2014) *Making the Education of Social Workers Consistently Effective. Report of Sir Martin Narey's independent review of the education of children's social workers.* London: Department of Education.

Narey, M (2016) *Residential Care in England. Report of Sir Martin Narey's independent review of children's residential care.* London: Department of Education.

National Health Service End of Life Programme Team (NHS) (2008) *Advance Care Planning: A Guide for Health and Social Care Staff.* Nottingham: University of Nottingham.

National Institute for Health and Care Excellence (NICE) and the Social Care Institute for Excellence (SCIE) (2006) *Dementia – Supporting People with Dementia and their Carers in Health and Social Care.* London: SCIE.

National Palliative and End of Life Care Partnership (2015) *Ambitions for Palliative and End of Life Care: A National Framework for Local Action 2015– 2020.* Available from: http://endoflifecareambitions.org.uk (accessed 23/3/17).

National Society for the Prevention of Cruelty to Children (NSPCC) (2014) *Culture and Race: Learning from case reviews. Summary of risk factors and learning for improved practice around culture and faith.* London: NSPCC.

Newman, T and Blackburn, S (2002) *Transitions in the Lives of Children and Young People: Resilience Factors.* Edinburgh: Scottish Executive Education Department.

NHS England *et al.* (2015) *Delivering the Forward View: NHS Planning Guidance 2016/17–2020/21.* London: HMSO.

Novak, T (2002) 'Rich Children, Poor Children', in Goldson, B, Lavelette, M and Mckechnie, J (eds) *Children, Welfare and the State.* London: Sage.

Obegi, AD and Natan Ritblatt, S (2005) Cultural competence in infant/toddler caregivers: Application of a tri-dimensional model. *Journal of Research in Childhood Education, 19 (3)*, 199–213.

Office for Disability Issues (2008) *Independent Living: A Cross-government Strategy about Independent Living for Disabled People.* London: Office for Disability Issues.

Office for National Statistics (ONS) (2013) *What Does the 2011 Census Tell Us About Older People?* London: Office for National Statistics.

Office for National Statistics (ONS) (2014) *Conceptions in England and Wales 2015.* London: Office for National Statistics.

Office for National Statistics (ONS) (2016a) *Families and Households in the UK.* London: Office for National Statistics.

Office for National Statistics (ONS) (2016b) *Women in Work.* London: Office for National Statistics.

Office of the Children's Rights Director for England (2011) *Messages for Munro: A Report of Children's Views Collected for Professor Eileen Munro.* London: Ofsted.

Ogbu, JU (1993) Differences in cultural frames of reference. *International Journal of Behavioural Development, 16*, 483–506.

Oko, J (2011) *Understanding and Using Theory in Social Work* (2nd edn). London: Sage.

Oliner, SP and Oliner, PM (1988) *The Altruistic Personality: Rescuers of Jews in Nazi Germany.* New York: Free Press.

Oliver, C (2010) *Children's Views and Experiences of their Contact with Social Workers: A Focussed Review of the Evidence.* Leeds: Children's Workforce Development Council.

O'Loughlin, M and O'Loughlin, S (eds) (2008) *Social Work with Children and Families* (4th edn). London: Sage.

Paludi, MA (ed.) (2002) *Human Development in Multicultural Contexts: A Book of Readings.* Englewood Cliffs, NJ: Prentice Hall.

Parker, J and Bradley, G (2014) *Social Work Practice* (3rd edn). Exeter: Learning Matters.

Parrott, L (2010) *Values and Ethics in Social Work Practice* (2nd edn). London: Sage/Learning Matters.

Payne, M (2014) *Modern Social Work Theory* (4th edn). Basingstoke: Palgrave Macmillan.

Phinney, JS (1993) 'A Three-stage Model of Ethnic Identity Development in Adolescence', in Bernal, ME and Knight, GP (eds) *Ethnic Identity: Formation and Transmission Among Hispanics and Other Minorities.* New York: State University of New York Press.

Piaget, J (1936) *Origins of Intelligence in the Child.* London: Routledge & Kegan Paul.

Piaget, J (1970) *The Science of Education and the Psychology of the Child.* New York: Grossman.

Priestley, M (2003) *Disability: A Life Course Approach.* Cambridge: Polity Press.

Prince, M, Prina, M and Guerchet, M (2013) *World Alzheimer's Report 2013: Journey of Caring: An Analysis of Long-tem Care for Dementia.* London: Alzheimer's Disease International.

Prior, V and Glaser, D (2006) *Understanding Attachment and Attachment Disorders: Theory, Evidence and Practice.* London: Jessica Kingsley.

Quality Assurance Agency for Higher Education (QAA) (2016) *Subject Benchmark Statements.* Gloucester: QAA. Available from: www.qaa.ac.uk (accessed 23/3/17).

Race, D (2002) *Learning Disability: A Social Approach*. London: Routledge.

Rathus, (2008) *Childhood and Adolescence: Voyages in Development* (3rd edn). Belmont, CA: Thompson Learning.

Ray, M and Phillips. J. (2012) *Social Work with Older People* (5th edn). Basingstoke: Palgrave Macmillan.

Ray, M, Bernard, M and Phillips, J (2009) *Critical Issues in Social Work with Older People.* Basingstoke: Palgrave Macmillan.

Ray, S, Sharp, E and Abrams, D (2006) *Ageism: A Benchmark of Public Attitudes in Britain.* London: Age Concern England.

Ready For Ageing Alliance (2016) *Still Not Ready For Ageing.* Available at www.cpa.org.uk/cpa/docs/R4AA/Still_not_ready_for_ageing.pdf (accessed 23/3/17).

Redmond, B (2004) *Reflection in Action: Developing Reflective Practice in Health and Social Services.* Aldershot: Ashgate.

Ritchie, JH, Dick, D and Lingham, R (1994) *The Report of the Inquiry into the Care and Treatment of Christopher Clunis.* London: HMSO.

Robinson, M (2011) *Understanding Behaviour and Development in Early Childhood: A Guide to Theory and Practice.* Abingdon: Routledge.

Ronen, T (2002) 'Cognitive-Behavioural Therapy', in Davies, M (ed.) *The Blackwell Companion to Social Work*. Oxford: Blackwell.

Roscoe, KD, Carson, AM and Madoc-Jones, L (2010) Narrative social work: conversations between theory and practice. *Journal of Social Work Practice, 25 (1)*, 47–61.

Rowe, JW and Kahn, RL (1987) Human ageing: Usual and successful. *Science* (Jul 10), *237 (4811)*, 143–149.

Ruch, G, Turney, D and Ward, A (eds) (2010) *Relationship Based Social Work: Getting to the Heart of Practice*. London: Jessica Kingsley.

Rutter, M (1981) *Maternal Deprivation Reassessed* (2nd edn). Harmondsworth: Penguin.

Schön, DA (1983/1987) *The Reflective Practitioner*. London: Temple Smith.

Schön, DA (1991) *The Reflective Practitioner: How Professionals Think in Action*. Aldershot: Ashgate.

Scott, S (1998) Intensive interventions to improve parenting. *Archives of Disease in Childhood, 79 (1)*, 90–93.

Seden, J and Ross, T (2007) 'Active Service User Involvement in Human Services: Lessons from Practice', in Aldgate, J, Healey, L, Barris, M, Pine, B, Rose, W and Seden, J (eds) *Enhancing Social Work Management: Theory and Best Practice from the UK and USA*. London: Jessica Kingsley (pp. 199–216).

Selman, R and Schultz, L (1990) *Making a Friend in Youth: Development Theory and Pair Therapy*. Chicago, IL: University of Chicago Press.

Shemmings, D and Shemmings, Y (2011) *Understanding Disorganised Attachment: Theory and Practice for Working with Children and Families*. London: Jessica Kingsley.

Shropshire, J and Middleton, S (1999) *Small Expectations: Learning to be Poor?* York: Joseph Rowntree Foundation.

Sidell, M (1993) 'Death, Dying and Bereavement', in Bond, J, Coleman, P and Peace, S (eds) *Ageing in Society: An Introduction to Social Gerontology* (2nd edn). London: Sage.

Siegler, R, Deloache, J and Esienberg, N (2003) *How Children Develop*. New York: Worth.

Slater, A and Bremner, G (eds) (2011) *An Introduction to Developmental Psychology* (2nd edn). Oxford: Blackwell.

Smith, PK, Cowie, H and Blades, M (2015) *Understanding Child Development* (6th edn). Chichester: John Wiley and Son.

Social Care Institute for Excellence (SCIE) (2008) *Research Briefing 25: Children's and Young People's Experiences of Domestic Violence Involving Adults in a Parenting Role*. London: SCIE.

Social Care Institute for Excellence (SCIE) (2013) *Personalisation: A Rough Guide – Adult Services Report 20*. London: Social Care Institute for Excellence.

Social Exclusion Task Force (2007) *Reaching Out: Think Family*. Norwich: The Stationery Office.

Social Work Reform Board (SWRB) (2012) *Building a Safe and Confident Future: Maintaining Momentum*. London: Department for Education. Available from: www.gov.uk/government/uploads/ system/uploads/attachment_data/file/175947/SWRB_progress_report_-_June_2012.pdf (accessed 20/02/17).

Social Work Task Force (2009) *Building a Safe and Confident Future*. London: Department for Children Schools and Families. Available from: http://webarchive.nationalarchives.gov.uk/20130401151715/ https://www.education.gov.uk/publications/eOrderingDownload/01114-2009 DOM-EN.pdf (accessed 20/02/17).

Steinberg, L (1993) *Adolescence*. New York: McGraw-Hill.

Stevenson, O (2004) 'The Future of Social Work', in Lymbery, M and Butler, S (eds) *Social Work Ideals and Practical Realities*. Basingstoke: Macmillan.

Sugarman, L (1986) *Life-Span Development: Concepts, Theories and Interventions*. London: Routledge.

Sugarman, L (2001) *Life-span Development: Frameworks, Accounts and Strategies* (2nd edn). Hove: Psychology Press.

Sullivan, HS (1953) *The Interpersonal Theory of Psychiatry*. New York: Norton.

Svejda, MJ, Campos, JJ and Emde, RN (1980) Mother–infant 'bonding': A failure to generalise. *Child Development*, 51 (3), 775–779.

Sweeting, H and Gilhooly, M (1997) Dementia and the phenomena of social death. *Sociology of Health and Illness*, 19 (1), 93–117.

Teenage Pregnancy Independent Advisory Group (TPIAG) (2009) *Annual Report 2008/09*. London: Department for Children, Schools & Families.

The Children's Society (2016) *The Good Childhood Report 2016*. London: The Children's Society.

The (Former) College of Social Work (TCSW) (2012a) *Professional Capabilities Framework*. London: The College of Social Work. London: BASW.

The (Former) College of Social Work (TCSW) (2012b) *Practice Educator Professional Standards for Social Work*. London: BASW.

The (Former) College of Social Work (TCSW) (2012c) *Professional Capability Framework – End of First Placement Level Capabilities*. London: BASW.

The Lords Select Committee on Public Service and Demographic Change (2013) *Ready for Ageing?* Norwich: The Stationery Office.

The Marmot Review (2010) *Fair Society, Healthy Lives*. London: Institute of Health Inequality.

Thom, B, Sales, R and Pearce, J (2007) *Growing Up With Risk*. Bristol: Policy Press.

Thomas, A and Chess, S (1977) *Temperament and Development*. New York: Brunner.

Thomas, A and Chess, S (1986) 'The New York Longitudinal Study: From Infancy to Early Adult Life', in Plomin, R and Dunn, J (eds) *Changes, Continuities and Challenges*. Hillsdale, NJ: Erlbaum.

Tinson, A, Ayrton, C, Barker, K, Barry Born, T, Aldridge, H and Kenway, P (2016) *Monitoring Poverty and Social Exclusion 2016*. York: Joseph Rowntree Foundation.

Turnell, A and Edwards, S (1999) *Signs of Safety: A Safety and Solution Orientated Approach to Child Protection Casework*. New York, NY: Norton.

Turney, D, Platt, D, Selwyn, J and Farmer, E (2011) *Social Work Assessment of Children in Need: Messages from Research*. London: Department for Education.

UNICEF (2011) *The State of the World's Children 2011: Adolescence, an Age of Opportunity*. New York: UNICEF.

UNICEF (2013) *The State of the World's Children: Children with a Disability*. New York: UNICEF.

UNICEF (2016) *The State of the World's Children 2016: A Fair Chance for Every Child*. New York: UNICEF.

UNICEF Innocenti Research Centre (2013) *Child Well-being in Rich Countries: A Comparative Overview*, Card 11. Florence: UNICEF Research Centre.

United Nations (2015) *World Population Ageing*. New York: United Nations.

Van Raak, A, Mur-Veeman, I, Hardy, B, Steenbergen, M and Paulus, A (eds) (2003) *Integrated Care in Europe: Descriptions and Comparison of Integrated Care in Six EU Countries*. Maarssen, NL: Elsevier Gezondheidszorg.

Vygotsky, LS (1962) *Thought and Language*. Cambridge, MA: MIT Press.

Vygotsky, LS (1978) *Mind in Society: The Development of Higher Psychological Processes*. Cambridge, MA: Harvard University Press.

Walker, L, Pitts, C, Hennig, K and Matsuba, M (1995) 'Reasoning about Morality and Real Life Moral Problems', in Killen, M and Hart, D (eds) *Morality in Everyday Life: Developmental Perspectives*. Cambridge: Cambridge University Press (pp. 371–408).

Watts, JH (2013) Considering the role of social work in palliative care: Reflections from the literature. *European Journal of Palliative Care*, 20 (4),199–201.

Wiggins, M, Oakley, A, Sawtell, M, Austerberry, H, Clemens, F and Elbourne, QD (2005) *Teenage Parenthood and Social Exclusion: A Multi-method Study*. London: Social Science Research Unit University of London.

Winter, K (2011) *Building Relationships and Communication with Young Children: A Practical Guide for Social Workers*. Abingdon: Routledge.

Wood, J, Ashman, M, Davies, C, Lloyd, H and Lockett, K (1996) *Report of the Independent Inquiry into the Care of Anthony Smith*. Derbyshire: Southern Derbyshire Health Authority and Derbyshire County Council.

Index